The Humanity Test

Disability / Therapy / Society

John Barton

First published 2022

PCCS Books Ltd
Wyastone Business Park
Wyastone Leys
Monmouth
NP25 3SR
UK

Tel +44 (0)1600 891509
contact@pccs-books.co.uk
www.pccs-books.co.uk

The Humanity Test: Disability, therapy, society

British Library Cataloguing in Publication Data.
A catalogue record for this book is available from the British Library

ISBNs   paperback 978 1 915220 12 7

           epub 978 1 915 220 13 4

Cover design by Jason Anscomb
Printed in the UK by Severn, Gloucester

Endorsements for *The Humanity Test: Disability, therapy, society*

This is a wise and fascinating account, written accessibly by someone who is a reliable guide to the worlds of disability and psychotherapy, because it's exactly where he lives. I trusted him immediately and recommend this book to all.

Tom Shakespeare, Professor of Disability Research, London School of Hygiene and Tropical Medicine

The Humanity Test is a great book. John Barton has found a balance between being candid and learned about disability. This book acknowledges the emotional aspects of disability in a sensitive and intelligent manner. Each chapter is an accessible primer on interesting and relevant topics relating to disability, while bringing everything together in a carefully structured argument for social justice. There are many different ways of thinking about disability – Barton manages to acknowledge this while finding universalities among all disabled people.

Josh Hepple, disability equality activist and consultant

Barton shows how disability exposes us to ourselves in all our vulnerability, loneliness, incompetence and fear of disappearing. His research demonstrates how this can paradoxically lead to a deeper, more soulful humanity – so lacking in our contemporary world. The Humanity Test should be part of all therapeutic training.

Professor Emmy van Deurzen, existential psychotherapist and writer, Principal of the New School of Psychotherapy and Counselling and Director of the Existential Academy

For Annie

About the author

John Barton is a UKCP and BACP accredited integrative psychotherapist in private practice in London, with a doctorate in counselling psychology, which he gained in 2019. His first career was as a magazine writer and editor in the UK and then for a decade in the US, before he returned to London and, after a stint as a Samaritans volunteer, trained to be a counsellor. He is also a father, writer, painter.

The Humanity Test:

Disability, therapy and society

Contents

Acknowledgements

I would like to offer enormous thanks, appreciation and gratitude to the many people who helped me write this book.

As well as family and friends, colleagues, comrades and co-conspirators, and the role models I pay tribute to in Chapter 2, I'd like to thank various teachers, supervisors, therapists, researchers and other wise people, including Mark Gullidge, Hette Los, Vanja Orlans, Werner Prall, Steven Smith, Paul Hitchings, Harbrinder Dhillon-Stevens, Lucia Swanepoel, Patricia Moran and Sofie Bager-Charleson. I would like to express my immense gratitude for my training towards becoming a therapist, a person with a disability, a human. You don't have to go to some remote mountain temple to find a beacon of enlightenment – the Metanoia Institute is just off the North Circular.

I'd like to thank some people who read early parts or drafts of the book and gave feedback and encouragement, especially fellow doctoral traveller Siona Bastable, my former managing editor when I lived in America, Lisa Furlong, and my lovely siblings and cousins.

I'd like to thank everyone at PCCS Books, especially its commissioning editor Catherine Jackson. On paper and in person, she destroys any careless, overblown or lazy words, thoughts and ideas with precision and grace, but always with immense kindness and encouragement, and humour too.

I'd like to thank the staff at the National Hospital for Neurology and Neurosurgery and at North London Neurophysiotherapy for keeping me reasonably physically well.

I'd like to thank all my clients for trusting, educating and inspiring me.

And I'd like to thank my daughter, to whom this book is dedicated, and the magnificent, beautiful and brilliant Dr Becky Barton for her love.

Preface

There is no one quite like you. Only you were born into your body, at that time, to those people, in that place; only you have had your complex web of relationships, encounters and experiences. You are a one-off prism that refracts and casts a unique light on what it is to be human.

So who are you?

This is a book about difference. The future of humanity depends on our ability to get along with people who are not the same as us. Disability is the most different of differences. How we respond to disabilities, illnesses, impairments – our own and those of others – is a test: the Humanity Test. Do you pass the test? Are you a humane human? Let the soul be our guide. United we stand, divided we fall.

This book is offered in the hope of helping people to live more soulful lives, pass the Humanity Test and contribute to bringing an end to ableism. It is also a book for those involved in the Advanced Humanity Test: people with disabilities and the therapists who work with them. And then there are those taking the Group Humanity Test – people involved with any kind of group who are interested in making it a force for good in this world. The Humanity Test is a lens through which you, your relationships, your family, community, society, or place of work, rest or play can all be viewed.

This is a book for anyone who wants to appreciate their life more, to understand their suffering and the suffering of others and to live more passionately, fully and meaningfully. It is for any human.

The book begins with my own story: a strange midlife transition from being a healthy, active golf and travel writer to becoming a qualified counselling psychologist and psychotherapist with two progressively disabling neurological conditions (Chapter 2). Chapter 3 is a necessarily abbreviated overview of disability, starting with all the different ways people with disabilities have been regarded and treated over the years – or, rather, disregarded and maltreated. I explore the research findings about the impacts of disabilities and present what I learned from my own research into progressive disability.

As well as requiring knowledge and curiosity about people who are different from you, to be fully human also requires some self-understanding, and one way in – therapy – is explored in Chapter 4. Here, I highlight 10 reasons why life can be hard, and offer 'humanity therapy' – a profound, unscripted, human encounter – as a means of discovery. Chapter 5 extends and transcends this process with an exploration of spirituality through suffering and ways to pursue a more soulful life. Chapter 6 broadens the focus to society at large, its sickness, selfishness and soullessness, and the closing Chapter 7 challenges us to reclaim our hard-earned birthright: our humanity.

Some portions of this book have appeared elsewhere, in college essays, papers, blog posts and magazine and journal articles I have written. It is all my own work, the product of my own experiences and explorations: my life and soul. What I present here is just one particular set of views from one particular vantage point. I inherited one neurological condition and acquired another in midlife. I do not wish or claim to speak for all people with disabilities, impairments, injuries and illnesses. I apologise in advance if I have made mistakes, inaccurate assumptions or misrepresented you.

And I offer this book as a tribute to all of us who are living with our varied disabilities. May the rest of the world learn to do so as well, and thereby pass the Humanity Test.

Terminology and language

I identify as 'a person with a disability', and I use this terminology throughout the book. Whoever you are, you are a person first. I acknowledge that some prefer to use 'disabled person' to emphasise that this is someone who is unjustly disabled not by their body or symptoms but by society. It's a good and valid point; it's just that for me, it's not the whole story. I do use non-disabled rather than able-bodied, because I see that as the key difference: some of us have impairments, diseases, injuries or conditions that disable us; most don't, and the rest of it flows from there.

1. Introduction –
Failing the Humanity Test

'The greatness of humanity is not in being human, but in being humane.'
Mahatma Gandhi

The secret to happiness, according to Australian comedian Jim Jefferies, is to be good looking. Everyone is somewhere on a bell curve of attractiveness; he rates them from one to 10.

'Ones are as rare as 10s,' says Jefferies, in a live stage show in Nashville. 'I've seen about five Ones in my life. Ones don't really leave the house. They know they upset the rest of us. The only time you catch a One is if they're going to a doctor's appointment or something. And it really is upsetting. You walk by, they're normally being lifted out of a minivan with a special crane onto a special chair. And when you see a One, it does ruin your day, doesn't it? You walk by the One and you're like, "Oh fuck me. Oh that's a fucking One if ever I've seen one." You get to work and you can't focus and your boss is like "What's wrong with you?" And you're like, "Argh, I saw a fucking One, didn't I".'

The audience laps it up. Jefferies has a good delivery; he is funny. But the segment reveals that it's still culturally okay to target disability; it is, perhaps, the last acceptable prejudice. If Jefferies had denigrated a representative of any other minority group in this way, it would have been career ending.

Joking aside, let us imagine life for the 'One' in this sketch. He – in my imagination, it's a man – has a severe disability. Let's say he acquired it in adulthood. This means he has experienced great loss in what he is able to do, impacting his ability to work, create, recreate and relate. Whatever fine qualities he may have, whatever he has achieved, however much he has loved and lived, these are all irrelevant to those who view disability through Jefferies' eyes. It's bad enough that the 'One' is having to contend with an illness or accident that took away some of his functionality. Now Jefferies is robbing him of his attractiveness, dignity, and even right to appear in public.

He might be your parent, child, uncle, teacher, partner, friend. He might be you.

Funny, huh?

§

A leading candidate for the worst word in the English language might be the noun 'invalid', which is defined by the *Oxford Languages* online dictionary as 'a person made weak or disabled by illness or injury'. The other meaning of invalid is as an adjective, with a slightly different emphasis in its pronunciation: 'not legally recognized because it contravenes a regulation or law; not true because based on erroneous information or unsound reasoning; not conforming to the correct format or specifications.' The online dictionary helpfully lists similar words, including worthless, illegitimate, incorrect, improper, unacceptable, cancelled, abolished, false, faulty, inadequate, wrong, unjustified, untenable, absurd, preposterous.

Non-disabled people are valid human beings.

Invalids, by definition in the English language, are regarded as invalid.

'Everyone who is born holds dual citizenship, in the kingdom of the well and in the kingdom of the sick,' wrote Susan Sontag in 1977. 'Although we all prefer to use only the good passport, sooner or later each of us is obliged, at least for a spell, to identify ourselves as citizens of that other place.'

People with disabilities – one in seven humans – are largely confined to 'that other place'. Anyone deemed 'disabled' is largely invisible, unwelcome in the non-disabled world, unless, as sociologist Erving Goffman says (1963), they can 'pass' for normal.

There are thus two worlds. In one lies power, privilege and validity; in the other, the supposed lack, shame and misery of the invalids. The barriers that separate the two worlds – physical, political and psychological – diminish us all. They cripple our societies. They are woundings to our shared humanity.

§

The key to happiness is to be good looking? No, it's not. If you define yourself in those terms, you will always feel ugly. The key to happiness is to live in a way that is true to your soul. For we are all human souls. Anybody can lead a soulful life. We can all aspire to be like Carl Jung's fantasy guru Philemon, who appeared to him in a dream, and who 'had a lame foot, but was winged in spirit' (Jung, 1961/1995, p.209): a perfect soul, despite an imperfect body.

Soul is your wise self, your larger self, perhaps your eternal self.

Soul is like a muscle for living: the more you exercise it, the bigger it gets, and the bigger it gets, the stronger you are.

Soul is where we return to when we finally, eventually, one way or another, get out of our tiny minds of rationality, logic, science and religion, and other dogmatic ways of being the world.

In his book *Care of the Soul* (1992), Thomas Moore identifies 'loss of soul' as the great malady of our times. It threatens all of us: our conversations, our families, our relationships, our work, rest and play. It cripples communities, organisations, institutions and nations. This is the true pandemic: humanity alienated from itself.

§

I used to live in the non-disabled world.

I have an inherited, degenerative neurological condition called Charcot Marie Tooth (CMT). It is named after the three neurologists who identified it in 1886. You lose strength and feeling in your feet and hands, but it usually progresses very slowly. Aside from having terrible balance, I was not really affected by CMT until my mid-40s. I could run, ski, dance and go for long hikes. I was privileged. I explored the world. I worked for glossy magazines. I wrote about golf and travel. I interviewed famous people. I stayed in the best hotels. I saw the sunrise illuminate the tip of Everest. I saw the sunset from the summit of Mauna Kea in Hawaii, revealing an astonishing night sky of dazzling infinitudes. I spent my 30s living in America. I was an Englishman in New York. I got married in Rome. I came home to London.

Volunteering at the Central London Samaritans in Soho changed everything, and I was inspired to train to be a counsellor, marking a switch from what Jung called 'the morning of life' to the very different afternoon, when people sometimes turn their attention from the outer world to the inner one (wrote Jung: 'Who looks outside dreams;

who looks inside awakes' (1992, p.33)). Today, I am a counselling psychologist and psychotherapist working in private practice.

During these years, my CMT symptoms progressed such that my walk became cumbersome, slow and uncomfortable, standing unaided became difficult, I experienced reduced manual dexterity, and my energy levels often flagged. My relationship with my environment, with others, and with myself – my identity – all changed considerably.

As part of my doctorate, I decided to research the experience of progressive disability through the voices of people who have CMT. Nine days before I presented my research proposal to my training institute's approval panel, in September 2013, I was diagnosed with an entirely unrelated and better-known chronic degenerative neurological condition, also without cure: Parkinson's. In the hierarchy of neurological conditions, the more challenging Parkinson's trumps CMT in severity (but is in turn trumped by amyotrophic lateral sclerosis (ALS) (also known as motor nuerone disease) and multiple sclerosis (MS)).

The Parkinson's diagnosis, though not a surprise when it was finally delivered, was devastating. I was the victor in some kind of cruel and grotesque anti-lottery – literally one in a million, a freak. Life would be much harder from here on in. And yet… I couldn't overlook the timing, the weird synchronicity of the diagnosis. After a while, this was something I was able to take as a kind of affirmation of my research: a sign that I was on the right track, that making sense of chronic illness is one of the things I was put on this earth to do – a purpose.

My Parkinson's diagnosis greatly amplified the importance to me and my life of my research. It facilitated a better acceptance of ill health, an accelerated individuation process, and an existential and spiritual midlife transformation. It has been good for my soul. I'd just turned 50 when I was diagnosed with Parkinson's. In many ways, this is when I began to live. Ill health is brutal, horrific, desperate at times. But it is not always a tragedy. Sometimes it heals.

§

Disability is the most different of human differences, the last frontier of prejudice, a challenge to polite, able-bodied society. It is a reminder, a rebuke, an affront, a horror, a terror.

One of the most difficult things about being diagnosed with a chronic health condition is sharing the news. No one wants to be the bearer of bad tidings. And in my experience, many people do not respond well.

Some act as if you have said nothing at all and quickly change the subject.

Some take the opportunity to tell you all about their own travails: when I tried to explain to a colleague why my walking was so bad, he responded by spending the next 10 minutes talking about a bump on his finger that was diagnosed as harmless and which, after a couple of months, disappeared. Some assume you must be devastated; others insist that you be positive. People will offer to pray for you. People you might have known for decades may not respond to your email and are never heard from again. It feels as if few people are particularly interested in your experience or what you might have to say.

Disability is a question. It is a test – the Humanity Test.

The way you respond to the test is very revealing – an instant measure of how humane a human you are on any given day; an X-ray of your humanity, a snapshot of your soul, a barometer of your being.

It tells you everything you need to know about your attitude towards people who are different from you.

Let's say it's you in the Jim Jefferies scenario above. You're walking down the street and you encounter someone with a disability. What happens? Perhaps it starts with a physiological reaction. Your body registers that here is something different. Perhaps you experience a visceral revulsion, or fear, or dread. These might swiftly be followed by a thought: 'Oh fuck me. Oh, that's a fucking One if ever I've seen one,' in the case of Jefferies. Others may have a different initial thought: 'Life must be hell for that poor bastard' or, 'I'm so glad that's not me' or, 'I wonder what happened to her' or, 'This could be awkward or embarrassing – don't get involved, keep away, look away.'

This will then be followed by a series of secondary thoughts and associated emotions. 'He's ruined my day,' in the case of Jefferies; 'That's my taxes paying for all his equipment and medical care' (anger); 'I'm not sure I could handle it if I were in that situation' (fear); 'She must've done something to deserve that, that would never happen to me' (self-righteousness); 'I'm just so happy it's not me' (gratitude); 'That poor woman, I really feel for her' (compassion). Or, 'I've been lucky – I don't do enough to help those less fortunate, those in need' (guilt).

Our bodies and our minds are designed to feed us this kind of information. These thoughts and feelings are perfectly natural. But now we come to the crux of the Humanity Test. At some point, usually just milliseconds after the first encounter, we arrive at a kind of closing thought. And each closing thought suggests an appropriate action. What do you need to do in the situation? For Jefferies, the conclusion is: 'He shouldn't be allowed out,' and he goes to work and complains about the 'fucking One' that ruined his day.

Others move beyond their own unease and consider the plight of the individual. But it seems too horrific, too unfair, so they arrive at a victim-blaming explanation: she deserves this in some way – this is bad karma, or the gods or God is punishing her for past misdeeds, or she made herself ill by not looking after herself or thinking bad thoughts. It's not your fault and nothing is required of you – walk on by. Perhaps they might make a small donation to a charity later in the day. Others may decide that they must Do Something, right now; they must 'help' (and some will insist on 'helping', regardless of whether such 'help' is needed or wanted). But in general, there is a broad consensus around the concluding thought and action: It is dreadful. Stay away.

In this way, most people fail the Humanity Test.

§

There is an Advanced Humanity Test, too.

Suppose in the Jefferies sketch, you're the other person, the 'fucking One', on your way to a doctor's appointment, 'being lifted out of a minivan with a special crane onto a special chair'.

What then? What is life like for you?

Perhaps it seems too horrific even to contemplate. Perhaps you imagine that life would not be worth living.

Life would undoubtedly be hard. Extremely hard. Maybe there would be physical pain. And the logistics of everyday life – getting around, eating, sleeping, washing, going to the toilet, shopping, working – would be extremely challenging.

Mobility is a fundamental part of being alive. It is how we separate and individuate as children. It is the means by which we encounter and commune with the world. It is a major part of how we participate in society. Restricting mobility is how we punish people: misbehaving children are confined to immobility on the 'naughty step'; unruly adolescents area 'grounded'; criminals are incarcerated. Any loss of mobility through bodily damage, disease or impairment can be devastating. Writes therapist Shula Wilson: 'Damage to the body, which is a source of self-identity and self-regard, can cause severe emotional upheaval, loss of identity and a diminished sense of self-worth' (2003, p.23).

According to the social model of disability, the problem exists not in you but in society – in a hostile, disempowering environment that fails to accommodate you. The Humanity Test can be fleeting – passing a stranger on a street. The Advanced Humanity Test can fill every waking moment. It is only for the chosen few, the warriors of living.

But it's not just the environment that's difficult; it's other people too, and other people, as Sartre pointed out, can be hell. Your very presence poses the Humanity Test to everyone you encounter. And you have to deal with all of their reactions, which can be violent, cruel, judgemental, strange, shaming, embarrassing, sometimes unintentionally unhelpful, and sometimes, just occasionally, really great.

Britain prides itself on being a 'tolerant' nation. But even if it were true, is that really the best we can do? It means we disapprove of others but we put up with them – all those other people who we don't know but don't like the look of. What a miserly, prejudiced aspiration it is to be merely 'tolerant'.

And it's not just the psychology of others that can work against you. There's your own, too.

People with impairments often internalise the negative social biases and stereotypes of others. This can manifest as feelings of shame.

Shame.

'Did you hear?' someone may say to you. 'She had a Down's syndrome baby. What a shame.'

'You know he was in a car crash? They say he'll never walk again. What a pity.'

'Apparently she got Parkinson's. Such a shame.'

There is shame, but it belongs more to the judger rather than the judged.

It belongs to the person who ghosts a friend once they become disabled. It belongs to the person who doesn't go to see the terminally ill relative because it might be uncomfortable. It belongs to the royal family, who locked up and neglected the Queen's cousins, Katherine and Nerissa Bowes-Lyon, because they had an intellectual disability. It belongs to all of us when we look away; when we fail the Humanity Test. It belongs to Jim Jefferies. It is not the disabled man who is ugly.

The ugliness is in Jefferies' reaction. In the words of John Lennon, you can't hide it when you're crippled inside.

In the movie *Shrek*, an ogre lives by himself in a swamp. Society hates him, fears him, comes to hunt him down. But they do not know him. He is strong, brave and principled. He wins the heart of Princess Fiona. His inner beauty shines through. The antidote to shame is love.

Life is hard enough with a disability without non-disabled people being weird around you and treating you like an ogre. People are afraid. Often they are not hostile. Often they are nice, decent people who worry about getting it wrong and causing offence or embarrassment. They have probably read those articles with headlines like: 'The 37 things not to say to someone in a wheelchair.'

Maybe it's not that hard. If you want to pass the Humanity Test and get along with a fellow human who is different from you, here's a suggestion: Don't assume anything. Don't assume someone's disability has ruined their life. Don't assume that it hasn't. Don't assume that they don't want to talk about it. Don't assume that they do. Don't assume that they need or want your help. Don't assume that they don't. Don't assume that they're miserable or happy, angry or enlightened, completely useless or possessed of special powers, such as being a pinball wizard. Don't assume that you know anything at all about why they are disabled, what you would do in their shoes, or what they should do. Don't say you know how someone feels – you don't. Any such assumptions are pre-judging another – the very definition of prejudice. It's important to learn about disability and be aware of the challenges people face, of course, and to be an advocate for social justice. But the billion people on our planet who happen to have a disability are first and foremost people. Like snowflakes, no two are alike; each one is precious and beautiful. If you want to know someone and understand their experience of life, it might help to talk less and listen more, and ponder why that is so.

§

There is also a Group Humanity Test.

People with disabilities are largely excluded from everyday life. There is an overriding picture of isolation, secrecy and invisibility. Society looks away – a kind of grand dissociation. The disabled are largely relegated to the disabled world, and kept there by discrimination.–They are denied the opportunity to participate, to have their unique skills acknowledged and used, appreciated and rewarded. Their opportunities for growth are now circumscribed.

Disability activist and academic Tom Shakespeare writes: 'Good societies enable people to cope... by removing barriers, providing supports, and by treating disability as part of normal human variation, rather than an abnormality to be discarded' (2018, p.22).

Such societies are rare.

Do you want to live in a place where the state sanctions the mass murder of people with disabilities, as in Nazi Germany? Or somewhere that enforces their sterilisation without consent, or has 'ugly laws' that make it illegal for persons who are 'unsightly or unseemly' to appear in public, as did lots of US states up until as recently as 1974? Or perhaps you'd support laws that forbid disabled people from procreating, like in China under Mao?

Does your country pass the Humanity Test? Does your town, community, neighbourhood? Your family? Your place of work? Your industry? Your children's schools? Your place of recreation? Or, if you have one, your place of worship?

Do you pass the Humanity Test?

Writes Watermeyer: 'The truth is that we all, disabled and nondisabled alike, struggle with the cultural phenomenon of disability... Difference is something we find hard' (2013, p.5).

Sooner or later we must all look in the mirror and ask: 'What sort of person do you want to be? What sort of world do you want to create?'

§

Do counselling and psychotherapy pass the Group Humanity Test? Therapy is often part of the problem, rather than a part of the solution. The profession is increasingly interested in working with difference and diversity in an enlightened way, especially in terms of 'race', sexual orientation, class, gender and age, but this multicultural interest does not seem to extend to disability.

Therapists can be quick to offer clients moralistic and shaming psychological explanations for their physical travails. Writes Sontag in *Illness as Metaphor*:

Psychological theories of illness are a powerful means of placing the blame on the ill... Nothing is more punitive than to give a disease a meaning – that meaning invariably being a moralistic one. (1977, pp.58–59)

This worrying trend, which I call *psychofascism,* appears to be on the increase.

Disability does not feature much in counselling psychology training programmes in the UK. The extensive reading lists provided for my counselling psychology professional doctorate a dozen years ago did not include a single book, article or other resource on disability.

The field of body psychotherapy, which could be enormously beneficial to those with impaired bodies, is almost entirely silent on disability. This totalitarian rejection of anything other than idealised, normative, healthy and pain-free bodies is disappointing.

Psychological research into disability is both sparse and often highly prejudicial.

The therapy profession is supposed to be enlightened, progressive and inclusive; our disciplines exist to serve the dispossessed, the alienated, the outsiders of this world. Yet people with disabilities – human beings often most in need of support, compassion and love – remain largely uncared for, untouched and untouchable.

§

One day I was watching an okapi at London Zoo with my daughter, who was about four years old at the time. I'm sorry to say I was rather making fun of the okapi. 'Look at him. What is he?' I said. 'He looks like he was made from leftover parts from other animals. He's got the legs of a zebra, the body of a horse, the head of a moose – ridiculous!'

'Daddy,' she scolded me. 'That's just how he be.'

Young children have still to learn how to fail the Humanity Test.

The philosopher Martin Heidegger said we are 'thrown' into existence (1927/1962, p.276). I think what he's saying is that we are born into this imperfect body, in this peculiar place, to these odd parents or caregivers, at this strange time.

We don't know why.

We didn't ask for any of it.

And living is not always easy.

What kind of okapi are you?

How do you suffer?

Because of your body? Or your mind?

Are you feeling stressed, frightened, excluded, unloved?

Is life hard because of poverty, your past, or all the losses you have had to endure?

Or just because it all seems pointless?

And yet restrictions, constraints, hardships and sufferings can inspire us to transcend them. They can spur vitality rather than hinder it. Health conditions and disabilities are not generally desirable, but they can be an invitation to respond, and in your response you may, if you're lucky, access and activate the best parts of you – parts you didn't know existed. They are like a shot of psychic penicillin; a little dose of death that brings you more fully to life.

There is no rainbow without rain, no rose without thorns. No ease without disease, no ability without disability.

§

Another time at London Zoo, again with my daughter, we're sitting at this little outdoor cafe, eating fish and chips, enjoying the sunshine, minding our own business, when suddenly, in this cage near us, a little monkey pops up and stares at us. My left hand is shaking as usual. The monkey starts mimicking my tremor, shaking his left hand so convincingly that he looks exactly like a monkey with Parkinson's. Is he laughing? Am I being ridiculed by a rare Vietnamese Francois' langur? Is this a bit of interspecies ableism? Or is it a message from one monkey to another: 'Hey you, lighten up.'

To pass the Humanity Test, you'll want to hang on to your sense of humour.

A couple of years ago, we were on a bus. My daughter was by now 11. A little old man who clearly had Parkinson's got up to get off the bus but then froze. 'I can't move,' he said. 'I'm stuck.'

A voice rang out from his wife, or carer – a voice of compassion and impatience in equal measure: 'Come on, Jerry.'

Jerry finally lunged forward and got off the bus. We found this little tableau highly amusing.

'That's you in a couple of years, Dada,' joked my daughter. 'Come on, Jerry.'

I am at first horrified that my daughter sees me this way, but I come to see the incident as heartening. Jerry seems okay. The woman's plea has become our rallying cry whenever we think someone is making a fuss – usually me – or a motivational mantra to the self when faced with a challenge.

We don't do victimhood

Or we try not to.

There is no humility or modesty in victimhood. It is a kind of narcissism.

Come on, Jerry.

§

We know that good news can come disguised as bad news, and vice versa. The Dalai Lama says: 'Remember that sometimes not getting what you want is a wonderful stroke of luck.' The same is often true of getting what you don't want – like a disability, disease or injury.

This is beautifully illustrated in the ancient Chinese tale of the farmer with one horse.

One morning the farmer wakes to discover his horse has vanished.

'That's terrible,' say the villagers. 'Your one horse is gone. What bad luck!'

The farmer replies, 'Good luck, bad luck, who can say?'

The next morning the horse comes back down from the hills and brings 10 wild horses with him.

'All those horses,' say the villagers. 'You are so lucky!'

The farmer replies, 'Good luck, bad luck, who can say?'

The farmer asks his son to break the horses in, tame them and train them. Out riding one of the horses the next day, the son is thrown to the ground and breaks his back.

'So sorry for your bad news,' say the concerned villagers. 'Now you have no one to work the farm. What bad luck.'

The farmer replies, 'Good luck, bad luck, who can say?'

The next day, the Emperor's men come and take every able-bodied young man to fight in a war in a distant province. The farmer's son is spared as he can barely walk.

Say the villagers. 'You are so lucky!'

The farmer replies, 'Good luck, bad luck, who can say?'

Disability and disease: Bad luck? Yes, actually. There's no getting around it. You can't paint a big smiley face on excruciating symptoms. But maybe these unpalatable confections come with some small measure of good luck, too.

2. Biography –
Getting on my nerves

'Today I consider myself the luckiest man on the face of the earth.'
Lou Gehrig

It is a Sunday morning in April 2015, and I am sitting on the sofa at home in London, surrounded by all my worries and disappointments and newspapers full of bad news, all gathered together in a pitiful, unholy congregation.

I am having a midlife crisis. My marriage has begun an inexorable disintegration. The couples counselling sessions over the winter are difficult. The descent happens slowly at first, then quickly, crash-landing two years hence with a bumpy divorce that would prove very costly, emotionally as well as financially. Our shared future, who we were in our youth, a sense of security, this very home – all would be gone. It is irredeemably sad.

My old career in journalism and I similarly have drifted apart. I am nearing the end of a long and expensive training for a career in psychotherapy that I didn't think I could do. I am thus caught between worlds: not belonging in either, anxious, unexpectedly emotional at inopportune moments, lost in space.

My body is giving up on me. I'd always struggled physically because of CMT disease, but then came Parkinson's disease too. Both conditions are starting to make their presence felt, turning me into a shuffling, shaking shadow of my former self.

My mother is starting to show signs of dementia, brought on by a brain tumour that in two years will kill her.

It is spring but everything feels like death.

The sounds of mournful, badly sung hymns enter from the church next door, doubling down the mournful dirge inside my head. 'How weary, stale, flat and unprofitable seem to me all the uses of this world,' says Hamlet. Life is 'an unweeded garden that grows to seed; things rank and gross in nature possess it merely.'

I put on the TV. The London Marathon is on. Great. The annual reminder of failure and regret. My personal Everest whose summit is beyond me.

Twenty-five years earlier, I ran it, but dropped out after 20 miles, in pain and semi-delirious. I always wished I'd finished the race. And I always intended to have another go. But the years rolled by, life got in the way, and my running days quickly became a distant memory.

I tell all this to my eight-year-old daughter as we watch the lycra-clad human gazelles on the TV, effortlessly breezing through the London streets. She has heard it all before, a year ago, and no doubt the year before, and the year before that. I am about to launch into a fatherly pontification about regret and the road not taken when she yawns and says: 'Do it next year, Daddy. You can just walk the whole thing.'

Antoine de Saint-Exupéry said: 'Grown-ups never understand anything by themselves, and it is tiresome for children to be always and forever explaining things to them' (1943/2018, p.86).

And so, a year later, on a gorgeous morning, I find myself in Greenwich Park, at the very back of the amassed 36,000 Marathon starters, alongside a man in a rhino costume, another dressed as a giant ear, and another wearing a cardboard lighthouse. There is said to be someone doing the marathon carrying a tumble dryer, but he is nowhere to be seen.

I am the only one with a walking stick.

I walk the Marathon in two days, accompanied at different times by various family and friends, stopping for fortifications at hostelries along the way, and for Sunday night at a hotel right beside Tower Bridge, the halfway point. By Monday afternoon, despite little sleep, a missed turn somewhere in the Isle of Dogs and an exploding blister in Poplar, I find my groove. My friend Stuart and I route-march along the Embankment in the rain. I feel stronger and taller with every step. The group grows, joined by my brother, sister and the mastermind of the whole operation, my daughter, with some of her school friends in tow. We all power along Birdcage Walk and the sun comes out, as if in benediction; then past Buckingham Palace, cheered all the way, and into the home stretch, the Mall, where a sea of blue and white balloons, banners and bodies awaits – Parkinson's UK has laid on a special finish. I have raised more than £17,000 for them and CMT UK. I have received so much support and love. I cross the line hand-in-hand with my daughter. I am last. I miss the world record by about a day. But it is my proudest moment. I feel like the champion. 'The time to live is now,' I say on the little film that Parkinson's UK made (46,000 views). 'I feel like I really lived today.'

The distance between my old life and my new life, from hopelessness to hope, breakdown to breakthrough, victim to victory, was 26.2 miles.

§

I am about four and Mum takes me to see a specialist doctor about my feet. I have no arch (flat feet from Mum) and am a bit slow at running (CMT from Dad, though we are decades away from knowing that). The doctor thinks exercising my feet will help. He recommends putting a toothbrush on the floor and trying to pick it up with my toes. When we get home, I put a toothbrush on the floor and try to pick it up with my toes. I can't do it. The exercise is abandoned. As are my feet, my *pes miserabilis*.

As a teenager, physical shame is never far away. At school, my CMT is sometimes dramatically and humiliatingly exposed. I am last to be picked for sports teams. PE lessons – usually taught by men in tracksuits who try to compensate for their shortcomings with a big whistle and random acts of casual sadism – are brutal. I am last or near-last, too, in 'The Steeps' – the annual, hideous, dreaded cross-country race for the whole school, in the dead of winter, through the rain, lagoons of mud and the stench of fear and adrenaline.

My dad almost never talks about CMT, but I did once ask if it affected him at school – a strict, regimented English boarding school, which he attended between the wars. He remembered having to do the hurdles at a sports day, and he couldn't – he kept crashing into the hurdle, falling to the floor, going round and trying again and again and again, his legs covered in blood. And he remembered hearing a parent saying, 'My God, that young man does keep trying doesn't he?'

Since school, my dad has strenuously avoided any exercise. 'Whenever I felt like exercising,' he likes to say, 'I would lie down until the feeling wore off.' He is 97.

At university, I foolishly agree to go roller skating with my friends. I clutch the wall and fall and fall again, and fall my way to the middle of the massive auditorium. Then there is an announcement on the loudspeaker: 'Clear the floor please, experts only for the next 15 minutes.' I am suddenly exposed, frozen, limbs awkwardly splayed, like Mr Bean. With everyone now watching from the sidelines, I walk, fall and then crawl all the way back to the exit.

Another day, in Cambridge, there's a similar misadventure involving punting. On my first ski trip, I spend a week falling on the bunny slopes; then, on the last day, in a bid for freedom, I fall and fall and fall again, at every turn, all the way from Tignes to Val d'Isere.

§

CMT disease – sometimes known as hereditary motor and sensory neuropathy or occasionally peroneal muscular atrophy – is a group of hereditary, slowly progressive neuromuscular conditions discovered in 1886 by Frenchman Jean-Martin Charcot, his assistant Pierre Marie, and their English counterpart Howard Henry Tooth. Charcot, Napoleonic in bearing, was a Parisian celebrity of the day, known for hosting high-society receptions at his private mansion at 217 Boulevard St Germain, and his famous lectures and demonstrations of 'hysteria' at the Salpêtrière hospital, where his students included Sigmund Freud and William James. He discovered ALS, MS and CMT, and clarified what Parkinson's was – and wasn't. He is known as the founder of neurology.

CMT affects either the axons or the myelin sheaths of the peripheral nerves in the feet and lower legs and hands and lower arms, causing muscle weakness, wasting, loss of sensation and fatigue; it also compromises mobility, dexterity and balance, and sometimes results in muscle cramps, pain and tremors. The progression of the condition is gradual and idiosyncratic; there are widely differing levels of severity, even among affected family members. Some people with CMT walk with a stick or use a wheelchair. It does not affect life expectancy or cognition. There is currently no cure.

According to some worldwide estimates, CMT is more common than MS. The latter has a median estimated global prevalence of 30 per 100,000 (WHO, 2008, p.14), or approximately 2.1 million people worldwide, whereas CMT has a prevalence of 1 per 2,500 people (Yale School of Medicine, 2013), or 2.8 million people worldwide. (There is a correlation between incidence of MS and distance from the equator – MS is comparatively rare in high-population areas such as Brazil, northern Africa and India.) Yet CMT is largely unknown, even among some medical professionals. 'It seems to be almost a hidden disorder and yet many live the experience,' says Dr Elizabeth Barrett, a New York psychotherapist and teacher who co-wrote the booklet *What It's Like to Live with Charcot-Marie-Tooth* (Barrett & Birdsall, 2008).

CMT is an unfashionable disease with a peculiar name, bereft of celebrity spokespersons. It turns its chosen few into people who are ungainly, clumsy and slow. It often comes with a lot of intrafamilial shame and blame. It isolates and excludes, and it only ever deteriorates. It affects every aspect of one's way of being in the world, and the only constant is change as the unstoppable condition unfurls. People with CMT suffer in silence.

I have lived with CMT from birth. My father has it, albeit with a mild presentation, as is the case with my brother, while one of my sisters has more significant symptoms.

I was formally diagnosed in 2002. I asked the neurologist at Yale whether he thought it was okay to have children. And he said, 'I wouldn't let it stop me. Everybody's got something, you know. There's ways of managing it, it doesn't affect your longevity, and there will probably be better ways of managing it in the future, maybe even a cure.'

My daughter, it would turn out many years later, has not inherited my CMT.

§

Fifteen years after my first, doomed attempt at skiing, I am back in the Alps, in Méribel. It's the end of a spectacular week among the endless web of trails that are spread out across three vast valleys (I did finally learn how to navigate my way down most slopes without falling so much). I am living in the US now and am here on my own, writing a travel story for *The New York Times* (Barton, 1998). My bags are packed and I am waiting for the coach and the long journey back to New York. Then something odd happens. I unzip my big ski-boot bag, remove my giant ski boots, and place them on a nearby wall – a kind of offering, or sacrifice, or cleansing; a disposal of the vanities. It is as if I am watching someone else perform this solemn ceremony. I am powerless to stop it. Having mastered skiing despite my CMT, my body appears to be making a unilateral decision to give it up (rather

than waiting for the inevitable time in the future when it gives up me).
I never ski again.

§

Little by little, embarrassing moment by embarrassing moment, my
physical decline opens up something else:

- At the start of a self-development workshop, the participants all
  stand in a circle and introduce themselves. After a few seconds, I
  realise with horror that I can't do this. The simple act of standing
  still, unaided, is now beyond me. I voice my confession and ask if
  I can sit down. A chair is provided. There is no fuss. I feel warmth
  from the teacher and the group throughout the day.

- I am covering the Open golf tournament in St Andrews, Scotland.
  I am walking on the golf course with a colleague but struggling,
  self-conscious and embarrassed. And I just blurt out: 'I'm really
  sorry but I'm not able to walk normally today.' I've never said that to
  anyone before. She is kind and curious. She says, 'Oh well, let's just
  walk really slowly. We'll walk together.'

- In class at the Metanoia Institute, where I am studying, I am about
  to make a presentation to my peers, outlining my doctoral research
  project. I am nervous. There is so much shame around CMT. The
  presentation goes well. Afterwards, there is a good discussion. I
  am choked up and unable to speak, because what is happening is
  simply revelatory: people are talking about CMT!

§

'The scan was abnormal,' says Professor Edwards, my NHS consultant.
'The results are consistent with Parkinson's disease.' The cells in one
small, dark area of my brain that are supposed to produce dopamine,
the rock star of neurotransmitters, are taking early retirement. They've
had enough. They probably started shutting down years ago, for
reasons unknown. The Parkinson's is entirely unrelated to CMT.

Professor Edwards has a gentle tone. He is smiling slightly as
he delivers the news, as if to say, kindly, 'Hey, you know, this is
going to be okay.' He has an optimistic outlook on management,
medications, prognosis, the race for a cure, life expectancy and living
with Parkinson's. The words are harsh but they fall softly. I thank

Professor Edwards, then stumble out of the neurology hospital, into the indifferent London streets.

In the afternoon, I return to my placement (what was I thinking?). I don't tell anyone my news. I see clients. There is an envelope for me at reception. Inside there is a card. 'All change,' it says on the cover. It is from one of my first clients here, a lovely person; our sessions ended a year earlier. They write: 'I was really struggling, and the time I spent with you has made a huge difference… I am so much more able to live the life I want to live… you really have made a significant difference to my life.' I have kept it together all day; this beautiful card does me in.

Much later, I lie awake wondering how I am going to tell everyone. What will people think or say? I am not expecting the outpouring of kind words and offers of help that comes from friends and family scattered around the world. A colleague in the US offers to raise funds to pay for treatment. Another in China says he will explore eastern remedies and herbal medicines. A friend in India invites me on a drive into the high Himalayas. A new term is about to begin at the Metanoia Institute. I send a group email with my news. In their kindness and presence, my colleagues show their true colours. They are Humanity Test champions.

David Tannenbaum, a New York City psychotherapist with quite severe CMT, sends me the most lovely email, which concludes:

> Since I know you personally, I feel very confident that you will come through this in time brilliantly. Faith to me is about trusting that we will eventually make our way through any difficulty. By allowing ourselves to go through all the feeling states of our conditions we are that much more in touch with ourselves and are so much more present with ourselves and others. I often need to remind myself that I am whole and perfect and beautiful just the way I am. I don't think I would have figured this out without my physical challenges. I have realized more and more that my sense of peace and tranquillity, which is really what is most important, does not depend on having a perfect body.

Of course, not everyone is so enlightened. People often don't know what to say, so they say nothing. Several friendships end in that silence. Or there is a mumbled sorry, or a story of some relative who suffered and died. In my experience, men are much more likely to fail the Humanity Test than women.

Around this time, the actor and comedian Robin Williams takes his own life. It emerges that he had recently been diagnosed with Parkinson's. There is a lot of commentary on social media. 'No wonder he topped himself,' writes one man. 'I'd do the same if I had Parkinson's, I wouldn't want to be a burden on anyone.' I find this quite upsetting. I write a riposte about giving up at the first bump in the road and I highlight some of the potential advantages of Parkinson's. A reply says I am guilty of 'New Age blue sky thinking'.

I decide that I am allowed to be positive about Parkinson's, or negative, too, for that matter, but people who don't have it are not entitled either to demand bravery or expect negativity from those that do.

Of all the many varied and sometimes baffling reactions from people to news of my neurological ill health, one of the oddest comes from Donald Trump. It's July 2014, a year after my diagnosis, and I am in his office in New York, high above Fifth Avenue, about to interview him for a magazine article (Barton, 2014). As I set up the voice recorders on his desk, my tremor – a kind of barometer of stress and nervousness – is quite noticeable. 'Sorry about my hand,' I tell him. 'I have Parkinson's.'

'Oh that's great,' says the future president. 'That gets better as you get older, right? Some of my friends have it – they do great with it.'

Norman Vincent Peale – a pastor and the author of *The Power of Positive Thinking* (1952/2012) – was a friend of Trump's parents. He had a huge influence on Trump.

Positivity is great – to a point. The positive thoughts can become tyrannical. They turn into exaggerations, spin, irrational optimism, delusions and lies. You start to believe your own bullshit. You malign and punish anyone who disagrees with you – anyone who dares to say that the emperor has no clothes. You become divorced from reality. Parkinson's is degenerative? Fake news. Such deluded, reality-denying, pathologically positive thinking might be fairly harmless for, say, a salesman or a gung-ho life coach. But in some jobs it could be problematic. President of the United States, for example.

§

A friend messages me: she has a spare theatre ticket. We meet for a meal and arrive in the upper stalls just before the curtain goes up. The only way to get to our seats is to walk up a steep aisle, then along the back, then down the steep aisle on the other side. The latter – a series of irregular, narrow steps with no handrail – is my downfall. I can't do it. But I set off anyway. I wobble and stumble. I feel under pressure: my performance is in front of an actual audience. This makes me even shakier, wobblier, weaker. I fall backwards and am sitting in a man's lap. He and an usher try to lift me to my feet. A woman with a clipboard and a walkie-talkie appears. I have created 'a situation'. When I finally get to my seat, rejoining my concerned friend, I feel shamed, embarrassed, exhausted. The overriding thought is: 'You don't belong here.'

Suddenly, where once I was welcome, I am now a misfit. 'Fitting' is 'a comfortable and unremarkable majority experience that often goes unnoticed,' writes Rosemarie Garland-Thomson; 'misfitting', by contrast, is a 'formative experience of slamming against an unsustaining environment'(Garland-Thomson, 2011, p.597).

I go home feeling sick and tired. I am sick and tired of feeling sick and tired. There's a strange ache of hopelessness in my abdomen, too. My teeth hurt. My mind is polluted.

There are many such misadventures. Another time I go to a spa. I have to sign a form saying that I don't have any health conditions ('You must sign or you can't come in,' says the woman at the desk). There are no accessible changing rooms. No handrails. To get into one of the thermal pools, I have no option but to crawl across the slippery marble floor. This spa – like so many gyms and swimming pools – caters to people who need it least: the young, toned, physically fit and non-disabled. The beautiful people. Those who need it most – the unkempt, disfigured, wheezing masses – are not welcome. Those who are deemed repellant will be repelled. Humanity Test result: fail.

§

Why did I get Parkinson's? I put the question to a private Harley Street doctor who specialises in it. 'Well, we know why,' he says. 'The cells in the *substantia nigra* region of your brain stopped producing dopamine.' This is a classic medical model answer: the machine stops performing, we identify which parts of the machine are faulty, and we try to fix them as best we can.

'Yes but why?'

'Oh,' he says. 'We don't know. Probably environmental.'

Most experts believe that it is precipitated by the presence of allergens, pathogens, a toxin or a virus in people with a genetic predisposition. Nutrition, inflammation and mitochondrial function are thought to play a role. Dairy products might be associated with an increased risk or progression of Parkinson's. A decreased risk or progression, by contrast, may be associated with fruit and vegetables, fish, soy, red wine, tea, caffeine. At the start of the year in which I was diagnosed, I gave up caffeine. And I later read that coffee drinkers – and smokers actually – are 40% less likely to get Parkinson's. So I thought I'd given it to myself. But Professor Edwards said that, by the time you're diagnosed, you've probably already had it for at least a decade.

From 1990 to 2015, the number of people with Parkinson's worldwide more than doubled, from 2.6 million to 6.3 million. By 2040 it is expected to have doubled again, to at least 12.9 million. Some call this a pandemic. They place the blame squarely on the relentless insistence of the Western world on continuing to use dangerous industrial chemicals and synthetic pesticides (Dorsey et al., 2020). They cite the solvent trichloroethylene, for instance, which has been linked to Parkinson's. The US Environmental Protection Agency (EPA) proposed a ban, but in 2017, after lobbying by the chemical industry, it was kicked into the tall grass – a craven and shameful decision. Something is being protected, but it isn't the environment.

Similarly, the pesticide paraquat, banned in many countries, and the nerve toxin chlorpyrifos, the most widely used insecticide in the US, are probably responsible for a great deal of human suffering in the shape of Parkinson's, yet the EPA does little to stop the proliferation of their use.

It is the case that Parkinson's occurs more frequently in rural areas. The evidence for a connection between a meteoric rise in Parkinson's cases and the growing industrial use of toxic chemicals and pesticides is, say Dorsey and colleagues, 'overwhelming' (2020, p.4). US ex-servicemen who were deployed to the Vietnam War are now thought to be at a greater risk of developing Parkinson's because of exposure to Agent Orange.

I have wondered about my own history of pesticide exposure – my previous career meant I spent a lot of time on those famous, fetishised, weed-free fairways of the top golfing resorts in the world. Years ago, on a snowy day in Washington D.C., I interviewed Jay

Feldman, co-founder and director of the non-profit pressure group Beyond Pesticides, for an article in *Golf Digest*. He spoke then of the vast sums of money the chemical companies spend on lobbying – a polite word for bribery – and on hiring or co-opting the best EPA officials. Gamekeepers turned poachers; public health and safety be damned. They have sold their souls. The Golf Course Superintendents Association of America was on the payroll.

Feldman remembers that meeting. 'Those were the days when we were really hopeful that golf would advance to organic practices,' he recalls now. They didn't. When the EPA announced it was banning chlorpyrifos in food production in 2021, Feldman quoted the Golf Course Superintendents Association saying that this chemical – known to cause brain damage in children – was a 'vital tool' in their work – essentially, the prettification of golf courses (Feldman, 2021).

As for Parkinson's, Feldman directs me to his organisation's impressive archive of research, papers and evidence linking illnesses and pesticides. There is plenty.

In 2021, hundreds of lawsuits were filed by people with Parkinson's against paraquat manufacturer Syngenta/ChemChina and Chevron, which previously held the rights to sell paraquat back in the 1960s. Syngenta denies the link but there are reports of a smoking gun: internal documents that indicate the company 'may have likewise known for years that paraquat caused Parkinson's disease' (Beyond Pesticides, 2021).

According to Bloomberg News, Syngenta disclosed in August 2021 that it had already agreed to pay out $187.5 million to resolve an undisclosed number of these cases. The number of claims is expected to swell into the thousands (Feeley, 2021).

Says Feldman: 'The amassed data on Parkinson's and pesticides is troubling.'

He does not drink tap water.

Paraquat use was banned in European Union countries in 2007 but Brexit has opened up the possibility of its return to the UK. The BBC reports that paraquat is currently manufactured for export at Syngenta's UK plant in Huddersfield (Marshall & Prior, 2022). A fifth of its exports go to the developing world.

§

The 'medical model' presents a mechanistic, technical, clinical view of disease. Another view, from the other side of the mind-body Cartesian divide, is that illness is a deeply psychological process and therefore something of one's own making, leading to a dogmatic, pernicious victim-blaming mentality that underpins much supposedly holistic healing. I call this *psychofascism*. Its high priestess is Louise Hay, whose book *You Can Heal Your Life* has sold more than 50 million copies. 'I believe we create every so-called illness in our body,' she writes (1984, p.1). If you only have joyous, loving thoughts, you will stay healthy, she says. If you already are ill, fear not: you can heal yourself. Hay claims to have had cervical cancer in the 1970s – the diagnosis has never been corroborated – and to have cured it exclusively with her thoughts.

In her book, Hay also claims that diabetes comes from 'Longing for what might have been. A great need to control. Deep sorrow. No sweetness left.' 'Accidents,' she opines, 'are no accident. Like everything else in our lives, we create them.' Moreover, the 'probable cause' of Parkinson's, according to Hay, and based on no evidence at all, is 'Fear and an intense desire to control everything and everyone.' She suggests a 'new thought pattern', presumably as a cure: 'I relax, knowing that I am safe. Life is for me, and I trust the process of life.'

I have of course entertained psychological explanations for my Parkinson's. My first therapist described me as 'Metal Man'. I launched myself into adulthood armed with a copy of Susan Jeffers' *Feel the Fear and Do It Anyway* (1987). There was fear. But I pushed myself. My way of being in the world was to 'grin and bear it'. The soundtrack to my 20s and 30s was a harangue of self-criticism. Metal Man was embraced by the capitalist machine. False selves can achieve much. But there is anxiety in a suit of armour. I felt disconnected and distant from my fellow humans. It all had to change. 'Me, I will throw away,' writes Patrick Kavanagh in the poem *The Self-Slaved* (2004, p.227): 'To go on the grand tour, a man must be free from self-necessity.'

I took a clumsy step towards a midlife career change by becoming a Samaritans volunteer – a leap into unchartered waters; a full immersion into the world of emotions, people, intimacy. I became more of a subject and less of an object.

Jung wrote:

Thoroughly unprepared, we take the step into the afternoon of life. Worse still, we take this step with the false presupposition that our truths and our ideals will serve us as hitherto. But we cannot live the afternoon of life according to the program of life's morning, for what was great in the morning will be little at evening and what in the morning was true, at evening will have become a lie. (1933/2014, p.111)

So maybe Metal Man literally got on my nerves, for a long time, and my nerves got fried, creating some kind of short-circuit in my brain that precipitated Parkinson's. Perhaps it's a uniquely human disease of disconnection. No other animals get it. Children do not get it either. Nobody ever gets better. Men are 50% more likely to get it than women – a ratio that is in line with the statistics on suicide and addiction. One twin study (Valdés et al., 2014) found that people with challenging jobs involving complexity are more likely to get Parkinson's. There are even pronouncements of a Parkinson's personality, as reported by Luca and colleagues (2019, original italics):

Since 1913 patients with Parkinson's disease have been described as particularly industrious, devoted to hard work, inflexible, punctual, cautious, and moralist. These psychological characteristics have been so constantly reported that the concept of '*Parkinsonian personality*' emerged.

Your body perhaps gets tired of being told what to do and harangued and neglected. Parkinson's might be an embodied manifestation of an intrapsychic schism; a lifetime of super ego-ordained fragmentation. Some of history's most fragmented people succumbed to Parkinson's, including Hitler, Franco and Mao – truly a monstrous trio of Metal Men.

At some point the brain cells that create dopamine – the neurotransmitter of love – simply give up. Perhaps they feel they are not needed: love is not wanted here.

But such an explanation strays into the realm of psychofascism. Any healthcare professional – especially a non-disabled one – who makes pronouncements like these when working with a patient is committing an act of violence.

Because we don't know. Maybe it's all just bullshit. Probably getting Parkinson's is triggered by exposure to neurotoxic chemicals, with a dash of pure dumb bad luck thrown in.

Regardless, even if Metal Man breeds Parkinson's, he does not survive its birth. Disease, vulnerability and mortality are real – a middle-fingered salute to false selves, vanity, narcissistic armour and polite conversations about the weather.

We will return to the subject of psychofascism in the next chapter. Incidentally, Louise Hay, in an interview with *The New York Times*, was asked if she really believes that people are responsible for their own deaths (Oppenheimer, 2008). Did victims of genocide, for example, or people killed in the Holocaust, get what they deserved?

'Yes, I think there's a lot of karmic stuff that goes on, past lives… it can work that way,' Hay said. 'But that's just my opinion.'

§

I am out for my usual Sunday morning bicycle ride around the quiet streets of London. It's been getting harder to do. I no longer have the strength to push off from a standing start or pedal at slow speeds. Somewhere near Notting Hill, I hesitate at a junction, start to wobble, then topple over: a spectacular crash.

I have enjoyed my adventures on two wheels. I cycled to Germany one summer with some school friends. Once I cycled from London to Madrid on my own. Another time, cycling in the Alps with a friend, we would spend the mornings heaving up a series of switchbacks to some summit or other, then freewheel at breakneck speed down the other side, leaning out around the hairpins, exuberant, elated, alive. But it's over. I sell the bike.

I can no longer play golf, either. It's just too hard physically to walk so far on numb, wasted feet; to hit a stationary ball when everything else is moving. I play my last game, alone, on the Isle of Wight, at the place where, four decades earlier, I played my first, with my dad.

'Accepting loss is hard,' I write in *Golf Digest*, in an article about my last round (Barton, 2018). The article is a farewell not just to golf and my career as a golf writer but to my relatively non-disabled youth. I get hundreds of messages from colleagues, friends and strangers.

In my work as a psychotherapist I meet all sorts of people who can't or won't. They cannot accept the death of a loved one, or a relationship, or a dream, or the image of the person they thought themselves to be. They cannot accept the troubled childhood they had, the life they have led, all the terrible things that have happened to them. Or, like King Lear, they cannot accept their mortality.

I call my dad from the 12th tee and tell him where I am. Many golfers have a special relationship with their fathers because of all the time they've spent playing together. My dad isn't a good golfer but has managed to pull off many miraculous shots, ridiculous hole-outs and, assisted by some extremely fortuitous bounces of the kind that often seem to favour him, what might be the worst hole-in-one in history. A life-long fan of Kipling, he always manages to treat the two imposters – good shots and bad shots – the same. 'You forget the bad ones anyway,' he says.

I thank him for all the golfing good times we've shared. Then I hit a booming drive, make my last par and walk off the course.

§

'Are we downhearted?'

In the daily assembly, the children on the ship crossing the Atlantic had been taught the required response: 'No we're not!'

It was 1940. The children had left their families to be dispatched across troubled waters – the ship behind them was torpedoed, 77 killed – to live with strangers in the US for the duration of the war. Among them was my mum. She was 10. There was one weekend visit from her dad, who was working as a medic on a troop ship, but otherwise, in five years abroad, she didn't see her parents at all.

She grew close to her foster mother. But when they said farewell in 1945, at the end of the war, her foster mother told Mum it would be best to cease all contact. For Mum, it was another inexplicable rejection. She told me this was like 'a wound that could not heal'.

For better and for worse, these childhood experiences shaped Mum's adult life in many significant ways. She was incredibly resilient. 'It's a great life if you don't weaken,' was one of her favourite sayings. She claimed she went into nursing not from any noble motives but because England felt so cold after the California sunshine, and she thought the hospitals would be warm. But she was a source of warmth for many. Generally, she was a champion of the underdog. She loved to watch Wimbledon and root for whoever was losing. There is barely a political party she didn't vote for. She loved the pomp and ceremony of the monarchy, but also took delight in ruffling feathers by saying it should all be abolished. She said OBE stood for Other Buggers' Efforts.

The last day she and Dad spend together, the last time they see each other, is their 63rd wedding anniversary. They are in the family home, on the white cliffs of Dover, on a beautiful summer's day. Mum thinks she is a prisoner of war. She's clutching a copy of Anne Frank's *The Diary of a Young Girl*. She explains to me and my sister how she plans to escape by jumping out of the bedroom window. When the transport finally arrives in the evening to take her to her care home, she joyfully greets the two paramedics as liberators. A couple of weeks before this, in hospital, she talked to me about her four children. 'You won't tell John what's going on, will you?' she asked me. 'Promise me you won't tell John what's going on.'

Later in the summer, one July morning, Mum gets up in the care home and has breakfast. It is a fine day. Then she goes back to bed, to sleep. At some point, instead of returning to wakefulness, she travels onwards. She leaves this world.

She was strong and unconflicted about death. 'I want to die!' she had loudly announced in the doctor's busy waiting room a few weeks earlier. After her appointment that day, she told me not to be sad after she'd gone. She'd had a hard life. She was tired. She was ready.

She had a great sense of humour. Born and raised in a house where an infamous murder once took place, Mum always had a fascination with serial killers, war, terrorism and human dramas like the OJ Simpson trial, the Elian Gonzales international custody incident, the rescue of the Chilean miners, the Costa Concordia cruise ship wreck, 9/11, the Boxing Day 2006 tsunami. Once, driving back from Scotland, we had to take a massive detour just to look at the unremarkable Lancaster house where, in 1935, a doctor – Buck Ruxton – murdered his wife and the housemaid and diced them up into disposable pieces. A couple of years before my mum died, my parents each chose one last summer vacation. Dad elected for a week in a nice resort on the shores of the Italian lakes. Mum chose a visit to Auschwitz.

She had a lot of soul.

She loved to travel but hated to fly – fellow travellers were blissfully unaware that the plane was held aloft by the sheer strength of her concentration and worry.

She loved her dogs. It was so awful when a dog died, and I always seemed to have to be there when the vet came with the needle. 'That's it, I'm not getting another,' she would say. But then, inevitably, she would. Because life goes on.

She felt guilty about CMT and my Parkinson's. 'I wish I could have it instead of you,' she used to say.

'Are we downhearted?' I would reply.

Then we'd shout out the refrain together: 'No we're not!'

I am glad she was my mum.

The portrait I painted of her hangs above my desk. As with my portrait of Dad, she is looking out of the frame at what the future holds. Her expression is rueful, wary perhaps, but her sense of humour is never far away.

Writes the poet Emily Berry (2017, p.56):

People you love can be removed from the world
(They can remove themselves)
They will be removed from the world
Didn't anybody ever tell you that.

§

I spend a week at the European Parkinson Therapy Centre in the spa town of Boario, in northern Italy. It's a few weeks since Mum died, and I feel that she is very much with me. When someone close to you dies, you are plunged into grief. The graph of wellbeing is then supposed to gradually rise and return to normal as you mourn and come to terms with the loss. For me, the graph is a mirror image of that: in Italy, I do not feel bereaved. Four years later, however, the loss has only grown.

I learn how to walk and talk and eat all over again. I learn that, in a way, everyone has Parkinson's: to be alive is to be ageing, and to be ageing is to have one's dopamine levels in inexorable freefall – mine are about the same as any 170-year-old. Life is fatal. We are all heading to the same destination, albeit by different paths. I learn that the number one symptom of Parkinson's is slowness. This helps me enjoy the Italian summer.

Doing things slowly affords the opportunity to do them mindfully and well. I stop wearing a watch. I can't be doing with those little strap holes and buttons and batteries. Suddenly, I seem to have so much more time. When I wore a watch, time had me. It had me handcuffed.

I make friends with the night. One of the Parkinson's symptoms is insomnia. (Wrote James Parkinson in 1817: 'The sleep becomes much disturbed. The tremulous motion of the limbs occur during sleep, and augment until they awaken the patient, and frequently with much agitation and alarm.') On holiday in the countryside, I am up in the wee hours trying something new: painting. It is absorbing, meditative, soothing. There is no tremor in my hands, or in my thoughts. I try to do a portrait of my dad from a photograph. I don't know what I'm doing. Trial and lots of error, night after night. And then something happens. I feel like I am tapping into some kind of sacred energy. It's as if an unseen hand is guiding me. The painting is shortlisted for the Summer Exhibition at the Royal Academy. In 2021, two of my paintings – a self-portrait and another painting of Dad – are selected for the show.

Another day, months later, another 3am moment. I wake from a deep, post-op sleep. The day before, I'd had a hernia operation – my second of the year. The first one didn't work. The problem was, when I was diagnosed with Parkinson's, I attacked it with exercise, and probably overdid it. When I had the hernia, for a while I gave up all exercise and went to the other extreme. Chocolate for breakfast? A red wine chaser? Sure, why not. Anger and self-pity are a volatile, toxic cocktail.

But right now, life is good. I feel a profound sense of wellbeing. Maybe it is from the kindness and care I received in the hospital yesterday. And the existential thrill of surviving, of being alive. And the drugs. Yes, my rapture is probably morphine induced. I put my music on shuffle and every track seems really intense, profound, numinous. All the hurt gently drifts away, out into the winter night. I am filled with gratitude. To an extent, this feeling remains to this day.

After a chaotic, rather adolescent post-diagnosis phase, I meet someone. Her name is Becky. She is a teacher and writer, with a doctorate in education. She is beautiful, clever and funny. In my first message to her, I tell her that I have Parkinson's, but that it does not define me. She replies: 'If you don't let it define you, there's no reason why I should.'

Normally, something good happens and then you feel grateful. But I think it can work the other way around, too.

§

In October 2017, in a back room at 10 Downing Street, Becky and I attend a reception for Parkinson's UK. Prime Minister Theresa May appears. She works the room, poses for photos and reads out a speech. She is taller than I expected, and has all the body language and charisma of a tree that has been struck by lightning. I wonder how many events like this she endures in a typical week, and whether there is any space at all for reflection and an inner life.

She highlights the work of Parkinson's UK, then adds: 'But as we draw inspiration from all of these things, so we should also renew our determination to step up the fight against Parkinson's. For two centuries on from Dr James Parkinson's Essay on the Shaking Palsy, we have simply not done enough or come anywhere near far enough.'

She says the government is investing more than £1 billion a year in health research. She does not mention her government's woeful treatment of people with disabilities.

It's good to be among fellow Parkinsonians. There is a sense of bonhomie. Nobody minds the spilled drinks and canapés on the floor. There is much handshaking and shaky hands.

Billy Connolly is there. He has been knighted earlier in the day. I tell him that I sometimes see him walking in Regent's Park. 'No, that's not me,' he says. 'I've heard about that guy. Can you believe, there's some poor bastard who out there who looks like me?'

He is smaller than I imagine, and his voice has lost its loud, brash edge. But he seems extremely soulful. He looks like some sort of wizard who is possibly several thousand years old.

I thank him for all the laughs. 'Ach, that was easy,' he says softly. 'Parkinson's is hard.'

§

A young man comes to see me. He is talented, handsome, popular, with a beautiful fiancé and a cool job. But he has all kinds of telltale symptoms of some kind of chronic underlying neurological condition. He has just completed a battery of diagnostic tests; the results are in, and they are devastating: he is completely healthy. He is convinced that a mistake has been made; he is paralysed by fear of an uncertain future, anxious to the point of incapacity. I cannot reach him; my words fall short and pile up on the carpet between us, to be disposed of, along with the used tissues, at the end of the session. Much is expected of this man; he perhaps unconsciously feels too small to inhabit his own life. The only words that will soothe him, that will give him an honourable discharge – 'Yes, you're ill' – I cannot give him. He does not return for another session.

I used to walk to the corner shop, trying really hard to look like a 'normal' person. Developing a disability divests you of the image of the person you thought you were, or were becoming, or who you think others want you to be. In its place emerges a progressive ability: to be and become you. My physical vulnerability can no longer be covered up. I can stop pretending. I can say what I mean, and mean what I say. I can walk as I walk. I can 'come out' as me. This is liberating.

I used to regard my body as a rather shameful contraption whose purpose was to carry my head around. Now I experience my existence mindfully and *bodyfully* – in the moment, present, alive.

If it's true that Parkinson's descends on people who are disconnected from themselves – people who push themselves too hard or too far, for example – then perhaps it's also true that Parkinson's contains some kind of a cure. It's a way for the body to get your attention.

§

A neighbourhood friend loses one of his three daughters to cancer. She is eight. For most of her short life, Vanessa Moss was a hospital patient. She endured countless rounds of chemo, radiation, operations, transfusions. Yet she never stopped smiling, singing, dancing and having fun. She charmed everyone. Hers was a rich life, full of joy.

I realise the importance to me of role models – not necessarily people I want to emulate, but people who subvert the doom and gloom, and especially those who refuse to internalise the mainstream, victimised view of disease and disability. I need confident, inspiring people who wear their physical challenges with style and ease and soul; people who show what is possible, who don't care what other people think. Often they are outsiders. The out-group is always more interesting than the in-crowd. Psychotherapy is a profession practised by and for those who live on the edge of town, on the edge of social groups, on the hard, sometimes cutting edges of their own self-knowledge.

There are many artists, musicians, poets, philosophers, teachers and therapists who have helped. People like Keats, Jung and Frankl are very much alive in these pages. Michael J. Fox, obviously. Legend. What a gift to humanity.

Clients are role models. Every day I admire, am inspired by and celebrate not 'celebrities', famous for being famous, but clients who face enormous struggles and sufferings of life, often alone, with courage and unheralded heroism. I salute them. The six women with CMT who were participants in my research into progressive disability are all my heroes. They have helped me and shown me how to be ill and how to live with disability.

My oldest sister, Diana, was misdiagnosed with Friedreich's ataxia at the age of 22. She went to the library and read that the life expectancy was 32. So she thought she had 10 years to live. She was thrilled to get the correct diagnosis a few years later: CMT. She knows how to live with style and confidence.

There's a portrait of courage that hangs on my wall. It's of a great uncle, Giles Prichard, a soldier in World War I, in uniform. He was wounded on the Western Front on 3 May, 1915. He was returned to London, to a military hospital next to what is now Tate Britain. In letters home, he made light of his major head injuries and was full of good cheer. He died on 9 August. He was 23. Giles' younger brother, Rowland or 'Rowley', was killed in action on 27 April, 1915. He was 19. There is no known grave. Their father, my great grandfather, a pastor, died of a broken heart in 1918 – my dad found out that he spent his final days in a nursing home just a few hundred yards from where I currently live in London. A whole generation, the brightest, healthiest, youngest men, marched into battle and were annihilated. Courage on a colossal scale.

Another of Giles' brothers served with the Royal Flying Corps in the Russian Civil War. He was shot down and interned and died of typhus on 1 February, 1920. There was one sister – my dad's mother. She died in 1963, 10 days after I was born. Two years later, the fourth brother, the sole surviving sibling, walked into the sea.

My friend Doug Sager had a rough start in life but went on to become a tireless advocate and campaigner for social justice, a filmmaker, poet, dancer, and always a stylish, snappy dresser. Doug would dazzle the dance floor for hours with his fancy footwork, still jumping and jiving long after men half his age had retired to the bar. The dancing days were halted because of late-onset CMT, then a stroke, but the passion, style and lust for life remained.

He was felled by Covid-19 in January 2021.

When I worked at *Golf Digest* in the US, I was privileged to have Pete Farricker as a fellow office colleague, writer, editor and friend. Pete was an ever-genial, gentle giant who always greeted the world with a smile, a quip and a radiant attitude. After his diagnosis of ALS,

Pete continued to grace the office, going to work every day until five days before he died. He wrote his own eulogy and had his wife read it out at the funeral. It began: 'I have started writing this the day after the Giants lost the Super Bowl so if I still owe anyone money for a bet, good luck trying to collect.'

ALS is also known as Lou Gehrig's disease, after the US baseball player for the New York Yankees. ALS forced Gehrig to retire at 36, and killed him two years later. He said farewell to baseball and the world on Independence Day 1939, in a legendary speech in which he listed the things he was grateful for in a life well lived: 'For the past two weeks you've been reading about a bad break,' he told a packed Yankee Stadium. 'Today I consider myself the luckiest man on the face of the earth.'

We cannot know who someone is from their resumé, social media presence, dating site bio, mental health questionnaire, personality test result or brain scan. We cannot know their formative experiences, the particular combination of sufferings they experience, or how they interact with them in their own unique way. Even members of your own family, or a partner you've walked with hand-in-hand through life for decades, can sometimes feel like strangers.

Everybody is a mystery. We've all been through a lot. Nobody gets out unscathed.

But in a sea of suffering, some people shine like beacons of humanity. When I am having a bad day, I think of those who have gone before. I often think of little lionhearted Vanessa.

Vanessa's father, Parker Moss, who is focusing his extraordinary talents on cancer research, writes:

So many people would ask us: how is it possible that Vanessa always smiles, that she always looks hopeful, is always excited by small gifts, is constantly besotted by babies, never complains… despite her life of constant pain, year after year surrounded by death in the narrow corridors of an oncology ward, and with each and every one of her childhood hopes crushed, one after another? In her darkest hour, Vanessa simply chose to sing. Vanessa had purpose from the very start. Vanessa knew who she was, she was confident and proud of her identity, and she chose happiness every day, in spite of her circumstances.

The only message that we can extract from the futility
and the outrage of the death of the innocent is that, when all
is stripped back, when there are no more words, when every
last hope has been extinguished, the only thing that remains
is a fragile yet certain revelation that there is pure goodness, a
profound and resilient thirst for happiness, at the core of our
children. As adults, we need not aspire to attain these things.
They are already within us. We just have to choose to reawaken
them.

§

Having been in a kind of denial for years, I start to explore the world
of Parkinson's more. I attend a Michael J. Fox Foundation webinar
on cognitive decline, dementia and psychosis. The US experts are
all excellent, well informed and earnest. But what they are saying is
dreadful. At one point, for instance, they are discussing how driving
becomes impossible as the patient's spatial awareness and ability
to perform complex tasks diminishes. The next day, driving out of
London to the country, I start to question myself. Suddenly I'm feeling
a little wobbly on the M2. The open exposition of symptoms from
the night before is becoming self-fulfilling. It's as if, however bad my
symptoms get, there is a medical Iago in a lab coat whispering in my
ear: 'Oh, it's going to get much worse than this.'

Sometimes denial is a very sensible strategy.

Luckily, somewhere near Faversham, my confidence returns.

Illness gets a terrible press. When you get ill, you are given a new
identity too, along with your diagnosis. Okay, you're a patient now, an
ill person. Parkinson's? You are that little old bent-over man, the one in
the illustration that's in every textbook and encyclopedia (he seriously
needs a makeover – the illustration was first published 1886). Take
your pills, don't make a fuss. Nothing more is expected of you. Shuffle
off home and sink into the warm embrace of the sofa, or under the
duvet of depression. Keep out of our way. One of my mum's old nursing
books states categorically that mental changes from Parkinson's will
include 'resentful attitude with emotional lability, depression, lack of
concentration, intellectual changes which may lead to dementia and
paranoid delusion. Becomes miserable and over-sensitive' (Koshy,
1977, p.169). Such a bleak, oppressive discourse creates and sustains
what Foucault calls a 'regime of truth' (1980, p.131) – one that removes

any agency or power or hope from the patient while reaffirming the authority and power of the medical system.

Yes, we get it. We realise that Parkinson's is an unfolding horror show. I know I am going to have to give up driving at some point, and much else besides. Cognitive decline, the possibility of dementia and psychosis – these are common occurrences in Parkinson's patients (though by no means a certainty, and those who are diagnosed when relatively young, like me, experience less cognitive decline than those who succumb to the shaking palsy in later life).

But all medical model approaches are focused only on alleviating and ameliorating deficits. No one ever talks about living a soulful life with them, let alone at times transcending them. People with health conditions can use them to live great lives and do great work. Parkinson's didn't stop Thomas Hobbes from writing *Leviathan*, for example, although it presents a rather grim, feral view of human nature (it was he who described life as 'nasty, brutish and short'). Beethoven did his best work while fighting deafness; similarly for Monet with blindness. Franklin Delano Roosevelt contracted polio at 39 and lost the use of his legs. He thought his political career was over. Instead, he became one of the greatest presidents of the US, steering his nation through the Great Depression and World War II.

At 21, in his final year at Oxford, Stephen Hawking was diagnosed with motor neurone disease, also known as ALS. He was told he had two years to live. But Hawking's was a rare, early-onset and slowly progressing form of the disease. He was gradually paralysed over his lifetime. He lost the use of his legs, his body, his voice. But how his mind soared. He became a brilliant physicist, cosmologist and writer. He lived a full, rich life with his disability.

'Don't be disabled in spirit as well,' he said (Dreifus, 2011).

Why aren't there webinars on using Parkinson's to live more authentically, socially, creatively, mindfully, spiritually, healthily, for example? With progressive disability comes the invitation to pursue *progressive ability*.

The late great British neurologist and writer Oliver Sacks wrote that illnesses and disorders 'can play a paradoxical role in bringing out latent powers, developments, evolutions, forms of life that might never be seen or even be imaginable in their absence' (1995).

In his later years he wrote:

I have seen hundreds of patients with various deficits – strokes, Parkinson's and even dementia – learn to do things in new ways, whether consciously or unconsciously, to work around those deficits. That the brain is capable of such radical adaptation raises deep questions. To what extent are we shaped by, and to what degree do we shape, our own brains? And can the brain's ability to change be harnessed to give us greater cognitive powers? The experiences of many people suggest that it can. (Sacks, 2010).

§

This body of mine is a strange, inexplicable piece of architecture. Its foundations are shaky; there is subsidence; the floorboards creak and groan; it will probably need some scaffolding at some point or the whole thing might collapse. There are holes in the roof; the antiquated plumbing system implausibly rumbles on; the wiring is shot to pieces. Yet the more it falls apart, the more I have come to appreciate this dear home and accept its gothic peculiarities. I am grateful for its refuge, its silent comfort. There were times when I kept the curtains drawn and the front door bolted, but these days the place is filled with light, and a fresh, calming breeze murmurs through the irregular rooms and passages, so familiar to me. I have lived here all my life, through all kinds of seasons. The day will come when I will cross the threshold and leave this place. It will be condemned, torn down and erased, leaving not a trace.

§

I take a class on *The Tibetan Book of the Dead*. It's a series of lectures livestreamed from the US to an audience scattered across many time zones but united in their interest in death. There are some experiential exercises, some Q&A sessions, and a social media forum to continue discussions after hours. It's full-on, hardcore Buddhism.

There are some disquieting aspects of the course. I get into an argument about karma and disability. There is a kind of spiritual elitism at play – some of these people, having put in the requisite hours of meditation, chanting and visiting remote Himalayan temples, seem quite sure they are entitled to a good death and a good rebirth. There is the insistence on presenting suppositions as facts.

One such is the assertion that, after you die, you enter 'the Bardo', where you are untethered and pass through a number of challenging stages and tests before you are assigned your next fate – a worker bee perhaps, or a sheep, or – for good Buddhists, my colleagues – an even more enlightened human, or Nirvana. The Bardo lasts for 49 days, apparently.

The Buddhists regard death as a letting go, and they believe you can make the Bardo easier by starting to let go of your ego attachment to your current human self in this life. Attachment to that self, they say, is what causes suffering. When your body dies, not everything dies. The teacher called the part that lives, the part that cannot die, 'the very subtle body'. I call it the soul.

It's all conjecture, but my takeaway from the course goes something like this: We are born with a body and a mind, but we already exist – as a soul. We can live a good life here in a way that honours the soul and further enlarges it, or we can live a soul-destroying Faustian life, driven by greed and material gain, bereft of spirituality or even love.

And a revelation: The soul is that part of us that isn't ever going to be ill, disabled or discriminated against. When I am doing soulful things – having a great conversation, or a meal, or being moved by nature, art, music, ideas, making love, learning, painting – I don't have Parkinson's.

Writes Eckhart Tolle: 'The condition that is labeled "illness" has nothing to do with who you truly are' (1999, p.182).

You can thus regard the ageing process as either very bad or very good; both can be true. Old age can be a deterioration, a diminishment, a decay: 'There's no fool like an old fool,' my mum used to say. Or you can regard it as a distillation. It's true things will be taken away from you during your life, and that can be very painful. But you will find other things, things you can do, and, like a blind person, the things you can do become intensified, and you will do them better and enjoy them more, until they too must go. You will simplify, slow down and be still.

British psychoanalyst Wilfred Bion famously said that therapy is best conducted 'without memory and without desire' (1970). Even the therapist's wish for their client to be, say, less depressed is, according to Bion, an imposition that will cloud that therapist's energy. He believed that in every session there had to be a genuine open-mindedness and freedom.

Maybe this ideal state of consciousness is only achieved when your memory and your desire have been taken from you, by disease, disability or death. Maybe you will lose your body and your mind, but a light-emitting, light-receiving soul will remain.

Some years ago, during a walking safari in Botswana, I saw a lame zebra. Abandoned by the rest of his non-disabled herd, he stood alone in a clearing, waiting for the inevitable moment when he would be attacked, killed and eaten by a predator, most likely a lion. He was entirely vulnerable. This was life for prehistoric man: short and violent. Early humans born with disabilities probably didn't live very long.

I often think about the zebra. Having a disability connects you to your animal vulnerability. You are sometimes just trying to survive. Yet this magnificent animal seemed calm and dignified. There was a sense of acceptance, courage, self-possession. His soul seemed huge. It was a powerful image, and it has stayed with me as I come to terms with my own unfurling physical impairments, more alive than ever in my slow but certain death.

Every day your soul matures and enlarges. It loses nothing. At the moment of death your body, often tired, broken and wasted, stops. But look at you. You're quite something. All the grit was necessary to make such a beautiful pearl.

§

I am on an expedition with my daughter to Foyles bookshop in London, where I once worked for about six months – my first job. I am telling her how one day the manager asked us to make a window display of a book that a friend of theirs had written. Despite our efforts to attract the book-loving hordes on Charing Cross Road, the book – a 900-page hardback called *The Art of Tunnelling*, by a Hungarian construction engineer – failed to become a bestseller.

This was but one of the many mad things about working at Foyles at that time. There was always plenty of fodder for the inevitable post-shift chats and carousings in the Cambridge Arms down the road or, many hours later, in what was then the rudest restaurant in London, Wong Kei.

In honour of *The Art of Tunnelling*, all these years later, my daughter and I decide to hunt for a worthy successor: the most boring book in the shop. The winner is *Advanced Biological, Physical, and Chemical Treatment of Waste Activated Sludge* (Prandota Trzcinski, 2018).

I didn't much like working at Foyles at first. I started out in the mail room. It was a kind of probation. I had to receive deliveries, lug heavy boxes around, unpack them and look busy if the manager appeared. I longed to be on the shop floor with actual customers, but also with bright young colleagues, especially the women – complicated, bookish introverts who might actually go for a coffee with me. The mail room days were interminable. There was often nothing to do. There was no escape. *The Art of Tunnelling* offered no practical advice. But of course, the day came when I was freed from the mail room and ascended to the relative heaven of the natural history department, where I sold books about animals. Everyone spends time in some metaphorical mail room or other: a place of hardship, exclusion and sometimes hard labour – a kind of waiting room or probationary period that we must endure, accept, appreciate and be changed by before real life can begin. A Bardo. Maybe life here on earth is just one big Bardo.

When I left Foyles, everyone wrote nice things in a big leaving card except a fellow called Ted, who amusingly wrote: 'Glad to see the back of you.' I tell my daughter this and then, moments later, working behind the till, there he is, someone I have not seen in decades – Ted! I remind him of the card, and we share a chuckle about it. For a moment it is 1986 again. I barely knew Ted. I was young and foolish then, and he seemed like an older, wiser man. I took his message to mean something like: 'Don't hang around here son, go off into the world and do your thing.'

Another time in Foyles, I hear a voice say, 'Hello, do you have Parkinson's?' I look up, and there, to my astonishment, is my doppelgänger. Rob is a bit older than me and has had Parkinson's for longer, but we look like twins, or at least brothers. My daughter wanders over and does a literal double-take.

I have been to quite a few CMT gatherings and a few Parkinson's ones too, and I have met some great people, but I've also met quite a few wearying types who are rather too invested in their own victimhood and make me feel like I am drowning. Rob, however, is terrifically upbeat.

One time, we walk through Trafalgar Square and Rob is telling me that he's been thinking a lot about his son. 'He's been in Iceland recently,' says Rob. 'And I'm not sure if he is back yet. I haven't seen him in ages.'

I look up ahead and see a lone seated figure, perfectly framed in a large window of a café.

And Rob says: 'Oh look, there he is.'

These odd, cinematic moments of synchronicity seem to be happening more and more.

One day, for no reason, I am thinking about a former client who left to go and live in Australia and have a baby. Some time later, I am walking through a packed King's Cross St Pancras Station, and it's as if the crowds part, and there she is. She tells me of her new life and shows me baby pictures. She seems happy. Another old client comes to mind, and practically the next day I get an email out of the blue, with an update and baby pictures. Any therapist will tell you of times when they have been discussing with their supervisor a particular issue they might be encountering with a client, and in the next session, it's as if the client had been listening in and has already moved on from where they were the week before.

There's also the saying, 'You get the clients you need.' In both quantity and quality, I have found this to be true. Many's the time I have been wrestling with a personal issue and a client comes for their appointment, unwittingly delivers the answer I've been looking for, and leaves. Obviously such transactions are supposed to be in the opposite direction, but we all learn from each other. Psychoanalyst Patrick Casement, whose first book was called *On Learning from the Patient* (1985), says the willingness to learn from each other is the very essence of the psychotherapeutic relationship.

Other strange happenings abound: glimpses behind the curtain. You go to look up something and, moments before you get to the relevant page, the answer comes to you. Doing a summer job in New York, in a premises with an L-shaped corridor, I found I was walking quickly when the abrasive boss was sitting at his desk, looking down the corridor, and slowly when he wasn't, but I was doing this *before I turned the corner and could be seen*. This unconscious ability to 'see' round the corner vanished as soon as I became consciously aware of it.

Once I participated in a séance, in a friend's parents' antique shop, on a dark and stormy night, and what happened was inexplicable. I had an astrological reading of my relationship from someone who I'd never met or spoken to, and who only had the time and place of our births to go on. His detailed written report was freakishly specific, accurate and helpful. Sightings of apparent doppelgängers, moments apart. Feeling a presence. Ghost stories.

The rationalists, those soulless automatons who regard humans in all their complexity as mere things that should obey the physical laws of science, deride this sort of thing. Western universities and academic journals, which by and large conform to this prevailing positivist orthodoxy, avoid going anywhere near these paranormal subjects for fear of censure or ostracism from their peers. Science is an echo chamber, a closed shop.

One who has made some such explorations is Rupert Sheldrake, who believes consciousness exists as a field that extends far beyond our physical, bodily boundary – a psychic reach akin to a gravitational or magnetic field or a wifi signal. He has used the scientists' own methods to explore things like telepathy – whether people can tell if someone is staring at them from behind, whether dogs know when their owners are coming home or cats know when their owners plan to take them to the vet, or whether one of the Nolan sisters can tell which of her many sisters is calling her. The results show a statistically significantly much better performance than chance alone would predict.

Schopenhauer is believed to have said: 'All truth passes through three stages. First, it is ridiculed. Second, it is violently opposed. Third, it is accepted as being self-evident.'

In his later years, Jung became increasingly interested in deeply meaningful encounters or significant occurrences that seem to go beyond being explained away as mere coincidences. Jung's term for these phenomena was 'synchronicity', which he described as 'the coincidence between an inner image or hunch breaking into one's mind, and the occurrence of an outer event conveying the same meaning at approximately the same time'.

Jung believed in a 'collective unconscious' that transcends time and space. Synchronicity thus contains echoes of Einstein's theory of relativity. It appears Jung was heavily influenced by Einstein, and also the physicist Wolfgang Pauli, a former client. Jung wrote that synchronicity is 'a necessary consequence' of the concept of relativity.

We are all connected.

Perhaps it's true that we meet who we're supposed to meet. My parents' eyes met across the room in a crowded pub in London, the Prospect of Whitby.

As a child, Oliver Sacks, like them, was separated from his parents for much of World War II. 'We evacuees sometimes recognise one other,' Sacks told Charlie Rose in a 1997 interview.[1] 'Maybe we never quite belonged. Something about a sense of belonging, I think or maybe bonding, has been shaken.'

How could my parents know in that instant that they shared so much, and would share so much? How to explain such a meeting of souls?

There is much that is strange and wonderful in the universe. In the last line of *The Minpins*, Roald Dahl warns: 'Those who don't believe in magic will never find it' (1991, p.48).

§

My partner and I are on holiday, driving around Scotland, visiting family and friends. It has been a rotten summer healthwise. I've been having more prolonged and pronounced 'off' periods when I can barely function, and they are completely unpredictable. This makes it hard to plan anything, go anywhere, drive or work. My functionality is all or nothing – either normality, more or less, or completely incapacitated. The drugs don't work, they just make it worse. Everything's fine; then it's as if, without warning, a hidden hand flicks an invisible switch.

The Scottish landscape is magnificent, as is the company. But there are some really difficult situations. These exacerbate the symptoms. And things spiral out of control. At such times, any sense of a comfort zone shrinks and then vanishes.

There is a psychological component to all of this. For various reasons, it's been a stressful time. Back in London, as autumn arrives, the pressure drops and the leaves fall. I change my medication and one of the new pills works miracles. I get my life back.

One night in Scotland though, at the height of the difficulty, high in the Highlands, Becky has a dream. We are in the car. I am driving. We are going uphill. Then the road gets steeper and steeper, and it is frightening. Our car is automatic; I shift into manual, and keep going. The road is almost vertical.

At one point Becky says: 'You know, I'm actually okay with this.'

And then we get to the top. We are relieved.

---

1. www.youtube.com/watch?v=XBZeipqo5UI

'Well done,' says Becky. 'I'm so proud of you. You drove so well.'

I can still do many things. From now on, though, I need to plan better, adapt, consider how it will be for me and for those around us. I need to trust my driving. To hope for the best but prepare for the worst.

We are on manual now.

At the end of the dream, we get out of the car. The view is spectacular.

§

It's not an easy thing to live a soulful life; to stay faithful to your higher, wiser, more eternal self. Again and again, we might find ourselves turning against our true nature, doing or saying something foolish or hurtful or inexplicable. From the cacophony of voices within – especially the more libertarian, id-driven, existential ones – catastrophically bad decisions sometimes emanate, especially when alcohol, exhaustion and mind-bending drugs – prescription or otherwise – are involved. We all walk a fine line between safety and danger, stagnation and growth, depression and anxiety. Sometimes we might go too far and inadvertently violate our own soul, perhaps so as to remind ourselves that we have one. There are bad souls sometimes pulling us off course, and we find ourselves in a bad situation. We get too close to the sun. Or something bad happens to us. There is a mess. There is shame and wretchedness.

For all the kindness and empathy that generous people bestow with such ease and grace, there are times and some dark places where a person might feel quite alone. You might have to let yourself be a little bit mad for a while. Keep plodding on. You will get through. You must be patient and, like a sunflower bowing its head through a long night, have faith that a new day will come and you will feel the sun on your cheek once more. You are human. Apologise to those you hurt. Forgive yourself, make amends, move on.

Disability and illness introduce us to alone-ness – or, to put it another way, to ourselves. If we can find peace there, everything else is alright and manageable. This is where we end up.

Virginia Woolf wrote:

That illusion of a world so shaped that it echoes every groan, of human beings so tied together by common needs and fears that a twitch at one wrist jerks another, where however strange your experience other people have had it too, where however far you travel in your own mind someone has been there before you – is all an illusion. We do not know our own souls, let alone the souls of others. Human beings do not go hand in hand the whole stretch of the way. There is a virgin forest in each; a snowfield where even the print of birds' feet is unknown. Here we go alone, and like it better so. Always to have sympathy, always to be accompanied, always to be understood would be intolerable. (1930/2002, p.11)

$

Today I get out of bed and I'm exhausted. I haven't slept well in years. I am running late. I am always running late. I have slowed down but my internal clock has the same factory settings as it did when I was 21. I totter and bounce off the walls and cupboards in the kitchen as I make a cup of tea that I don't feel confident about carrying to my desk. It takes me 10 minutes to put on my shoes and the foot/ankle supports with all their straps, buckles and strips of Velcro. Buttons are a daily wrestle, as are the stubborn blister packs that contain my morning medley of meds.

For all the profiteering and cynical marketing of big pharmaceutical companies, I am grateful for my morning cocktail of pills: synthetic dopamine, agonists, enzyme inhibitors, drugs to mitigate the side effects of other drugs, vitamins, herbal who-knows-whats, what-the-hecks and why-nots. The dopamine agonists in particular can add some lively if discordant notes to the melody of the Parkinson's experience. They are not dopamine, but they tickle the dopamine receptors with a kind of chemical feather boa. If you are psychotic, they give you dopamine antagonists, which is why you sometimes see people on psychiatric wards showing Parkinsonian symptoms. So people with Parkinson's are essentially given pro-psychotic medication. Common side effects, it says in the small print that comes with the pills, include 'strong impulse to gamble excessively… altered or increased sexual interest… uncontrollable excessive shopping or spending… binge eating'.

These pills are blunt instruments and there is a concern that Big Pharma's muscle might inhibit the development of other approaches. Many Parkinson's professionals remain silent about, or even at times so vehemently denounce non-pharmacological treatments such as healthy food, exercise, meditation, acupuncture that you wonder if in some way or another they are on the payroll.

But regardless, I am grateful. No amount of journalling, chanting, crystals, hypnosis, meditation or yoga will change the fact that I have CMT and Parkinson's, but medical science might.

A great unlearning is taking place: things that children struggle with – tying shoelaces, say, or handwriting – have become a struggle once more, only this time I am descending the mountain of mastery, banished against my will, rather than heading excitedly for the summit. I am systematically being divested of basic life skills. Every day, huge chunks of human experience slide out of my reach, never to return. I am losing the use of my legs, and it is frightening.

I glance at my notes from yesterday's supervision session. They are entirely unintelligible.

I head outside into the street with my walking stick, to join the fast-flowing river of commuters elbowing their way to the office. I am slow. I am in the way. My walk is clumsy, weak, shaky today. Wrote James Parkinson in his marvellous, original 1817 essay that introduced the shaking palsy to the world:

> Walking becomes a task which cannot be performed without
> considerable attention. The legs are not raised to that height, or
> with that promptitude which the will directs, so that the utmost
> care is necessary to prevent frequent falls.

A jogger runs past. There is an astonishing beauty in the way she moves: a kinetic ease, a graceful efficiency that she perhaps isn't even aware of. She does not yet know that this can be taken away. Will be taken away.

CMT has wasted my feet, systematically diminishing their strength, support and shock-absorption. It is like having one's feet and lower legs injected with muscle relaxants and then having to wear lead boots. Add to that the effect of Parkinson's on the commands from the brain – flickering, like a series of intermittent power cuts – and I am sometimes barely able to walk at all. The decline is progressing, the clock is ticking, the bell is tolling.

On the tube, a woman offers me her seat. Sitting down is easy; getting back up is not. I only have a few stops. I thank her but decline. She glowers at me, infuriated by my apparent ingratitude.

I meet a friend. We catch up over breakfast. We talk about work, partners, mothers. It feels good. I walk all the way home. The rest of the day is filled up with clients, naps, admin, reading, messing about on my phone and – much later, much too late really – writing this. I am typing painfully slowly with one finger. It is weak and inflexible. I can't really use a computer mouse anymore.

Some nights my flat is busy with an assortment of blurry, translucent, humanlike shapes. Sometimes they are just passing through. Some approach me and try to attract my attention by making vigorous movements with their hands and arms. Some simply stand and watch. They are silent. Often they will suddenly all leave together, as if summoned by a spiritmaster's bell that only they can hear. Hallucinations and delusions are well-known side effects of Parkinson's medications. I am, however, willing at least to entertain the possibility that these shapes are not simply the epiphenomena of a disordered brain chemistry but are, in fact, real – a glimpse beyond the primitive, restrictive human doors of perception. I have experienced enough strange things and heard such tales from clients to believe that there are perhaps spirits among us.

I doze in front of the computer. The night deepens and falls silent. The weary motorists return to suburbia with a sigh; the last wheelie suitcase comes to rest in the corner of a flophouse hotel room; drunks pass out in doorways. The rats emerge from their lairs. The restless city surrenders to a fitful, begrudging semi-sleep for a few hours.

Now I am inexplicably wide awake. And still fully clothed.

I am alone. I'm terrified of disappearing.

I make tea. The objects in my flat, once so comforting, have turned against me. The kitchen appliances, proud and beautifully designed for normal people, are embarrassed; they can't believe how useless and clumsy I have become. My shelves are filled with unread, half-started or misunderstood books that whisper their disappointment and disapproval to each other. Even my clothes have turned hostile. They are trying to kill me. Only after a long struggle do the buttons let go, and then with a hollow, mocking laugh. In trying to disrobe, my shirt manages to get me in a half-nelson and I am trapped and can hardly breathe. By the time I get to bed, it's getting light again already. Soon it will be a new day.

The US comedian Steven Wright has a line about how he avoids thinking about the past because 'it just brings up all these memories'. For me, grief is an ongoing process of letting go, a kind of forgetting. I am forever saying farewell to the me I used to be; every day some more doors close behind me. There isn't much capacity to reflect wistfully on the passing of a non-disabled past or worry about a drooling, incapacitated future when there is such vibrancy in the present. There is a fresh, raw and challenging nowness to engage with – my disability keeps me living in the moment.

I meditate. I relax. Despite it all, I feel good in spirit anew. I had a good, rich, full day. There is music in my head, a little wine in my heart.

Since I was diagnosed with Parkinson's eight years ago, I have become a psychotherapist, earned my doctorate, finished the London Marathon, become an artist with work exhibited at the Royal Academy, written this book, met Becky.

Confucius: 'You get two lives here on earth, and the second one begins when you realise you only have one.'

3. Disability –
Who and what is disabled?

'I am not an animal. I am a human being. I am a man.'
John Merrick ('The Elephant Man')

Definitions

The official British definition of disability is: 'You're disabled under the Equality Act 2010 if you have a physical or mental impairment that has a "substantial" and "long-term" negative effect on your ability to do normal daily activities.'

'Substantial' is defined as 'more than minor or trivial, eg. it takes much longer than it usually would to complete a daily task like getting dressed.' 'Long-term' is defined as '12 months or more, eg. a breathing condition that develops as a result of a lung infection' (UK Government, 2010).

Impairments may be physical or mental, visible or invisible, congenital or acquired through accident, illness or old age. People who qualify as having a disability may or may not regard themselves in that way.

In the US, the Americans with Disabilities Act defines a person with a disability as someone 'who has a physical or mental impairment that substantially limits one or more major life activities, a person who has a history or record of such an impairment, or a person who is perceived by others as having such an impairment.' Major life activities include, but are not limited to, caring for oneself, performing manual tasks, seeing, hearing, eating, sleeping, walking, standing, lifting, bending, speaking, breathing, learning, reading, concentrating, thinking, communicating, and working (US Department of Justice, 1990).

The social model of disability, however, upends these definitions. The 'problem' is no longer the impairments in people's minds or bodies;

it is located in societies that fail to make the necessary adjustments to enable those with impairments to enjoy their full citizenship and human rights. The UK's Union of the Physically Impaired Against Segregation redefined disability in 1976 as 'a particular form of oppression... the disadvantage or restriction of activity caused by a contemporary social organisation which takes no or little account of people who have physical impairments and thus excludes them from participation in the mainstream of social activities' (Shakespeare & Watson, 1997).

The United Nations' 2006 Convention on the Rights of Persons with Disabilities does not explicitly define disability, but states:

> Persons with disabilities include those who have long-term physical, mental, intellectual or sensory impairments which in interaction with various barriers may hinder their full and effective participation in society on an equal basis with others. (United Nations, 2006)

According to their report, this marks a paradigm shift in attitudes and approaches:

> Persons with disabilities are not viewed as 'objects' of charity, medical treatment and social protection; rather as 'subjects' with rights, who are capable of claiming those rights and making decisions for their lives based on their free and informed consent as well as being active members of society. The Convention gives universal recognition to the dignity of persons with disabilities. (United Nations, 2006)

I define disability as the combined debilitating effects of unjust, prejudicial physical, cultural and psychological barriers in society, organisations and individuals that together mean people with impairments are treated as invalid humans, bereft of souls, thereby crippling humanity and shaming us all.

Statistics

These definitions pigeonhole a vast number of people with an extraordinarily wide array of challenges.

- There are 14.1 million people with a limiting long-term illness, impairment or disability in the UK – 20% of the population. The most commonly reported impairments are those that affect mobility, lifting or carrying. About 1.5 million people in the UK have a learning disability. Approximately 8% of children, 19% of working-age adults and 44% of pension-age adults have a disability (Department for Work and Pensions, 2020). An estimated 11 million people in the UK (one in six) are living with a neurological condition (Brain Research UK, n.d.).

- In the US, there are 57 million people with disabilities – 19% of the population (US Census Bureau, 2014). Approximately one in five has a chronic illness or disability (Livneh & Antonak, 2005). The most common disabilities are difficulty walking/climbing stairs (30.6 million people); requiring assistance for everyday tasks (12 million); vision difficulty (8.1 million); hearing (7.6 million); using a wheelchair (3.6 million); Alzheimer's or dementia (2.4 million).

- There are more than a billion disabled people on the planet (WHO, 2020).

- Approximately 80% of people with disabilities live in developing countries (WHO, 2020).

- In countries with life expectancies greater than 70 years, individuals spend on average about eight years, or 11.5% of their lifespan, living with disabilities (Disabled World, 2021).

- The World Bank estimates that 20% of the world's poorest people have some kind of disability, and tend to be regarded in their own communities as the most disadvantaged (Disabled World, 2021).

- 90% of children with disabilities in developing countries do not attend school (Disabled World, 2021).

Ways of thinking about disability

Since time immemorial, people who are 'different' have been excluded, shamed, pitied, patronised, punished, attacked and killed. History reveals that our species has a great propensity for flunking the Humanity Test. Each epoch and set of beliefs carries with it various attitudes, practices and policies towards people with disabilities, all of which continue to exert their influence on the experience of disability. The complex and troubled ways that disabilities have been regarded and responded to have coalesced and crystallised into a number of theoretical models or ways of thinking about disability today. There are three principal ways that disability is viewed (Oliver, 1996; Olkin, 1999): the moral, medical and social models. Here I have added a few more. They are listed roughly in chronological order.

The evolutionary model: Survival of the fittest

This is the most primitive of viewpoints. The evolutionary model believes that humans are no different from animals, and the law of the jungle prevails. By this reckoning, infanticide, neglect and violence against people with disabilities are all simply manifestations of the human and animal drive to survive – survival of the fittest.

Charles Darwin's *On the Origin of Species* (1859/1909) was co-opted and misinterpreted as a justification for creating human hierarchies on genetic lines. Those with power – 'the European' – of course placed themselves at the top of the hierarchy, and placed those without power – 'the African' – at the bottom, along with anyone who was disabled, gay, had a criminal record, or did not speak with a plummy accent.

Darwin's half-cousin Francis Galton took this 'social Darwinism' a step further by naming and championing the practice of eugenics – controlling the breeding of the unfortunates to preserve the supposed white supremacy of the elite.

The misappropriation of Darwin was amplified by much spurious anthropological 'research,' new fake 'sciences' like craniometry, and the dissemination of extremely large amounts of propaganda about differences in intelligence and the supposed perils of 'miscegenation' (it was well known that genetic diversity – the notion of heterosis or 'hybrid vigour', the opposite of inbreeding – was a good thing).

All of this was claimed as justification for imperialism. Poverty, war, the late-19th-century 'scramble for Africa' and the genocide of indigenous peoples by white Westerners were all seen as the result of an inevitable, scientific, natural law, devoid of any moral responsibility. Domestically, too, the eugenics movement allowed the elites to justify their wealth, power and privilege. The National Association for the Care and Control of the Feebleminded was created in 1896 to campaign for the permanent and lifelong segregation of disabled people.

The British Empire collapsed, but beliefs in eugenics didn't. The remnants of the discredited, antique ideas on which it was built lived on, and not just in some cobwebbed recess of the colonial psyche; they positively thrived in many places around the world. 'Eugenics belonged to the political vocabulary of virtually every significant modernizing force between the two world wars,' writes Dikötter (1998, p.467).

The British invention was exported and enthusiastically embraced and adopted far and wide. Many US states enacted laws prohibiting marriage and procreation by those deemed 'unfit'. There were bans on inter-racial marriage too, and more than 30 US states allowed compulsory sterilisations of so-called undesirables – between 1907 and 1963, more than 64,000 people in America were forcibly sterilised under eugenic law. What came to be known as the 'Mississippi appendectomy' (sterilisation without consent of women deemed 'unfit' to reproduce) was disproportionately inflicted on black women. As noted in the previous chapter, there were so-called ugly laws, too, that banned blind beggars and others deemed to be 'unsightly or unseemly' from appearing in public.

In extreme conditions, when power imbalances pass a tipping point in unconstrained totalitarian regimes, people abandon their humanity in droves.

The evils of eugenics reached their logical conclusion in Nazi Germany. One of Adolf Hitler's first acts when he came to power was to pass the Law for the Prevention of Hereditarily Diseased Offspring in 1933: sterilisation was mandated for anyone with any undesirable attribute that might be considered genetic, such as physical deformity, epilepsy, blindness, deafness, mental illness, learning disabilities, and severe alcoholism.

Nazi propaganda described disabled people as 'useless eaters' who were a drain on the state. One famous film – *Ich Klage An*, or *I Accuse*, released in 1941 – told the story of a doctor who killed his disabled wife, portraying it a 'mercy killing'.

Between 1934 and 1937, the Nazi regime forcibly sterilised an estimated 400,000 people who were variously disabled. The killing began in 1939. People with disabilities were injected with poison, starved, sent to the gas chambers or otherwise murdered in one of six death camps. The covert operation, codenamed T4 – headquartered at Tiergartenstrasse 4 in Berlin – took the lives of an estimated 275,000 people with disabilities.

It's a sin: The moral model

This perspective, which is as old as humans, regards the disabled person as inherently sinful, evil or guilty of some supposed moral lapse, and thus deserving of their fate. As with illness (Sontag, 1977), the victims of disability are blamed, often with a religious, supernatural, psychological or political rationale. In more collective societies, the entire family tends to carry the shame and stigma. Religion is the biggest source of moral judgement of disability, dictating how disabled people are treated not just in Western societies but also in the Hindu and Buddhist faiths, with the concept of karma.

In the long distant past, in Ancient Greece, children with birth defects evoked great fear. They were considered as both the cause and effect of the gods' anger, and the common practice, usually agreed by community elders, was exposure: the newborn would typically be taken out into the wilderness and left to the will of the gods. Return to sender.

The tale of Oedipus in Greek mythology is a cautionary one: born with a club foot, he survived such an abandonment but went on unwittingly to murder his father and marry his mother, bringing ruination to the kingdom. Many cultures have similar stories (Stiker, 2017, p.149).

Infanticide was popular with the Romans, too: the Twelve Tables of Roman Law, published in 449bce, stated that deformed children must be put to death, and that the patriarchs of Roman society were allowed to 'discard' infants at their discretion, usually by drowning them in the Tiber.

Turning to the Abrahamic religions, people with disabilities make lots of appearances in the Old Testament. For example, if you disobey the Lord, the book says:

> The Lord will afflict you with madness, blindness and confusion of mind. At midday you will grope about like a blind man in the dark. (Deuteronomy 28: 1&28–29)

> For the generations to come none of your descendants who has a defect may come near to offer the food of his God. No man who has any defect may come near: no man who is blind or lame, disfigured or deformed; no man with crippled foot or hand, or who is hunchbacked or dwarfed, or who has any

eye defect, or who has festering or running sores or damaged testicles. (Leviticus 21: 16–20)

Do not offer to the Lord the blind, the injured or the maimed, or anything with warts or festering or running sores. Do not place any of these on the altar as an offering made to the Lord by fire. (Leviticus 22: 22)

People with disabilities are thus presented very much as second-class citizens: unclean sinners who are to be denied access to places of worship, social groupings and the wider community. They are among the very long list of people subjected to exclusion, punishment and even death over the centuries under antiquated Christian lore, and justified by reference to the Old Testament in particular. People who worked on a Sunday, for instance, or had sex with someone they weren't married to, or had parents who weren't married; women who had sex, or who talked in church, or defended their husbands, or were menstruating, or who were just women; people who were gay or who masturbated or ate bacon (Leviticus 11: 27, in case you are wondering).

The big fork in the road for the Abrahamic religions and the treatment of people with disabilities was when Jesus appeared. He welcomed the halt, the sick and the lame, soothed and supposedly cured them, and, says Stiker, 'quite decisively breaks the connection between disability and individual fault... Jesus says explicitly that the sick, the disabled, the marginalized, are the first in the Kingdom of God' (Stiker, 1997, pp.33–34).

The Judaism of the Old Testament calls for a strict religious prohibition of anyone afflicted by disability, without possibility of appeal. The written law of the Torah regards people with disabilities as abnormal, impure and not deserving of full inclusion in society. Abrams (1998) argues that this Orthodox position is discriminatory and in need of reform. The Torah, however, is open to interpretation (Jones, 2007).

Meanwhile, Islam has long been denigrated in the Western world. As early as the 12th century, many European writers were attacking Islam itself as 'heretical, immoral and irrational', arriving at a consensus that bore little relation to what Muslims actually did or believed (Richardson, 2004, p.9). 'Islamophobia' has intensified latterly, in a new Cold War (Mamdani, 2004) in which Muslims have become 'a kind of scapegoat for everything we do not happen to like about the world's new political, social, and economic patterns' (Said, 1978/2003, p.lv).

Yet Islam is perhaps the most enlightened religion with regard to disabilities. They are not seen as a punishment, the result of a divine moral judgement, but more as a kind of test. The Prophet preaches: 'No reproach to the blind, no reproach to the lame, no reproach to the sick.' The Quran emphasises that all human beings have inherent worth and dignity (Saeed, 2013).

A fundamental tenet of Hinduism, Buddhism and Jainism is the concept of karma, which dates back to the oldest religious texts: the Upanishads, a collection of Vedic philosophies that were first written down hundreds of years before Jesus. If something bad happens to you – like acquiring or being born with a disability – it's because of your own bad karma. Perhaps, for instance, you carried out immoral acts in a previous life. Karma is not a punishment administered by a vengeful deity. Nor is it fate. It's simply the result of your own actions. Bad karma can be reversed by good deeds, righteous actions and healthy living.

As one of the earliest known philosophers, Yajnavalkya, explains:

> According as one acts, according as one behaves, so does one become. The doer of good becomes good, the doer of evil becomes evil.[1]

What is meaningful about karma – it is Sanskrit for 'action' – is the idea that our behaviour matters, and that we should act with love and kindness in everything we do. But a simplistic cause/effect model that ascribes blame for suffering to the past misdeeds of the sufferer – the greater the suffering, the greater the supposed misdeeds – is deeply problematic.

Gupta writes:

> … belief in karma may sometimes cause negative coping by evoking feelings of guilt in the person with a disability who may be blamed for having brought on the disability by doing misdeeds in the past. Parents may be blamed for causing congenital abnormalities of their children. These reactions may

---

1. www.britannica.com/biography/Yajnavalkya

cause discord and evoke shame, stigma, and dishonor to the family's honor. (2011, p.74)

What a pity: The charity model

Returning to the influence of Jesus and the New Testament, in the 11th century St. Francis of Assisi burst upon the scene. A young scion born into wealth and privilege, he renounced it all to become a holy man and perhaps did more than anyone to promote the idea that people with disabilities should not be reviled and should instead be supported, praised even, for their courage in the struggle with everyday living.

St. Francis, canonised in 1228, two years before his death, wrote:

God allowed me to begin my repentance in this way: when I lived in sin, seeing lepers was a very bitter experience for me. God himself guided me into their midst and among them I performed acts of charity. What appeared bitter to me became sweetness of the soul and body. (Acocella, 2013)

Thence, the disabled became 'charity cases' – objects for those more fortunate to pity and to remind them of their good fortune. The latter's salvation came to be seen to be dependent on the hospitality, succour and alms they gave to the former. For much of our more recent history in the UK, there was no provision for people with disabilities by the state, or any concept of their having rights. You either lived with your family or were reliant on the kindness of strangers seeking to buy their way into heaven. Monasteries and convents took you in, acting as non-statutory asylums and also offering occupation, if not employment. It is a model that still prevails in many developing countries without a national statutory infrastructure of health and social care.

Arguably, it was the Victorians, with their flamboyant manifestations of piety, their robust moralism, their confident expectations of heavenly bliss and their creation of the workhouse and the asylum, who perfected the art of charitable giving and created the notion of the deserving and undeserving poor. If disability pricked the conscience of the non-disabled, charity offered the default response – an attitude that predominates today. But woe betide the object of pity who dares to have an opinion, expects to have independence and choice, fails to show due gratitude or appears to expect equal access to what the non-disabled person enjoys as their human and citizen's right. They can rapidly become undeserving and cast into the wilderness of their Ancient Greek forebears.

We will fix you: The medical model

In 17th- and 18th-century Europe, with advances in medicine, science and philosophy, disability came to be seen more as a technical challenge and less laden with religious or supernatural connotations. In this optimistic Age of Reason, it was assumed that any impairment or deficit could be diminished or eliminated through education, physical therapy, prosthetics and medical science.

The person with the disability was now to be regarded clinically, as like a broken machine. The physical defect was to be identified, labelled, treated, fixed, managed or accepted, and some steps taken to accommodate disabled people, for which they were expected to be grateful. There was less judgement and moral interpretation. The person was entitled to assistance, to full citizenship, to an education – the first special education schools opened in the 1770s. Thomas Blacklock, a blind poet, philosopher and cleric, wrote *On the Education of the Blind* in 1774, citing examples of when blindness can be a spur to great achievement – a 'less is more' possibility that upended previous negative conceptions of disability.

In *What Psychotherapists Should Know About Disability*, Rhoda Olkin, a polio survivor, writes:

> The main contribution of the medical model is its repudiation of the view of disability as a lesion on the soul. Further, the medical model has spurred medical and technological advances that have improved the lives of people with disabilities. (1999, p.26)

The medical model remains the prevailing orthodoxy in Western healthcare provision today. But it is a normative model. It promotes a binary us/them split, in which the 'us' people project all their fears, anxieties and horrors onto the 'them,' as Wilson (2001, p.679) points out. The disabled person is pathologised, aberrant if not abhorrent. Many times I have sat in a lecture room full of people with CMT while a CMT-free CMT expert explains what our 'abnormal' axons, feet or gait look like, and what they 'should' look like.

> Thus, the individual with a disability, regardless of personal
> qualities and assets, understands that he or she belongs to a
> devalued group. (Smart & Smart, 2012, p.63)

The person with a disability or disease becomes invisible, their subjective experience irrelevant. Patients are passive recipients of both disease and treatment. Aside from a brief description of symptoms, they are largely silent. Clinics and clinicians aren't much interested in a patient's own phenomenology, their somatic history, knowledge and meaning-making, or in contextual details about what else might be going on in their lives.

Foucault – the son of a doctor – was highly condemnatory of what he termed 'the medical gaze'. He wrote:

> The presence of disease in the body, with its tensions and
> its burnings, the silent world of the entrails, the whole dark
> underside of the body lined with endless unseeing dreams, are
> challenged as to their objectivity by the reductive discourse of
> the doctor. (Foucault, 1963, p.xi)

Hospitals became increasingly clinical and stripped of hospitality – garages for a medical machine that oftentimes can feel acutely bereft of soul. Any demonstration of humanity by the more soulful doctors and nurses is generally discouraged, although it can live on in the personal warmth and small acts of kindness of individuals, which can almost feel subversive. A nurse once told me she was reprimanded for spending too much time attempting to comfort patients who were about to undergo an amputation.

Some regard the medical model of illness as deeply flawed. Illich opened his critique with the words: 'The medical establishment has become a major threat to health' (1976/2010, p.3). We are plagued, he wrote, by a society-wide epidemic of iatrogenic (doctor-induced) disease and death; modern medicine has become a rapacious commercial machine, one that sustains itself through its production of clinical damage, its political furtherance of an unfair, sick society, and its tendency 'to mystify and to expropriate the power of the individual to heal himself and to shape his or her environment.'

All in the mind: The psychological model

Then we come to the vexed question: is it the body that rules the mind, or the mind that rules the body?

The medical model goes all out for the former; the pendulum has swung too far. But more latterly the pendulum has in some quarters swung too far the other way, fuelled perhaps by Western flirtations and interpretations of Eastern thought, the 1960s and a spiritual hunger born of a surfeit of materialism. The psychological model regards physical symptoms as indicative of something unresolved in the unconscious, a problem in the psyche, a sickness of the spirit. One result is the kind of cultish New Age quackery that can sometimes become dogmatic and extreme – psychofascism. For these kinds of evangelical positive thinkers, angel therapists and other self-appointed psychics, faith healers and metaphysicists, individual power and responsibility are inviolable; they see health and illness as a psychological choice. The 'mind' advocates can be just as dogmatic as the 'body' medical-model types they seek to critique. Many are widely accepted as balanced and reasoned yet offer victim-blaming explanations or unhelpful metaphors that all too often can be moralistic and punitive.

One such is Gabor Maté, the widely respected Hungarian-Canadian doctor, writer and public speaker. He declares on his website:[2]

> It's my belief that diseases like cancer, ALS, multiple sclerosis
> and so on, that cause so much suffering for people, all come
> along to teach something – and that if the lesson is learned,
> with compassion for oneself, then the 'teacher' has done its job
> and can then take a hike. That's not a guarantee, but I've seen
> many examples of people who have taken on their illnesses
> in this way and either survived or far outlived what medical
> science would have predicted, or at least greatly improved their
> own quality of life while alive.

So show me some of those people who got Parkinson's, learned their lesson and then got better. It has literally never happened. People do sometimes get better from cancer, it's true, but many do not. Ten million people around the world died from cancer in 2020. Did they all fail to learn the 'lesson' that had been offered?

---

2. https://drgabormate.com/

That's a cruel thing for anyone to say, especially a medical doctor who presumably believes in the Hippocratic Oath and really should know better. It is barely short of saying that we people with such conditions 'brought them on ourselves' by some failure of character and attitude.

A call for justice: The social model

The Industrial Revolution saw a huge rise in workplace injuries. Men, women and children suffered horrendous harms in the factories and mills, to say nothing of the appalling diseases engendered in the overcrowded cities that grew to serve the industrial machine. This sparked a corresponding demand for statutory responsibility, which was greatly increased by the vast numbers of injured servicemen returning home from the two world wars. In 1951, 800 members of the British Limbless Ex-Servicemen's Association travelled to 10 Downing Street to participate in a 'silent reproach' to a government that had all but forgotten them. Two MPs who had been injured in World War I, double amputee Jack Brunel-Cohen and the blinded Ian Fraser, championed the cause, as did MP Jack Ashley, who was deaf. There was a growing recognition that, in a civilised society, everyone should have the chance to benefit from education, employment and a health service that offered treatment, rehabilitation and repair to all, in equal measure. From the 1942 Beveridge Report onwards, legislation was implemented to ensure that these things were offered (and also to then cap them, and remove them, as the realisation hit that providing an effective health service also ensured that more people lived longer but sicker lives). By the 1970s, disability was becoming a largely secular phenomenon, but also a growing one, as children became more likely to survive into adulthood and adults lived longer into older age.

Disability rights groups emerged, driving a shift away from segregation and towards integration, perhaps accelerated by the elevation of anti-discriminatory consciousness from the civil rights era and the lingering memory of the Holocaust. From the backdrop of horror at what Hitler's Nazi fantasies of white supremacy had wrought emerged a host of campaigning and fundraising charities for different marginalised groups. Asylums and long-stay hospitals, where many people with disabilities were warehoused in dreadful and sometimes abusive conditions, were decommissioned. 'Community care' became a political mantra rather than a description, and sadly failed to materialise as it became increasingly obvious that the community didn't care, didn't want to care and preferred the caring to be done for it by others, somewhere else.

In 1976, however, the UK's Union of the Physically Impaired Against Segregation radically reframed the traditional disability debates with their formulation of a social model (Hahn, 1985), which located the problem not in a person's body or mind but in the prejudiced, unfair and inhospitable environments around them (Smart, 2001; Terzi, 2004). Disability suddenly got political; disability studies emerged as an acknowledged academic field of enquiry on its own merit. People with disabilities were now to be regarded as an oppressed minority that was being denied basic access to education, work, transport and social groups, and representation in culture and media. According to Olkin (1999), people with disabilities are united by their shared experience of the difficulties, barriers and prejudices they face in the non-disabled world, not by their physical or mental impairments. Their commonality is their systematic exclusion from society; the prejudice and discrimination they face is more enduring and pervasive than that experienced by any other group (Smart & Smart, 2012, p.69).

The social model rejects pity and charity and instead demands justice. It has been used to great effect by many courageous, dedicated disability activists to bring about great political change. The United Nations released the Declaration on the Rights of Disabled Persons in 1976, declared 1981 the International Year of Disabled Persons, and in 2006 issued the global Convention on the Rights of Persons with Disabilities.

But disability is an atypical demographic for a minority group. By entirely focusing on a presupposed monolithic oppression and ignoring the contribution of any physical impairment to a disability, individual differences and identities are potentially erased.

The nature of the disabilities themselves – and their attendant challenges – are extremely diverse. Even within one family affected by a single condition – such as my own, with CMT – there may be a variety of presentations. Within the world of disability at large, however, the quality and quantity of differences are so broad in scope as to render the catch-all term almost meaningless. I have enormous empathy for, say, someone who is blind, deaf or intellectually impaired, or who uses a wheelchair or is in unending pain. We share our humanity and soulfulness and vulnerability. We share the experience of being excluded and overlooked. But each of our stories is unique; I do not presume to know how other disabled people feel or what their specific challenges, abilities and needs might be.

Furthermore, branding everyone with a disability with the same label serves to exacerbate the very them/us division, the 'othering', that disability activists want to destroy (Owens, 2015, p.389; Shakespeare, 2018, p.19); it highlights difference in a bid to be treated just the same. The social model, like other minority liberation movements, thus has the potential to reinforce the barriers it seeks to abolish and, by reinforcing and drawing attention to negative aspects of group identity, it can induce victimhood,.

In this way, Fraser (2000) says identity politics can become inward-looking and sectarian, homogenising its members for the purposes of advocacy and political change. Fraser prefers an individual, 'identitarian' approach that highlights autonomy. Owens (2015) proposes a more nuanced, pluralistic conception of disability based on the writings on power and plurality of Hannah Arendt. This:

> allows for an elaboration of the complexities, contradictions and common aspects of disabled people's experiences, instead of incorporating them into one collective understanding that excludes aspects of each person's experience. (Owens, 2015, p.394)

Levitt proposes an 'active' model (2017) that focuses on the agency and actions of the disabled person, empowering them rather than challenging the disabling environment. Also of note is the human development model of disability (Mitra, 2018), based on economist Amartya Sen's work on the role of human individual capability in poverty reduction. These post-social model ideas vary in scope but are all enabling in their foregrounding of the agency, capability and participation of disabled people – who have, of course, many varied abilities.

Current reality: The apartheid model

There is an inherent tension between the philosophy of the medical model (as operated by our government and statutory health service), which locates a disability within the human body, and the experience of a disabled person, who experiences society as disabling. It's as if the government points a finger at people with disabilities and says: 'You lot, you're a problem,' and the people with disabilities reply, in a loud, rousing, united response: 'No, you are the problem!'

Attempting to bridge the divide with a commonly-used hybrid of the medical and social models is the World Health Organization's International Classification of Functioning, Disability, and Health (WHO, 2001). This sees each person as unique and their level of disability as dictated by the dynamic interactions between their health condition and their socioeconomic and psychological context – what Lewin (1935) called their total 'life space' (Chan et al., 2009).

All of the above models seem to be either cruel, misguided or incomplete. In Chapter 7, I present yet one more model, which is the one I hope we're heading towards: the humanity model of disability.

For now, in my view, most of the world today operates largely under a system of *disability apartheid* – an unholy interaction of the medical model, the social model and human psychology, inflected by the moral model and the evolutionary law of the jungle.

I realise that using the Afrikaans word 'apartheid' – literally 'separateness' – might seem inflammatory. In no way do I intend to equate the horrendous sufferings of black Africans crushed by monstrous, overtly white-supremacist governments with the experience of people with disabilities in the Western world. But there are equivalences. Racism and ableism are widespread, pernicious and crushing to the human soul – and body. Black people and people with disabilities are united in being judged solely because of their appearance; being subjected to deeply-ingrained prejudice and discrimination from individuals, groups, organisations and governments, and being relegated to 'that other place', that other world – a para-world. And, as with South African apartheid, these two worlds are a very long way from being 'separate but equal', which is itself a long way from together and equal.

At its simplest, the disability apartheid model depicts a world where anyone deemed 'disabled' is largely invisible and unwelcome in the non-disabled world unless they can 'pass' for normal (Goffman, 1963). The non-disabled live in 'abled world': a land of growth, a land of potential hope and glory. The disabled by contrast inhabit 'disabled world', which can be a place of solidarity, support and political activism, but also a place of lack, victimhood and powerlessness.

There is a hard border and a soft border between the two. The hard border is physical (and political). It has a red light of segregation and a green light of integration. The soft border is psychological, with a red light of shame and a green light of acceptance. Both borders are porous; lots of movement does happen.

I have classified the population of the two worlds into four broad archetypes. They are, of course, very crude. The non-disabled I call either dividers or multipliers. Dividers (red light/shame) approve of the apartheid system. They might be prejudiced a little or a lot, consciously or unconsciously. They judge, criticise, moralise and laugh at jokes about disability. Sometimes they act as freelance enforcers of disability apartheid, questioning and policing people with disabilities (people with invisible disabilities face inquisitions on both sides of the border (Kattari et al., 2018)). The dividers are part of the problem. The multipliers (green light/acceptance), on the other hand, are part of the solution. They have respect for difference, empathy, tolerance, open-mindedness and an appreciation of diversity.

People with disabilities I have characterised, equally crudely, as either subtracters or adders. Subtracters (red light/shame) take themselves out of the game. They can be self-critical, maybe sliding into self-pity, and trapped in victimhood and depression. All very understandable, given the prevalence of divider attitudes with which we contend. Adders (green light/acceptance), through luck, genes, family, opportunity, whatever, are better equipped, better able to accept the givens of their situation. They go out into the world and live their lives.

Which ones pass the Humanity Test? Which one are you?

Of course, these characterisations are highly simplistic. Sometimes people can speak or act in a way that supports apartheid; at other times – sometimes in the same breath – the exact opposite can be true.

The physical border is the nexus of activism, chipping away at dismantling the border wall with improved disability rights and legislation, better wheelchair access, universal design, integrated schools, inclusionary workplace employment practices, public transport for all and a fair system of benefits. Kleinman states that images of chronic illness and disability are bad PR: capitalist ideologies want to represent health and success as they try to encourage consumption or mobilise enthusiasm for governmental campaigns (1988, p.47). The UK government was roundly condemned by the United Nations in 2017 for the way it has treated people with disabilities in the current era of austerity (Butler, 2017).

Disability rights activists and the social model of disability have successfully highlighted the way individuals and governments treat the most vulnerable members of society. A great many gains have been achieved over the past several decades, transforming the lives of millions.

The psychological borders are perhaps more enduring.

People with acquired or progressive disabilities have experienced losses that already take them out of the 'normal' world. Often they have had to say goodbye to beloved careers, activities and places. But there's the bigger problem of the psychological walls of the non-disabled – the subtle and not-so-subtle aversion, hostility, bullying, prejudices and acts of discrimination that make disabled people feel unwelcome and unsafe in the non-disabled world. It also makes it hard for people to accept their disability if no one else does. On the other hand, it's hard to be accepted if you don't accept yourself.

A well-known quote often attributed to Abraham Maslow states: 'In any given moment we have two options: to step forward into growth or to step back into safety.' For someone with a disability, safety is obviously enormously appealing, given how vulnerable we can feel in non-disabled land. We all need sometimes to be subtracters – to retreat from the world, or to hang out and do things with other people with disabilities in disabled land. But we must not give up on growth.

It's all too easy to see oneself as a victim. Anyone who has ever lived has probably been there, done that, at some time. I certainly have. I hope this book in some way helps the process of victims becoming victors. We can do better. We can individually and together reclaim our soul.

The Humanity Test is for every body.

In search of research: The 'disability paradox'

Maybe you or a client or a family member has just received a terrible diagnosis of something incurable or terminal. Maybe you have had a horrible accident that has smashed your body. Maybe you have just had a child who was born with a disability. Maybe you've had a disability your whole life but you just can't do it any more; it's too hard. Perhaps you're perfectly healthy and have no impairments but are haunted by the possibility of one of these things happening to you – you don't think you could cope.

How do people cope, actually? What sense can possibly be made of what has happened? Meanwhile, some people you know seem to be living effortlessly healthy, satisfying lives. They grin at you in Facebook selfies snapped in exotic hotspots. The lucky ones, the beautiful people. It's not fair. Why is this happening to me?

I'm really sorry for these slings and arrows that have come your way. They are horrible. They are not what you deserve. I don't believe they are the result of some moral failure or bad karma from a past life. They are not 'God's way'. They just are. I'm sorry. But, hey, you're still here. If you're reading this, you're alive. So what are you going to do? What can you do?

How are you going to live?

In looking for answers, we turn to research. When I chose to study disability – or, more accurately, when it chose me – I was genuinely shocked to discover there was so little research and how prejudicial and ableist it was.

The first problem is that much of the research is quantitative rather than qualitative. Quantitative research is fine when it comes to measuring things in the physical world. But for the understanding of the inner life of humans, numbers are insufficient. As the sign said to hang on Einstein's wall said: 'Not everything that counts can be counted and not everything that can be counted counts.'

This obsession with numbers began in Victorian times, in the aftermath of the Enlightenment and the Industrial Revolution, when psychology increasingly strayed from its philosophical roots and attempted to don the respectable robes of hard science. J.B. Watson's manifesto of radical behaviourism recognised 'no dividing line between man and brute' (Watson, 1913, p.158); humans were presupposed to be entirely logical and predictable. Watson was only concerned with observable, measurable inputs and outputs. There was no consideration of a soul; a ghost in the machine was silenced.

Quantitative research, it is true, has made many useful contributions to psychology, but in general our species refuses to conform to a worldview that seeks to understand and explain the human condition in terms of loveless, soulless, hard science, biological determinism, statistics, mental health questionnaire scores, IQ tests and diagnostic labels.

And it's not even true that quantitative researchers live up to their own ideals. Time and again, published research produces findings that conform to researchers' biases, sponsor preference or cultural difference, or are career enhancing or politically self-serving. All research is political. In 90% of studies of antipsychotic drugs, the best-performing drug was manufactured by the pharmaceutical company that sponsored the research (Cooper, 2008, p.4).

If we look at the example of research into CMT, you find first of all that there is very little research. And what there is tends to be quantitative, pathologising and riddled with biases and prejudices. Typically, these unedifying studies will give a depression inventory or quality-of-life questionnaire to people with CMT and people without CMT and then compare the scores. These 'randomised control trials', which reduce human complexity to numbers, are considered to be the last word on research by para-governmental agencies such as the UK's National Institute for Health and Care Excellence (NICE).

Vinci and colleagues (2007), however, point out that the questions found on standard psychometric measures can lead to biased results when applied to the CMT population. They write:

> For example, 'I get tired more easily than I used to', 'I am worried about physical problems such as aches'… bias the score toward depression when, in fact, easy tiring and pain are real symptoms of the disease.

Vinci has CMT.

And sometimes people with CMT, who are supposed to be suffering, can score quite well on quality-of-life measures. Carter et al. (1995) did not find elevated depression among people with CMT; Vergili et al. (2007) found that quality of life and depression were poorly correlated with the severity of CMT; Vinci et al. (2009) found no difference in psychological distress between 53 people with CMT and the general population. Shy and Rose (2005) are surprised when such 'unexpectedly high levels' of quality of life are reported in studies of chronically ill and disabled people, which they describe as 'the disability paradox' – a 'discrepancy between the person's perception of his or her ideal state and his or her *real state*' (2005, p.790, my italics), as though people with disabilities must be delusional to imagine they have a good quality of life. The 'objective' researchers are baffled that people with disabilities don't conform to their negative prejudices.

This phrase, 'disability paradox', is invoked whenever people with disabilities don't agree to be miserable and depressed and lifeless, as they've been told. The real paradox is that researchers, who presumably have an interest in finding out stuff, can be so hard wired in their prejudices yet seemingly completely oblivious to them.

Fortunately, the philosophical approach has not been defeated by positivism and the blind faith in numbers. A descriptive, subjective, phenomenological psychology lives on, requiring for Merleau-Ponty 'a foreswearing of science', which he regarded as 'always both naïve and at the same time dishonest' (1945/2002, p.ix).

Qualitative research rejects objectivity not only as not possible, but also as not desirable. The unique histories, qualities and biases of the researcher and participants are not denied; they are embraced, as are constructivist and social constructionist approaches that claim no grand narratives or fixed absolutes and instead see reality as temporary, partial, local. For McLeod, 'the primary aim of qualitative research is to develop an understanding of how the world is constructed' (2001, p.2).

Not all qualitative research, however, is good research. Olkin (1999, p.314) and Olkin and Pledger (2003) identify two broad kinds of disability research. What they call 'Paradigm I' research tends to be static, pathology oriented, and about but not by people with disabilities. These studies reflect either the 'moral model' or the 'medical model' – research into what 'we' think about 'them': attitudes toward the disabled person (e.g. Jabin, 1987), the countertransference of therapists with disabled clients (e.g. Segal, 1996), or client transference towards a therapist with a disability (e.g. Anisfield, 1993). A recent study (Ashworth, 2017) found that therapists working with people with neurological conditions can be unsettled and worry about their own health; the clients are present only as mute vectors of therapist unease. Legions of researchers apparently assumed that people with disabilities would have nothing interesting to say about disability; better to rely on their own prejudices.

'Paradigm II' research, by contrast, inquires about health and resilience as opposed to deficit. Paradigm II reflects the social model of disability: it highlights the agency, voice and lived experiences of people who are affected by disability and actively strives to improve their conditions, services and place in society. It is often conducted by disabled researchers.

There is precious little research on disability. And, argues Olkin, of the disability research that is conducted, the vast majority belongs squarely to Paradigm I. Such work, she says, often not only fails to produce any positive changes but also reinforces unhelpful stereotypes (1999, p.308).

Researchers form a negative hypothesis about a pathology that they don't suffer from, and then construct research around verifying that hypothesis, which then becomes a *fait accompli*. This kind of research assumes that a pathology causes suffering:

> Researchers then use a pathogenic filter which looks for and inevitably finds pathology… Prejudices, stereotypes, and myths about disability are infused into every stage of the research process until the inevitable outcome is to verify these misconceptions. (Olkin, 1999, p.311)

What is glaringly absent from most research into disability is the voice of the people who experience it. There are very few studies that are even remotely interested in that voice.

My research

I was interested in hearing the experiences of people affected by disability and comparing their phenomenology with my own. I ended up conducting an interpretative phenomenological analysis (IPA) study of six women with CMT, interviewing each one at length in two separate sittings, and having a colleague interview me twice, too.

I believe that it is in the subjective interplay and tension that exists between phenomenology and interpretation that truths – as opposed to *the* truth – are discerned: truths that are rather more modest, provisional and contextual than anything purporting to be factual. (A saying widely attributed to Socrates goes, 'The only true wisdom is in knowing you know nothing.') IPA is a rich, engaging process that respects and honours the inherent complexity, changeability and mystery of human life. Indeed, its focus on understanding and making sense of experience (Smith, 2019) is the very essence of an existential life: a human search for meaning.

The interviews were extraordinary encounters. None of the participants had spoken about CMT in such depth before; some had never discussed their feelings about CMT with anyone. Additionally, the fact that I too have CMT generated an enormous sense of kinship. The interviews were not just a meeting of minds but of bodies too – bodies that shared the same peculiar kind of brokenness. These were deeply intersubjective, embodied encounters. Merleau-Ponty wrote: 'It is through my body that I understand other people' (1945/2002, p.186); it was through the shared physical vulnerability wrought by CMT that I and my participants connected.

The recorded interviews totalled 22 hours and 38 minutes of testimony. How are truths best uncovered? For Heidegger, unconcealment and concealment are conjoined twins: you cannot have one without the other (Heidegger, 1927/1962). Truth is thus always a mystery, shrouded in untruth.

Considering multiple viewpoints, stages of interpretation and shifts of the camera lens allowed meaningful overarching themes to come into sharp focus. I found this to be an organic, iterative process that crystallised into three main themes: the body and loss; identity, and discrimination. Each had attendant subthemes that reflected participants' lived experience. I added a fourth theme – growth – from later reading and discussions. On countless discarded pages of scribbles, the four main themes eyed each other nervously at first, then began to interact and make sense of each other, before finally taking their positions: four pillars of disability around which an imperfect house of understanding and therapeutic philosophy was constructed.

The body and loss

Strict adherents of the social model of disability see no place for discussions about loss. If what is disabling is a hostile environment rather than any individual's impairment, then there has been no loss. The person with the disability is presumed to be whole.

Yet there are losses aplenty for those with an acquired disability. For someone like me with progressively degenerative conditions, the losses come hard and fast, and just keep coming. One day can you can stand unaided, carry a cup of tea from the kitchen to the living room, or write something down that you can actually read later. Inexplicably, the next day, you can't; another door closes behind you. Then there is the loss of that other you, the one who is just like you but without the impairment or illness. Who might you have been? What might you have done? Given the choice of a cure for Parkinson's and CMT or a less ableist society that was more welcoming of my symptoms, I'll take the cure every time, thank you.

Impairments can cast a shadow on everything: work, social life, romantic relationships, autonomous sense of self. They can rob you of people and activities you once loved. They can make you a stranger to yourself. You can lose your dignity. You can lose hope.

When I sat down with one of my research participants for her first interview, she handed me two sheets of paper, stapled together. She had typed at the top 'How CMT affects me…' Under the headings of Dressing, Hygiene, Mobility, Pain, Household Chores/Cooking and Miscellaneous, she had identified 56 symptoms that challenge her. She wanted me to know that her disability was a constant, unwanted presence in every facet of her life. For her, there was no respite, and no grounds for optimism either, given the progressive nature of her condition. She could only walk short distances, with a cane. She also used a wheelchair and a mobility scooter. She had to give up her work in a children's care home and many beloved activities – swimming, dancing, going for long walks, exploring castles – were no longer possible.

Another participant was somewhat distressed when I met her for her second interview. The day before she'd met with a physiotherapist who supplied her with a new, bulky lower-leg and foot splint to help her walk. She had suffered a lifetime of physical decline and loss, but this new piece of equipment – which did indeed help her mobility – felt like a fresh affront, yet another 'new normal' to adjust to, one more chunk of physicality chipped away. You are always on shaky ground with a progressive disability.

Her disability had forced her to take early retirement from a job at an art gallery that she greatly enjoyed. But her biggest regret was having to give up hiking. She told me:

> It's been really important to me over the years, because I wasn't
> any good at sport, but also, I've got a very strong feeling for
> nature and being outside, and I've had that all my life. Walking
> in nature was what I did with friends. Now I can't. There is a
> part of me that is very unhappy about it.

Another participant used to love drawing and painting, but now struggled to do anything much that required manual dexterity. Another had to give up her dream of being a famous singer.

As disabling conditions go, CMT is relatively benign. It is a slowly progressing, non-life-threatening condition, the symptoms of which can be mild and often don't start to bite until adulthood or midlife. This means diagnosis is often slow. Or it doesn't happen at all – someone with undiagnosed CMT might have their difficulties explained as just having 'funny feet' or not being 'sporty'. Some people with CMT report relief at receiving their diagnosis, to finally have a concrete reason for their fatigue, ungainly walk or clumsiness. Some feared or had been told they had something much worse. Nevertheless, diagnosis for many is a brutal, traumatic introduction to the kingdom of sickness. There are too many tales of bad news delivered badly.

Said one participant:

> My first memory, and I think it is the hardest one to cope with, is when I was 15. I remember going to the doctors, and they're saying to my mum and dad, in front of me, that by the time she's in her 30s she won't be walking. But then nothing else was said to me about it. And Mum and Dad, um, it was very quiet at home. No one said any more to me. It was like I'd done something really wrong. I got very good at burying my thoughts and feelings.

Another's experience of diagnosis was similarly painful:

> So I was in the hospital, um, and, I remember one morning about 7 o'clock I woke up, and the doctor came and sat on the bed, he said, 'Er, right we've got your results back, and I can confirm that you have got hereditary motor sensory neuropathy otherwise known as Charcot-Marie-Tooth. It's a progressive disease,' he said, 'Er, er, that's it.' Then he said, 'The best thing I can advise you is to never have children.'
>
> And then he just went. All I ever really wanted was to have kids, to have a family, and I felt CMT had snatched that away. I was 21, and I'd just lost my dad, and my mum wasn't around, I didn't know anybody, I was just, I suppose I was dumbstruck.

The message inherent in the doctor's advice was that it would be better if people with a neurological condition had never been born. Such a view, such disregard for ethical standards, has no place in medicine.

Post-diagnosis, participants experienced an ever-changing kaleidoscope of responses to living with the losses wrought by disability. All reported times of low mood and anxiety. Perhaps the commonest reaction was anger: We can no longer do what we used to be able to do, the everyday things that other people take for granted, and we lose patience with our failing bodies, and we snap.

Said one participant:

> I get pissed off really. You can't grip your credit card, you can't
> get your change out properly, and you can't… you can feel
> something down in your bag and you can't actually grasp it to
> get it out. And we live in a world where people don't notice you,
> they practically knock you over if you hesitate or you're fiddling
> round with your money. There are times when I get really upset
> about little things I can't do. When I see people walking down
> a staircase, not holding the bannister and maybe carrying
> something, well, it looks like a miracle.

The physical vulnerability that disability confers often necessitates a degree of psychological protection. One of my research participants described this as 'the wall.' She kept her emotions away from others but, to a significant extent, she kept them away from herself, too. Anger gets internalised and numbed into submission, depression. She said:

> I don't feel things. People can tell me things that for them
> would be upsetting, and I don't understand why they're upset. I
> would like to feel more. I should feel more feelings but I don't.
> I'm odd. Sometimes I think I'd like to cry and then straight
> away tell myself no, that's not gonna happen.

The 'wall' also means that people with disabilities can sometimes be reluctant to ask for help. My research participants' desire to keep their struggles to themselves made them all enormously self-reliant and resilient in managing their day-to-day challenges. Disability can be the mother of invention. They were experts in living. They cherished their independence and privacy, but to varying degrees all sought help at times, from family, friends, strangers and healthcare professionals. All felt ambivalent about help. Few found helpful help. Said one:

I've had tons of help, you know from professionals. All of them. Recently I've had special hand people look at my hands and give me suggested exercises and suggested bits of kit and gloves, special gloves for the winter and all this, you know, because when your hands get cold, everything goes a lot worse. I've just had so much help, but there's a certain point where the help can't go any further.

Another did not regard herself as someone in need of help. She said:

I can be sad, I mean I can, I can sit there and cry my eyes out sometimes, but then you realise that it doesn't matter, you get to the stage where, you realise that it doesn't matter how much you cry, or how frustrated you get or how bad it is, no one's going to do anything to help. If you don't pull yourself out, you've lost it, it's your life gone, so you've got to do it. No one does help, no one's gonna help. There's no one out there that can help. I just want people just to accept that I'm me, this is me. And get on with it.

§

These testimonies reveal the extent of the losses that disability has wrought: careers, relationships, beloved activities, the image of the kind of life they hoped to live – all gone. And they never know what is coming next: CMT is progressive, with an inexorable, gradual, linear degeneration of nerve and muscle. But loss of functionality often happens in discrete, quantum stages. Someone might one day wake up to discover that buttons or keys or signing their name are suddenly a problem, or the seemingly simple act of standing still is now impossible. The progressive disability journey includes many such landmark moments along the way. At each stage, a process of adjustment takes place, parameters are revised, and the sense of one's self and one's life shifts once again. The losses accumulate: People experience a never-ending cycle of loss, grief, adaptation, acceptance, along with an ever-present anxiety over what the future holds.

Thomas and Siller (1999) liken the effects of disability to the mourning that Freud described as resulting from object loss (1917/2001): a gradual withdrawal of libidinal energy from what has gone, the integration of the loss with the new reality so that life can go on, and the resulting continued survival of the ego – an ego that, as Freud stated, 'is first and foremost a bodily ego' (1923a, p.25). Life thus carries with it the possibility of an ongoing, never-ending series of mourning processes as function continues to decrease. For some, such mourning may slide into pathology – what Freud called melancholia, which 'behaves like an open wound', or perhaps, to borrow a phrase from the literature on parents of children with disabilities, 'chronic sorrow' (Olshansky, 1962). Psychological support therefore needs to be tailored to facilitating this mourning process, for which 'progress is long drawn out and gradual' (Freud, 1917, p.255). For many people with progressive disabilities, this is a lifelong process of 'working through'.

Livneh (1984) proposed a five-stage model that consolidated prior models of adaptation to disability. The first stage, 'initial impact', consists of two substages: shock and anxiety. The second stage is 'defense mobilization', which consists of bargaining and denial. The third stage, 'initial realization' or 'recognition', consists of mourning and/or depression and internalising anger. The fourth stage, 'retaliation' or 'rebellion', includes both direct and indirect methods of externalising anger and aggressiveness. The fifth and final stage, 'reintegration' or 'reorganization', is composed of a cognitive substage of acknowledgment, an affective substage of acceptance or assimilation, and a behavioural substage of adjustment, adaptation or reconstruction.

Livneh's model bears a striking similarity to Kübler-Ross's 'five stages of grief' in her seminal book *On Death and Dying* (1969), based on her psychiatric work and interviews with terminally ill patients. You start with denial ('If I pretend it's not there it will go away'), move into anger ('It's not fair – why me?'), bargaining ('Okay, fine, I'll exercise, take my meds, live a good life and then maybe it won't be too bad'), depression ('This is terrible, what's the point of living?') and finally arrive at acceptance ('This is part of my life, I can cope, it will be okay').

The book became a roadmap of dying, and then of mourning as the model became applied to the latter process as well. An orderly procession from stage to stage, arriving at the final destination – a cheerful accommodation to your loss, much to the relief of family and friends, who might have tried to usher you along on your journey as expeditiously as possible. The model also provides a useful lens for research into how people respond to progressive physical disability. The six participants in my research had experienced all of these 'stages' at different times and with different intensities. While the experiences in their stories were all unique, anger and denial in particular were reactions they had in common. All of the participants had periods of depression or low mood but there was no way of knowing to what extent this was attributable to disability. As we have seen, a common response was withdrawal. CMT is an awkward condition, embarrassing, hard to explain. You don't want the parent who gave it to you to feel bad. The world out there is a minefield. Better not to talk about it. Better to stay home.

The notion of 'adjustment' to disability is contested as it puts all the onus on the person with a disability to change – in a manner that is acceptable to the non-disabled – rather than on an environment or attitudes of the non-disabled that fail to accommodate them (e.g. Wright, 1983; Olkin, 1999, p.44; Dunn, 2015, p.28).

Furthermore, grief is an idiosyncratic process that does not follow a predictable pattern. Each person's response to a loss is their own, and no one has any right to question that. Certainly, I do not want to live in a world where people with disabilities are pathologised unless or until they are able to demonstrate a sufficient level of cheerful, meek acceptance. This 'requirement of mourning' – that a person's reaction to their disability must conform to the non-disabled person's assumptions and expectations – is oppressive (Wright, 1983). I have had non-disabled people tell me they would kill themselves if they had Parkinson's; congratulate me 'for not giving up'; praise me 'for doing so well in the circumstances'; inform me that, if I'm not really angry at having two neurological conditions, then clearly I must be 'in denial'. Others have demanded the opposite extreme: that I be 'positive' or 'brave' or 'fight' the onset of symptoms. Mostly people just don't go there – they don't mention the elephant in the room because, well, elephants are big and scary and unpredictable.

Instead of making ridiculous assumptions, why don't they just ask me what my experience is?

In a later review, Livneh and Parker (2005) identified further models for adjustment to disability, beyond linear, orderly 'stage' models: 'linear-like models' (Livneh, 2001, p.153), 'pendular models' (Charmaz, 1995), 'interactive models'. They also proposed a 'chaos and complexity model', in which adaptation to disability is 'nonlinear, unpredictable, and discontinuous'. The clinical implications for this model are that it:

> suggests the supremacy of an eclectic approach that
> incorporates multifaceted, yet nonrigid, views of the human
> experience… Such an approach recognizes the complexity,
> uncertainty, transformation, and ever evolving dynamics
> of the human spirit, especially as it seeks to transcend the
> constraining barriers imposed by chronic illness and disability.
> (Livneh & Parker, 2005, p.26)

This postmodern approach is a reminder not to make any assumptions or generalisations about the phenomenology of people with disabilities, and always to be open to the possibility of being surprised. The life of each person is unique.

Identity

When the Olympics came to town in 2012, I went to number of events with my daughter. One of them was a paralympic basketball match. Before the opening whistle, all we saw was wheelchairs. Five minutes into the game, we had completely forgotten about the wheelchairs as the players' personalities shone through: the aggressive attacker, the huge defender, the fast one, the sneaky one, the tactical thinker, the flamboyant, stylish one, and so on.

It was a thrilling match, the highlight of our Olympics.

And we don't even really like basketball that much.

People with disabilities vary greatly in their attitudes towards their physical impairments. Those at the negative end of the spectrum regard themselves as helpless victims of a completely incapacitating body. Their expectation of themselves is low. At the other end, people can be relentlessly positive, either denying that there is anything wrong with them at all, or else denying that it impacts them negatively in any way. They will only reluctantly ask for or accept help from others. These different reactions can be observed between different people with disabilities, but also within those people: our mindsets can fluctuate within a day or even within a sentence.

The participants in my research were no different in manifesting this ambivalence : 'I'm okay, I don't need help, I can exist in the world just fine'; 'I'm not okay, I struggle, I'm vulnerable, and I need help,' and toggling back and forth between them, as the following extracts reveal.

One of my research participants described how she might look forward to a night on the town, a charity walk, or a backpacking trip to Cambodia. She wanted to be included. But she didn't want to hold anyone else back.

> Yeah, that's kind of the fine line isn't it? You want to be treated the same as everyone but, then when you're treated the same in some situation, you find yourself getting into difficulty, which is quite common. But you don't want to go to the other extreme of always telling people about your disability and then being treated only like a disabled person. I don't want to be defined by it, I don't want to be one of those people that like, they become their illness or disability, not that that's wrong, but I don't, I don't find that particularly attractive nor do I want to be that person.
>
> 'Disabled' is a funny word that I don't really like. Am I disabled? Um. Probably… yeah. But I don't think of it as a really clear sort of stamp. I have a disabled blue parking badge, but I feel guilty about that as well. It is part of me but I don't want it to define who I am. I know I am weak, and sometimes I feel like it affects my femininity. But then sometimes I think that's really ridiculous, like, some people can't walk. I don't know.

Another participant similarly sometimes felt her disability was not serious enough to warrant any special attention:

> Well, when I see other disabled people, I think well, at least I can still walk. I got a disability parking badge, and I don't use it sometimes. My mum says why on earth don't you use it? I just think someone else might need that space more than I need it.
>
> Once I'd parked and put my badge up and I got out of the car, and this woman behind me turned round and said to her husband, 'What on earth's she got a badge for? There's nothing wrong with her.' You know, and that's why I think, that's why I feel guilty when I use my badge a lot of the time. You know, if someone's thinking that, because they can't see that you've got your AFOs [ankle-foot orthoses] on, I just feel guilty. It's

invisible, and that is, I think, a very big part of the problem.
Yeah, I feel guilty. Because there's people a lot worse.

We can see from these passages how people with a disability sometimes deny and disown it, but at other times, especially when it becomes more severe, they have to accept it and own it in order to be accommodated in the world at large.

This interview exchange with another participant further exemplifies the ambivalent mindset about needing help yet denying those needs because to admit to them would be to 'give into' them:

Me: Is it difficult to ask for help?

Participant: Yeah, yeah.

Me: What happens?

Participant: I just, I dunno, I would sooner go without getting some food rather than ask other people to help me get it. I don't know, I think it's because I'm quite an independent person.

Me: Right, so if you ask for help, what does that mean?

Participant: I'm giving in to it.

Me: Giving in?

Participant: Giving in to it. It's silly because I always say to my daughter, if you need help, you know, you've just got to ask someone to do it for you. So I'm trying to push it on her that she mustn't be frightened… I'm quite a shy person and I just don't like asking for help.

Me: Don't want to make a fuss?

Participant: Yeah, yeah, because then people are thinking, well, why does she need help, what's her problem? I don't know.

Me: So you can't take your own advice, in other words.

Participant: No [*laughs*].

Me: Why is it one rule for your daughter and another one for you? What kind of person would you be if you were somebody who needed help and asked for help and got help? What would that say about you?

Participant: I don't know, it's my silly rules, I think.

Me: We so often feel like we have to present a smiley face to the world.

Participant: Yeah, I'm very good at doing that.

Me: But if, if all we ever all of us ever do is walk around with a smile on our face, we never actually really connect.

Participant: No.

Me: Have you ever asked for help?

Participant: Er, not really. The only time I did ask for help was when I ended up going to Mind because things got so bad. I got to the stage that I didn't want to be here anymore.

She was imprisoned in a kind of fortress of her own making. Her disability was unacceptable, and it was unacceptable for her to be vulnerable and in need of help, so no one was allowed in. At one time, her isolation was such that she became suicidal. Today she has plenty of people and love in her life, not in spite of her disability but, in part, because of it. Where once she withdrew, now she reaches out.

Sometimes people with disabilities cover up or minimise their struggles – and sometimes the people closest to them do likewise, as this exchange illustrates:

Participant: If I tried to talk to people about it, I'd quite often make jokes about myself. So I may say something in a joke but actually inside I mean it, but I don't know how to express it seriously. So I'd always laugh at myself. But inside I want to say, I'm sad because I can't run and jump anymore.

Me: And why did you do that do you think? Make light of it.

Participant: To protect me, because I don't like people seeing me sad, or that it gets to me. It's comments, you know, oh, you're always tired, you're always going to bed, you're always so slow. You know, I said to my friend yesterday my feet are hurting. She went, well my feet hurt – I've got hard skin and a bunion. And I thought, you just don't get it. You haven't got a clue. You have no idea. You've got no clue.

And you know, sometimes you really feel like you're taking a risk telling somebody about it, and when you don't get the right kind of response, you just sort of think oh well, you know, I'm not gonna bother. I mean, I don't want sympathy, I just want understanding.

A lot of people who are ambivalent about their disabilities inevitably project their doubts onto others – especially partners or potential partners. They cannot imagine their disability is acceptable to a partner as it is not always acceptable to themselves. Said one of my research participants:

> I mean, to accept me, the way I am… I'm not a normal girl am I? Who'd want to date someone with a disability? In 10 years, 20 years you know, do they want to be with someone who they might have to be looking after, when they could have a woman that they don't have to? You know, who would choose to look after somebody? But then my head says, I would do that for someone, so there are people out there, you know there are going to be men out there that think like that.

§

Whenever someone with a medical concern accesses healthcare services, some kind of drama ensues. If you're on the list for a hernia operation or an NHS counsellor, it's *Waiting for Godot*. A trip to A&E becomes *Long Day's Journey into Night*. All those tests you had when you were stressed and thought your heart was giving out? *Much Ado About Nothing*.

Every medical room is a kind of theatre. There is often suspense, tragedy, mystery. There is rich dialogue; there are some fine soliloquies. There is comedy. Everyone knows their place, their lines, their props. Everyone seems to be playing a role according to NHS dramaturgical guidelines.

In general, these roles polarise the cast into us and them: the well and the unwell, the sane and the insane, the okay and the not okay, the glad and the mad. In a sense, the staff have a vested interest in keeping the patients as far away from them as possible. It's hard for the two camps to reach each other across the great divide, within which lies a welter of fear and despair, with death never far away.

Goffman (1959) says this is how identity works. We each get a sense of ourselves from how we perform – and how we are expected to perform – in various social settings. We are aware of how our performance is received by others and we are alert to the reciprocal and interdependent performances of others, too. Erikson's theory of psychosocial development (1968) similarly says we learn a sense of ourselves through our interactions with others. This process takes place especially during adolescence, when someone with a disability might typically be experiencing bullying at school.

Social identity theory (Tajfel, 1969; Tajfel & Turner, 1986) suggests that we derive a lot of our personal sense of identity from our roles within social groups, and that perceived group identities lie at the heart of discrimination.

Identities can be seen to play a key role in creating and sustaining social interactions and cultural practices. They are generally adopted unconsciously within social structures and accepted as part of the natural order, as a given. But they are not fixed. Sometimes we act as members of a particular social group, but we can also make choices to do things differently. Indeed, it is in the dissonance between personal identities and different group identities that individual, social and cultural changes can happen (Giddens, 1991; Jenkins, 2008). There has been an enormous rise recently in interest in and the study of intersectionality, defined as:

> the interconnected nature of social categorizations such as race, class, and gender as they apply to a given individual or group, regarded as creating overlapping and interdependent systems of discrimination or disadvantage. (Cyrus, 2017)

Acting as an individual, in defiance of your assigned or expected group identity – going against traditions, institutions, moral codes, and established ways of doing things – is not always easy. You might find opposition from hegemonic power networks, and from discourse and ideologies within family, community or at state level (Althusser, 1971; Foucault, 1988; Butler, 1990; Brewer, 1991; Stangor, 2013).

Perhaps up to now you have told yourself a certain story about your life: one that integrates past and present selves and considers possible future ones, too. Such a narrative identity (Ricoeur, 1984; Markus & Nurius, 1986; Bruner, 1987) is, however, profoundly impacted by ill health. In *The Wounded Storyteller* (1995), Frank describes how, as patients, we must surrender our own narrative of our 'dis-ease' and submit to the narrative provided by the expert. And it's usually a thoroughly damning, prejudicial narrative that only considers the deficit.

A diagnosis is not the end of the story however, although I have met people who have responded as though it were. But how is something like a chronic, degenerative illness to be integrated into one's narrative? How does one manage what Goffman (1963) calls a 'spoiled identity'? You have a stigma now; you are 'not quite human' (1963, p.15).

Whatever the new happenstances – a diagnosis, a death, a divorce, for example – they will change the whole story. The past is revisited in the light of the present and the present in the light of the past (Bakhtin, 1981; Ricoeur, 1984; Bruner, 1987); different 'possible selves' are foreshadowed for the future (Markus & Nurius, 1986). We experience, then interpret; we interpret, then experience. The formation of a sense of self is a lifelong reflexive process of hermeneutic phenomenology.

The perceived group identity of people with a common illness is so pejorative – and constantly reinforced by the daily insult of prejudice and discrimination – that it's no surprise group members are ambivalent about adopting it. Goffman says the afflicted man 'can neither embrace his group nor let it go' (1963, p.132). CMT generally has fairly mild symptoms in the early years, allowing other, healthier identities to be established first. As an unwelcome guest arriving late to the party, it's understandable that the illness identity will initially be turned away at the door – some studies suggest that early onset of disability leads to better adjustment (e.g. Barker & Maralani, 1997); Charmaz's longitudinal study suggests the opposite (1995). Then there is the fact that, for many years, sometimes for a whole lifetime, some disabilities can be largely invisible. For many, it is possible to travel among the well disguised as one of them; to 'pass' for 'normal' (Goffman, 1963, p.92). Finally, CMT identity itself is ill-formed. It is a largely unknown condition, lacking a culture of its own. It is understandable that one's CMT-ness is frequently denied or disavowed. My six research participants were all members of the national charity CMT UK and all had thus reached some kind of accommodation of their condition, but even they were highly CMT ambivalent at times. CMT is like a big heavy cloak that we wear: it can't be removed, but it is sometimes invisible, and we do sometimes completely forget we are wearing it.

We should all wear our cloaks proudly. We should not deny, hide, feel ashamed by or apologise for an essential part of us. Ill or not, we all hold the transformative power of being able to choose our own story, which in turn can then disrupt the accepted discursive and cultural norms. We can dance to the anthem provided, or we can write our own music, and in so doing change the anthem. In this way, a society's narratives can be mediated by the 'small stories' of individuals (Bamberg, 2006, 2011; Georgakopoulou, 2006).

How we wear our cloaks matters. Writing about gender, Butler (1990; 1993) sees identity as a performance – one that reflects the interplay between who you are and what you do. Individual performance is a choice; it can challenge and confront societal norms and expectations and thereby alter them. Butler named these 'queer' performances: 'Queer is by definition whatever is at odds with the normal, the legitimate, the dominant' (Halperin, 1995, p.62).

If you have CMT, or Parkinson's for that matter, your assigned role now is perhaps to be somewhat helpless, benign, a bit dim, but also noble in your quiet suffering, and brave. While queer theory and disability studies have their differences (Sherry, 2004), a *queering of disease and disability* might be to refuse to accept all that and simply do it your way. There is a subversive thrill in defying expectations. These are not even diseases – they are conditions. And they need not diminish the appetite for and engagement with living. Quite the contrary.

The alternative, unattractive identity to adopt is that of the victim. It's a get-up that is always in my psychic wardrobe. Sometimes, alas, I can't help but slip it on.

Chronic victims see their life as harder than anyone else's, their suffering greater, their losses more significant. They are sponges of negativity. Seemingly minor events are mined for nuggets of bad feeling. If you ask them how they are, they will give you a lengthy exposition on all their aches and pains and doctors' appointments.

The victim will find a way to insert themselves into events that have nothing to do with them, insisting on their right to feel personally victimised. The victim will often claim that, if only all these terrible things hadn't happened, if only they weren't so unlucky, they would have achieved all sorts of amazing things and be living a life full of courage, success and fun.

Being a victim is an enormously powerful position. In a way, it offers a kind of defensive safety.

Victims will often go to therapy for years to prove that they can't be helped, that their problems are insurmountable, that they can't do anything and thus don't have to do anything.

Victims live as 'misers and complainers', writes the poet David Whyte, 'reluctant and fearful, always at the gates of existence, but never bravely and completely attempting to enter, never wanting to risk ourselves, never walking fully through the door' (2014, p.172).

Nothing changes until, one way or another, a choice is made to live a different way. This involves giving up the victim mentality, taking an honest look in the mirror, admitting your vulnerabilities, and accepting and loving oneself. And then, afraid but resolute, you step through that door to life.

To be clear, I am not characterising people with disabilities as lazy, needy benefit cheats, as some of our nation's odious media channels do. If someone with an acquired disability or chronic condition wants to spend some time hiding under the duvet, I understand. If you think it's hard and it's not fair and nobody understands – yes, you're right.

But eventually, we all have to face the most famous six words in literature: 'To be or not to be?' That's the question Hamlet asked himself. Stricken with grief over his father's death, unable to avenge the murder or his mother's betrayal, incapacitated by indecision and fear, he chose to be, but as if he wasn't – a kind of living death, a walking shadow – until actual death chose him. The rest is silence.

If only Hamlet had found a good therapist, he might have chosen to live; perchance to dream.

The answer to Shakespeare's question is 'Be'.

With pride.

Discrimination

A client who is blind is riding an elevator with her personal assistant (PA). The elevator stops, the doors open, and a woman gets on and addresses the PA.

'Is she blind?' she says.

My client smiles and replies: 'Yes, I am blind, but I'm not deaf. I can hear you.'

'Oh!' says the woman. 'Well, you're not very gloomy are you?'

My client is exasperated. 'Do you want me to be gloomy?' she says. Silence.

All the participants in my research have a sorry abundance of experiences of being ignored, excluded, denied, ridiculed and even attacked for having CMT. Instances of discrimination can be ever present or intermittent, large or small, active or passive, conscious or unconscious, subtle or unsubtle (Deal, 2007; Ostrove & Crawford, 2006). Sometimes it's the physical environment that presents the obstacles. Very often it's other people.

People with disabilities often first become acutely aware of their difference in school. Many find that their vulnerability attracts the interest of bullies. In those fragile years when children are building a sense of self, those with disabilities find that self can take a battering – sometimes literally. It's understandable from these experiences that people often try to keep their disability hidden, cut themselves off from their emotional reactions to it, and deep down develop a sense of shame.

Here are some of my research participants' testimonies.

I was always picked on at school, because I was different.
Because people could see that I walked differently, I couldn't
wear the shoes that everybody else wore, I couldn't do sports.
I was bullied a lot. There was one particular girl who was really
popular in school, and she knew she could get at me. She knew
she could bully me. She used to pull my hair, you know, she
used to come up behind me and push me, because she knew
I hadn't got very good balance. Or you know, when I was
walking past, people would deliberately put their foot out
and trip me up.

They used to call me Forrest Gump and laugh at me, or they'd
say, Oh you walk like you know, you've been to the toilet. Just
cruel things that kids would say. I used to not be able to say
CMT without crying. I'd cry instantly. And then over time I got
stronger, so when they used to call me names I just used to tell
'em to do one. And it didn't really bother me any more and that
is the truth.

It was mainly PE. PE I found very very difficult. They just
thought I was clumsy and not trying. I always remember them
trying to make me jump over this big horse thing. And I just
said, 'I can't jump,' and they said, 'Course you can, everyone can
jump.' I just remember sort of running up to it and just sort of
leant over it, and I said, 'I can't jump, I can't jump.' I remember
one PE teacher particularly trying to make me do hurdles and
I was just like, 'I can't jump, so how am I gonna be able to jump

> over a hurdle?' And she was like 'Don't be stupid, everyone can
> jump over a hurdle.'
>
> You got bullied and accepted it. You just did other things out of
> school that they didn't do. If girls wanted to be bitchy in school,
> I got on with it.

At work, too, participants experienced discrimination and even bullying. It's certainly hard enough battling disability at work, but this is cruelly amplified by having to battle the prejudicial attitudes of fellow employees too. This is one participant's story:

> I sometimes have to go and get a chair out of another room when
> I'm tired, you know. And if I do, I just feel a bit guilty again then
> because someone says, 'Oh, you're sitting down again, what's up
> today? You're sitting down a lot lately.' Then I had a new manager,
> and he took the chair away totally. I weren't allowed to sit down
> at all. I said, 'I need the chair because I've got a disability,' and
> he just dismissed it totally, he said, 'No and that's the end of
> it.' And I went to my HR and um, they sort of sided with him.
> It was horrible. Obviously, I was very stressed. I thought they
> were going to use it as an excuse to get rid of me. It sort of got
> personal, and I couldn't do anything right and my confidence just
> went right down to nothing. He just made me feel totally useless
> at my job. I got to the stage I didn't want to go into work.
>
> After about a year, I won. We were in an office and I had
> two of the senior management there, and I'd just found out so
> much information and I'd researched everything, and I just
> blurted it all out in front of them, and he just sat back. After the
> meeting, they told me to put a chair right where I needed it. It
> shouldn't have ever got to that stage. Not long after that, he left.

Experiences from healthcare providers in the NHS are a typically mixed bag. At their most extreme, discriminatory attitudes can even extend to questioning the right of someone with a disability to exist. The participant who was advised on diagnosis to 'never have children' ignored the oppressive advice and many years later found herself pregnant: her beloved daughter is now a teenager. She was asked to have amniocentesis to check if her child also had CMT. 'I'm not doing it,' she told the doctor:

It wouldn't make any difference. You can write all the referral slips you like, I'm not doing it. There were these two nurses. They were so vile to me. They were really, really horrible to me. The one lady said, 'Well, don't you want to know if the baby has what you have? Would you really want to bring a child into the world that's disabled?'

The participant later heard from her partner, the baby's father, that members of his family were expressing similar sentiments. 'They went, "Well, we just don't think it's fair if there's a chance that this baby's gonna come out disabled".'

One grandmother in the family told her, 'Well, if that child is disabled or deformed in any way, I don't want nothing to do with it.'

Discrimination is not always so overt and explicit. It can happen anywhere. One participant described the horrors of simply going out to a restaurant:

I went for a meal the other day and I couldn't use the knife properly to cut my food up. My elbows go out and I end up elbowing someone, and then the food flies off the plate. There's anxiety in situations like that. I don't really like eating in front of people. Then I got locked in the toilet. I didn't have the hand strength to unlock the door. I only feel safe at home. I'm becoming a bit of a hermit to be honest.

Said another:

Yeah, socially it does limit you. Recently in a restaurant I was sitting there trying to cut a roast potato and I couldn't hold my knife properly and then you think well everyone's looking at me, because I can't hold my knife, and it's just things like that you know that um… [*sighs*]. People ask if you want go roller-skating or something. I'm not gonna be going [*laughs*]. You know, you need to know your limits. It's okay. I think the only thing that has always really got to me, probably true for every woman that's got CMT, is shoes. You get a nice dress, and you're going to a wedding or whatever, and you're thinking, what on earth am I gonna put on my feet?

Disability has a major impact on romantic relationships, too. Said one participant:

> In relationships I get really worried about my CMT – has that
> been the reason why people have broken up with me, or will it
> have an effect on relationships in the future? I don't know.

Another saw her symptoms worsen during her 12-year marriage and her husband become increasingly unsupportive, critical and emotionally abusive. Finally, she divorced him, some three years before I interviewed her. She said:

> So obviously now I'm single. And the actual thought of dating,
> or being with anybody else – I can't see that. Because of the
> CMT. So, yeah, that stops me getting too close with anyone.

Another recounted her experience of being ejected from a relationship and her home:

> We had a relationship for five years, and, um, he came home
> one day and said, 'I've had enough, you, you need to pack your
> bags and go.' And it was his house, and it all came out of the
> blue. I went, 'I don't understand, you know, what's going on?
> What have you had enough of?' You know? And he said, 'Well,
> I don't want to upset you, but it's there and I can't get away from
> it, I can't, I can't live with you, knowing that you may end up in
> a wheelchair, or that you're going to be crippled. I can't live with
> that, because I don't want that. I don't want to be looking after
> you.'

Not surprisingly, a lot of the negative views that non-disabled people may harbour towards disability can become internalised, magnified and projected. Shame is a common, overriding response to discrimination. People with CMT often say they don't like walking in public, for example, because their ungainly gait makes 'people think you're drunk', although few can offer any evidence for this supposition. One research participant, a singer, recalled:

> I was selected to go and do this masterclass with a top
> singer. I sang an operatic aria that required quite a lot of

physical strength and stamina and this lady, who was in her 70s, was critiquing me in front of this whole audience in this very posh venue.

'Oh come on,' she said, 'I need you to support your body, sing into your back, use your muscles – put some strength into it, girl.' And I was like, oh God, oh no. And then she was trying to pull me and then she was dragging me across the stage. And she was like, 'Oh come on, that's pathetic.' Like I'm an old lady. I was 22. I just felt like, completely ostracised and humiliated. I actually physically couldn't do it, but I couldn't say in front of a whole, like, room full of people. And then as soon as I sat down, I was just, like, choking up with tears. And as soon as the masterclass was finished, I was just uncontrollably crying. I was humiliated.

Another research subject had 'worked through' the shame and humiliation and come out the other side:

I'm not gonna be embarrassed about it. I've worked all through that. My mantra has always been that whatever someone's got wrong, you look at their eyes, and you get through any physical disability. You talk to them and it's not a problem. You treat them like humans. I don't want to feel sorry for them, and I don't want anyone to feel sorry for me. I don't want pity. I want someone to accept that, just, I'm me, this is me.

Her other rule was that any help should be offered, not imposed. People could do as much as she needed them to do, and always on her terms. She had no handles on her wheelchair. 'Don't like being pushed,' she said, 'Don't do with being pushed.'

§

We human beings like to regard ourselves as rational and logical and good, but our motives, instincts and behaviours are not always noble. Allport (1954) said prejudice was not some rare evil but a part of being human. Our survival has depended on a certain level of anxiety, vigilance and distrust towards the unknown, the Other, and an affiliation with the safety of the known: this has been our evolutionary process (Schaller et al., 2010). We navigate through life with the help of 'thin-slicing' (Gladwell, 2006): we use our senses, our experience and our beliefs to process a given situation very quickly, largely unconsciously, and act. Sometimes the red warning light flashes completely unnecessarily; we have an immediate physiological reaction to each other (Macrae & Quadflieg, 2010). White (2011) writes that non-disabled people experience disgust and 'dissmell' when they see her in her wheelchair. The outcomes of such bad intelligence can be devastating, especially if poor light and police firearms are involved.

This is not to say we are inherently prejudiced. One review of research into attitudes towards people with disabilities concluded that they are ambivalent rather than uniformly negative (Söder, 1990). But discrimination is an undeniable fact. And it can be contagious, too – thin-slicing draws heavily on groupthink. Tajfel's social identity theory (1969) suggests that we categorise members of a group as being all the same. Such prejudice 'creates or maintains hierarchical status relations between groups' (Dovidio et al., 2010, p.7).

A number of studies have shown just how easy it is to create 'in groups' and 'out groups' based on the most meaningless of differences, and the hostility towards the out group can escalate with depressing ease. Examples are the Robbers Cave experiment with two arbitrary groups of 12-year-old boys (Sherif et al., 1961), which bore a depressing resemblance to Golding's fictional account, *Lord of the Flies*; Jane Elliott's classic schoolroom blue eye/brown eye exercise (Peters, 1971), and Zimbardo's Stanford prison experiment (Zimbardo et al., 1971), though these are now being reconsidered and reinterpreted. The archives of these experiments have now been opened up and, on closer inspection, writes Bregman:

> It turns out we had it back to front all along... Most of these
> people, it seems, just wanted to help out. And if anyone failed,
> it was the people in charge – the scientists and the lead editors,
> the governors and the police chiefs. They were the Leviathans
> that lied and manipulated. (2020, p.199)

We are suggestible: we are hardwired to be on the alert for danger, to be full of doubt about 'the Other.' We are Othello, and there is no shortage of Iagos whispering in our ear, casting aspersions, pointing the finger of blame. In this way, discrimination becomes political.

Edward Said called this 'Orientalism' – a process by which dominant cultural, professional, national, political and economic powers establish versions of 'knowledge' and 'truth' about themselves and those over whom they wish to exert power (1978/2003, p.273).

People who are physically impaired are at the bottom of the ladder – polar opposites of the 'beauty-is-good' stereotype (Dion et al., 1972). They are looked down upon by everyone else on Fiske's vertical hierarchy of power (2011). They are not regarded as whole people but as damaged goods. Typically, disabled people are perceived as warm but incompetent, eliciting pity and help (whether wanted or not), but also neglect (Fiske et al., 2007).

The medical model dictates that only the defective body part is seen, and it is assumed to be an enormous burden. This 'correspondence bias' or 'attribution error' (Pettigrew, 1979; Gilbert & Malone, 1995) is commonly applied to whole groups – wheelchair users, for example. And Foucault's 'medical gaze' (1963) is not confined to doctors.

It is my view that the medical model that treats people like dysfunctional machines inevitably stigmatises people with health conditions and exacerbates the psychological challenge of coping. As shown in the testimonies of my research participants, particularly around diagnosis, there is sometimes an almost wilful lack of empathy in some healthcare professionals that borders on cruelty – and which, anecdotally at least, can exacerbate symptoms. At the same time, the system does not care to offer any professional psychological care.

People with disabilities often harbour prejudices against the non-disabled (Monteith & Spicer, 2000; Johnson & Lecci, 2003). But they also typically internalise the negative social biases and stereotypes of others (Johnson et al., 2000; Ellemers et al., 2002; Morris, 2014). This can manifest as feelings of shame.

Guilt over something you've done is bad enough, but shame over who you are is far more pernicious. It is an unchanging message that runs to the very core of your being; 'an inner wounding' (Wurmser, 1994) to accompany the physical deficits and impairments that you and society find so unacceptable. Shame makes us want to hide. Jung described it as a 'soul-eating emotion' (1957, p.23). The shamed live in 'silence and secrecy' (Sanderson, 2015, p.25). I believe this is true of many people with disabilities.

My research project participants were very open about their feelings of inferiority and shame. At the same time, I was struck by how incredibly resilient and strong they were in the face of discrimination.

Growth

For much of the 20th century, the prevailing approach to psychological thought and practice was inflected by modernist ideas of science. The belief was that, if only sufficient experiments could be performed, all the laws and truths of human behaviour and the human mind – absolute, universal, objective truths – could be known. This belief came under fire in a postmodern revolution that saw a new 'second science' of psychology emerge from under the shadow of academic psychology, one based on practice rather than empiricism and on subjectivity rather than objectivity.

Yet unhelpful aspects of old thinking persist today. Positivist psychology – for Kvale, an irrelevant 'museum of modern thought' (1992, p.48) – is still taught widely in universities and directs much industry research that is influential but of limited practical value to psychotherapists. The tiresome debate about whether or not psychology is a 'real' science festers on. And the cause-effect-treatment medical model of clinical psychology that applies uniform, pejorative labels to those in psychological distress predominates.

The medical model sees nothing good in disease or disability. The goal is to usher the inert, passive and preferably silent patient in the direction of a normality from which they are so very clearly deviant, mostly through pharmacological, surgical or prosthetic interventions. It is recognised that there is such a thing as psychology, but the medical model dictates that the solution to problems in this area is more drugs and, if you insist, some therapy to correct faulty, aberrant thinking and behaviour through psychoeducation.

But what if, rather than being seen solely in terms of deficit, illness and disability could be regarded as potentially transformative experiences that may, in the person's struggle with them, catapult the individual into a whole new, richer and more interesting way of living?

I asked all six of my research participants if there was anything good about having a disability. They all said that it had made them the strong person they are today. One spoke for all when she said she had learned to be herself and not care what other people think, while at the same time she felt much greater compassion and connectedness in interactions with fellow humans. Another said:

> You have to live in the moment. I breathe. I am present. You can't undo what's done, you've got to move forward. You can't let obstacles get in your way. I'm a firm believer that things are sent because they're there to try you. You've got to get on with it. When we've been on cruises, sometimes they've said people with wheelchairs can't get off at this stop because the gangplanks are the wrong width. And I just say, 'Watch me.' And he [husband] takes the wheelchair and he holds it above the gangplank and he walks down and I go down the gangplank on my arse. I've been up a glacier on crutches. If I wanna do it, I'm gonna find a way.

I quote here from John O'Donohue's poem, 'For a friend, on the arrival of illness' (2007, p76):

> May you learn to use this illness
> As a lantern to illuminate
> The new qualities that will emerge in you
> May the fragile harvesting of this slow light
> Help to release whatever has become false in you.
> May you trust this light to clear a path
> Through all the fog of old unease and anxiety
> Until you feel arising within you a tranquillity
> Profound enough to call the storm to stillness.

§

If you give small doses of poison to mice, they live longer than a control group of clean-living mice who are kept poison free – this is the principle of hormesis (Mattson, 2008). Something that produces harmful effects at moderate to high doses may produce beneficial effects at low doses. More than a third of entrepreneurs in America are dyslexic (Logan, 2008); they regard their disability as an 'advantageous disadvantage' or a 'desirable difficulty' (Bjork, 1994). Many successful people faced huge obstacles or traumas in their youth, such as the early loss of a parent (Gladwell, 2013). Many go on to use their wounds to heal others by becoming brilliant therapists (Farber, 2017).

The straight edges of the artist's canvas, the conventions of a musical score, the requirements of a haiku or sonnet, the rules of a game or a sport – creativity flourishes under strictures.

We go on monastic retreats in spartan conditions, in search of spiritual advancement.

The Covid-19 pandemic forced us into lockdown where, in our isolation, we discovered the importance of connecting, opening up.

Much of the world's best medicines come from poisonous plants.

Everyone falls or is felled by life to some extent, but it is in the suffering, struggling and rising that growth happens. Similarly, Wright (1983) argues that disability does not have to equate only to suffering – successful adaptation to loss, she says, can sometimes facilitate the development of greater individuation, integration and mental health than the person experienced when not disabled. Marinelli writes:

> Disability is increasingly viewed as an enabling experience.
> This has allowed for the development of personal growth in
> life domains and contributions to the lives of others that were
> previously unavailable. (2007, p.xxii)

The New York therapist David Tannenbaum, who wrote me such a comforting message when I was diagnosed with Parkinson's, wrote in another message that our physical challenges 'can accelerate emotional maturity and a shift toward a more spiritual approach to life. A healthy life is not about having healthy legs'.

There are times when the 'dose' seems too high, the suffering too great, and positive, healthy psychological growth a fantasy. Growth cannot be guaranteed or demanded. But the potential is always there. There is always hope.

Related to this, the literature on post-traumatic growth explores the remarkable irrepressibility of the human spirit. Tedeschi and Calhoun describe post-traumatic growth as 'a change in people that goes beyond an ability to resist and not be damaged by highly stressful circumstances; it involves a movement beyond pre-trauma levels of adaptation… it has a quality of transformation' (2004, p.4). Typically, post-traumatic growth takes place in three areas: in improved relationships, from reaching out for help (Tedeschi & Calhoun, 1996); in an improved sense of self from trusting that you can survive, and in an improved appreciation and philosophy of life (Tedeschi & Calhoun,

2004). In a qualitative study of people with disabilities, Boswell and colleagues (2007) found spirituality played an important role in their lives in five overlapping areas: purpose, awareness, connections, creativity and acceptance.

One model of post-traumatic growth that is easily applicable to the arrival of disease or disability is the 'shattered assumptions' theory (Jannoff-Bulman, 1992). Everything you held true about your life, the 'certainties' that you relied upon for your sense of security and wellbeing, are gone. From the wreckage, you pick up the pieces and build a new life that – like the Japanese broken vase art form *kintsugi* – is stronger, more interesting and more beautiful than the original.

In many such narratives in fact and fiction, however – *The Elephant Man*, *Children of a Lesser God*, *My Left Foot*, *The Diving Bell and the Butterfly*, *Wonder* (all of them books and films of the book) – the disabled person is cast in a heroic light, their suffering conferring upon them wisdom, heightened awareness and often supernatural powers, highlighting 'our need to impose order and purposefulness on random events such as incurring a life-threatening illness' (Olkin, 1999, p.25). This 'halo effect' is the flip side of the moral model of disability: although the conception is a more positive one, it can be as limiting and prejudicial as stereotypical negative depictions. The person with a disability is thus the reluctant recipient of projections of either sin or saintliness; both do a disservice to their actual lived experience.

4. Therapy –
The search for a soulful life

'The unexamined life is not worth living.'
Socrates

The ancient and sacred ritual of therapy is a means to living a better life through the curative powers of knowledge and love. We harvest awareness, understanding and meaning from our pain and struggles with existence; we learn to feel more accepting and compassionate towards ourselves and others; to know and to be known; to love and to be loved; to rediscover our humanity.

Change is not always easy. Unhindered, it happens naturally: we're born, we grow, we ripen. We can't help but grow – it's what we do. We are fluid, like a river, as Heraclitus argued two-and-a-half thousand years ago. Nothing will ever again be quite the same as it is right now. But sometimes our growth can be stunted, stuck or skewed. We don't get the optimum psychological light, water, nutrients and nurturing that we need. Life's troubles, stormy weather and other obstacles find us, or sometimes we find them.

Therapy is an attempt to be free from the shackles and to live better. (Ideally) in a quiet, sequestered room, one unique humanity encounters another in a spirit of acceptance, growth and change. Through the conjoined twins of knowledge and love – intellect and emotion, Logos and Eros, yin and yang – we open our minds and hearts. There is a whole universe in there.

The self

The great British psychoanalyst Wilfred Bion wrote that therapy is the process of introducing clients to themselves. Very often, they are surprised by the self they meet – they are not who they thought they were; they are not who they have been trying to be all these years. Clients discover that they are not one but many. We are each like a perpetual committee meeting, with all kinds of dissenting voices from the backbenches. Some on the committee are always hogging the metaphorical microphone – they are well known to the client. Others haven't been heard from in years – they were long ago bound and gagged, or otherwise silenced. It can be hard to discern a sense of self amidst this cacophony that's going on in our mind. All the voices are encouraged to speak in therapy.

There are no bad selfies here.

Writes the 13th century Persian poet, Rumi (1995):

This being human is a guest house.
Every morning a new arrival.
A joy, a depression, a meanness,
some momentary awareness comes
as an unexpected visitor.
Welcome and entertain them all!,
Even if they're a crowd of sorrows,
who violently sweep your house
empty of its furniture,
still, treat each guest honorably
He may be clearing you out
for some new delight.
The dark thought, the shame, the malice,
meet them at the door laughing,
and invite them in.
Be grateful for whoever comes,
because each has been sent
as a guide from beyond.

Freud's great discovery was the unconscious. Our stated, conscious desire 'comes from the Other,' according to Lacan (in Fink, 1999, p.207); our unconscious wants and motivations might be quite different. Heidegger said we discover our intentions through our actions rather than the other way round (1927/1962), and neuroscientific studies have reinforced that (e.g. Libet, 1981; Libet et al., 1983). Damasio says: 'We are always hopelessly late for consciousness' (2000, p.127).

We humans like to regard ourselves as rational and logical, able to make conscious, optimal choices. In practice, however, we're walking contradictions, not always sure what we really want. Our actions can betray our words, and vice versa. We can be at war with ourselves. We preserve and protect our neurotic symptoms, said Freud, 'like a lioness defends her young'. He identified 'the wish for an unsatisfied wish' (1899/1955, p.148). Through psychoanalysis we can make the unconscious conscious and feel less like a passenger in our own life. For Freud, however, the unconscious is a dark, Gothic place of primitive instincts, base desires and eroticised childhood experiences.

Human motivation

Our motives are not always clear, and not always noble. We have an immense propensity for good… and for bad, as various infamous social psychology experiments from the 1960s have demonstrated. We don't have absolute free will. But nor is everything predestined. I prefer the Buddhist belief in a middle way: we are neither free nor not free.

We are powered by five different engines:

- We are **biological** creatures. We are motivated by survival. Freud (1913/2001) said we had natural instincts for sex and aggression and death. Many years later, Dawkins (1978) wrote that we're at the mercy of our 'selfish genes'. The behaviourists believed that, like rats in a maze, we simply respond optimally to external stimuli.

- We are **psychological** creatures. Maslow (1943) said we each have an innate tendency towards psychological growth, which happens via a 'hierarchy of needs', culminating in 'self-actualisation'. These ideas were taken up by Rogers (1961), May (1967) and other humanists. Some critics say this focus on individual autonomy gave rise to a selfish 'me-generation' of narcissists, concerned only with their own personal growth and 'success' (e.g. Rieff, 1966; Lasch, 1979).

- We are **relational** creatures, born to connect, whether that's from an 'object-seeking libido' (Fairbairn, 1952), a need for mirroring and idealisation (Kohut, 1971), or 'attachment' (Bowlby, 1991). Buber declares: 'All real living is meeting' (1958, p.26).

- We are **societal** creatures. We exist as individuals within complex cultures that in subtle and not-so-subtle ways dictate the rules of the game. We are presented with a double bind: we are told to be true to our self, to find our own way, yet we are also expected to comply with our society's laws, customs, rituals and beliefs.

- We are **spiritual** creatures. Many people yearn for communion with some kind of higher meaning in a world 'devoid of intrinsic meaning' (Yalom, 2002). Being a psychotherapist is, for me, much more than a job. It is a transpersonal, spiritual practice; a 'daring to open up', as Rowan puts it (2005).

All of the above are at play in a dynamic, complex interplay of 'motivational systems' (Lichtenberg et al., 2011). We are motivated by self and others, nature and nurture, the conscious and the unconscious, thoughts and feelings, by past, present and future (Drozek, 2010).

Given the complexity of our various selves and motivational systems, it's no surprise that, in an ever-more complex world, people can lose their way. They lose connection with their soul; their inner-life satnav falls silent, or starts giving conflicting directions, or spouting nonsense.

General principles of humanity therapy

Body, mind and soul

Is disease a random occurrence brought on by phenomena like infections, inflammations, changes in bodily chemical levels, compromised immune systems and genetic predispositions? Or are symptoms an expression of a deeper malaise, an inarticulate howl of a suffering soul? Which is more likely to make you ill: a poor diet or social isolation? Why are placebos often just as effective as drugs with active ingredients? Does someone develop tumours in their lungs because they smoke or because they have a 'cancer personality'? Do they need to be 'strong' to 'fight it'?

The axis around which these kinds of debates revolve has been in place for millennia. According to one of Plato's dialogues in *Charmenides*:

For the greatest failure in the treatment of disease is that there are physicians for the body and physicians for the mind when the body and mind cannot be separated. But the Greek doctors overlook that fact and that is why so many diseases elude them. (Quoted in Schoenberg, 2007, p.13)

Descartes, by contrast, regarded his mind as entirely distinct from his body. 'I think therefore I am,' he wrote – he would still be Descartes even if he had no body (Russell, 2013, p.517). A central philosophical conundrum of Descartes' *Meditations on First Philosophy*, written in 1641, was how a non-physical entity, the mind, could have an effect on something physical, the body (Westphal, 2016). In sickness and in health, the union of mind and body is curious, complex and contested.

In the previous two chapters I have written about the oppressive dogma of psychofascism. Cancer is the disease whose victims are most commonly subjected to this kind of judgement. They are told they brought it on themselves by being too emotionally repressed; it is then demanded that they think positively and be 'strong' to beat the disease. Ehrenreich eloquently describes her experience of this in *Smile or Die* (2010). How many people with cancer have died believing their death was down to personal weakness?

Not so many years ago, I attended two body psychotherapy CPD workshops. I asked the presenters a question from the floor: what sense did they make of bodies that stop working or succumb to sickness? One, Michael Soth, replied that physical symptoms invite 'psychological explanations'. The other, Nick Totton, said they were 'an invitation to do some work on yourself'.

In follow-up emails, I challenged their responses, citing Susan Sontag's critique of such victim-blaming explanations in her 1977 landmark work *Illness as Metaphor*.

Soth replied by agreeing with Sontag's argument, highlighting the guilt-inducing and shaming moralistic implications prevalent in how holistic contemporary therapies approach illness, but adding that, despite the dangers, he believed an experiential 'bottom-up' psychological exploration of meaning was possible, to open up conversations rather than shutting them down with rigid cognitive certainties.

He wrote: 'Whilst I agree with much of Sontag's critique of some kind of over-zealous omnipotent psychological interpretation, I also see her falling into the opposite, polarised conclusion. The problem is not psychological meaning-making in relation to illness *per se* (every human and every patient's psyche cannot help but do that unconsciously in the background, anyway), the problem is the one-dimensional (rather than multi-dimensional) relational stance that drives or dominates that meaning-making procedure. However much we fight *against* the symptom, a part of the client's psyche lives *within* it, and speaks *through* the symptom. But it does not speak the language of left-brain, mental representation and interpretation – the symptom is a poet, communicating via imagination, symbol and bodymind metaphor. To engage with the psychological meaning of illness, we need to join its – imprecise, associative, unfathomable – language.'

Totton directed me to a paper he had more recently written (Totton, 2019), titled 'Different bodies: The problem of normativity in body psychotherapy'. In it, he states that 'the fact that we as therapists will no longer be allowed to get away with our normative assumptions is perhaps the least significant reason for abandoning them. Much more importantly, they are unjustifiable, and also deeply cruel.' He concludes that therapy 'should align not with the normative ideal, but with the particular, imperfect, damaged, material, wounded and inadequate nature of human existence'.

We don't actually know precisely the reasons for the arrival and progression of cancer or any other disease. Cancer is common in all mammals, too, with a few exceptions: mole rats, for instance, almost never get it (Pennisi, 2013). Are we to assume they are better at expressing their anger than their fellow rodents? Did they have better attachment experiences in their youth? This is not to deny psychological processes, but sometimes we are 'thrown' into disease and there is no reason. With life comes disease, disability and death. No one is to blame.

In my case, I got CMT because a genetic mutation, a duplication of a segment of chromosome 17, was passed on to me by my father, who in turn received it from his father. Beyond that, the ancestry of our peculiar family heirloom is unknown. I got Parkinson's because, at some point in my 40s, for reasons unknown, the cells in the *substantia nigra* region of the brain that manufacture the neurotransmitter dopamine started to take early retirement and shut down. I believe mind and body are both completely involved in these conditions – in their arrival, expression and progression. Instead of the thesis of the medical model that ignores the mind, or the antithesis that too often degenerates into fatuous psychospiritual new-age quackery, what is needed is synthesis. I reject the black-and-white thinking of Cartesian dualism. Merleau-Ponty says Descartes was mistaken: living, our sense of the world and who we are, our subjectivity – these are deeply embodied experiences. Of course they are.

Says Merleau-Ponty: 'The body is our general medium for having a world' (1945/2002, p.169).

The mysterious marriage of mind and body does not submit to certainties. In the words of Suzuki and colleagues:

> Our body and mind are not two, and not one… Our body and mind are both two and one. (2010, p.7)

Writes Oken:

> Psychological and biological factors are involved in all aspects of human function – healthy and disordered. All disease and health is psychosomatic; there are no 'psychosomatic disorders' because there are no 'non-psychosomatic disorders'. (2007, p.831)

In *Why Do People Get Ill?* Leader and Corfield similarly argue:

> No single major illness is exclusively caused by the mind, just as few illnesses will always be completely exempt from the mind's influence. (2008, p.3)

They advocate holistic treatments that may include traditional medicine but that also engage with the individual, the soul. In my experience, such a truly holistic approach is rare.

Professor Mark Edwards, the doctor who diagnosed me with Parkinson's, is an expert in what are called functional or psychogenic movement disorders (FNS), also sometimes known as 'medically unexplained symptoms'. These are symptoms without a known underlying cause; the effects of a disease without us knowing what the actual disease is. Reportedly they account for around 20% of all medical consultations in primary and secondary care, and manifest in myriad different ways.

And things can get complicated when a patient with an actual disease with expected symptoms develops additional psychogenic symptoms as well. Professor Edwards has researched this phenomenon, and reports that upwards of 15% of people with 'organic' neurological problems have additional functional symptoms.

I put it to Professor Edwards that 100% of people with Parkinson's have symptoms that are profoundly affected by psychogenic machinations that can be long term or sometimes very short term. I know that my physical symptoms go hand-in-hand with my overall psychological state at any given time. They affect each other. They are intimately intertwined. They are, perhaps, indivisible.

This complex interplay of mind and body was very apparent to me as an observer some years ago on an NHS neuropsychiatric ward. The treatment programme consisted largely of medication, plus a token amount of cognitive behavioural therapy (CBT) and physiotherapy. Psychotherapy was rarely considered or even mentioned. Other approaches that considered the emotional or spiritual needs of patients were dismissed as 'diversionary therapies'.

Here are some examples of these kinds of patients – I have fictionalised the details to preserve confidentiality:

- A man has a history of chronic balance symptoms, dizziness and crippling headaches. It happens whenever there's an academic, personal or employment-related challenge on the horizon. An obvious, underlying diagnosis might be unrelenting, unattainable high standards and fear of failure. This is not mentioned. He is sent to an ear clinic.

- A woman in a wheelchair is looked after by her two adult sons. She has abandonment issues from childhood and hates being alone – which she would be, if she got better. The medication, physio and CBT make little difference to her mobility.

- A woman reports convulsions, weakness and paralysis, which she describes in a flat, affectless tone. The doctors seem irritated by her – her symptoms are thought to be 'behavioural'; one consultant says she clearly has a 'personality disorder'. She experienced extreme trauma as a child and fled war in her native country. She arrived in the UK with her mother, who subsequently died, leaving her young daughter alone, frightened and homeless in a foreign country. There is no mention of trauma or PTSD. She is medicated.

- A young man, educated at boarding school, was bullied, and responded with a massive defensive narcissistic compensation. He spends hours in the gym every day, attempting to hone a perfect, invincible physique. But he has a constant insatiable hunger. He binges, bloats, then goes back to the gym. This super-bright, super-fit young man is completely isolated and starved of love. He is medicated.

- A man who works as a lab technician has developed unexplained pains, weaknesses and paralysis in his legs, resulting in long periods off work. He lives alone. His work mainly involves testing products on animals and then killing them. He often has vivid, disturbing dreams. His bosses accuse him of malingering. He is medicated.

The medical and health professionals on the ward seemed to me to have almost no interest in unconscious processes and the possible meaning of symptoms. Yet to me, the variety and apparent ingenuity of the symptoms begged to be explored as potential unconscious attempts at solutions: a way to prevent the person from having to do something difficult, or keep them safe, or feeling cared for or loved. For a lot of the patients, I felt that, if they could have been helped to find their voice, their body would not have had to do all the talking.

Patients are often wary of psychological explanations of physical difficulties because they fear being judged as weak or accused of making it up and malingering. That fear is real: one doctor described the neuropsychiatric ward to me as 'cheerful people in wheelchairs'.

So the pendulum swings the other way. A decade ago, doctors and researchers who even suggested that there might be a psychological aspect of chronic fatigue syndrome, otherwise known as myalgic encephalomyelitis, received death threats and hate mail; some were physically attacked.

So now doctors have an almost complete aversion to exploring anything psychological at all (beyond the usual cursory 'How's your mood?' question).

There's so much that could be done in helping patients come to terms with a diagnosis like Parkinson's and use it as a springboard for a whole new life – perhaps a life of healthy living, growth, community, creativity, spirituality.

There must be more that can be offered than just pills.

Professor Edwards emailed back: 'You are absolutely right in what you say regarding the indivisibility of the body and mind, and the way in which the human aspects of being ill are consistently ignored or downgraded in healthcare. But I would also extend this to people in general, including many of those who are ill – there is a consistent pattern of mistrust when human factors, beyond the biological facts of an illness are discussed in medical consultations, and negative experiences of this sort make many doctors and other health professionals wary of going beyond the strict biological grounds of medical science. I commonly see this in the consistent misuse of the word "psychological" as a slur to mean "not real" or "not important".

In a powerful essay in the journal *Brain*, Professor Edwards writes:

> *Consciousness breathes life into pathology*, as it does to the physical and social environment. This process, mediated by individual bodies and brains, gives birth to a feeling, an experience, occurring in a place and time and which is in turn changed and given new life through interaction with others who are conscious. The true paradox is that we continue to act as though a relentless and single-minded focus on improving the tools we have for measuring disease and altering the associated pathophysiological state of the body will solve all the problems of people who are ill. (Edwards, 2021, original italics)

He goes on to call for 'a new paradigm in medicine' – one that considers the whole person rather than atomised bits of their body; one that offers a truly integrated multidisciplinary service. He concludes:

> The aim is not to create a cuddly version of biomedicine, a rebranding exercise where we expect change to happen by installing a few aromatherapy diffusers and inserting the word 'wellness' into our mission statements. Instead, it is to recognise and invest in the science and expertise that will truly allow us, as scientists and clinicians, to become partners with the patient. Partners in understanding, moulding and finally re-creating in a better form what it is, personally, to be ill. (Edwards, 2021)

Kleinman, a medical doctor, bemoans how the medical care system:

> ... does just about everything to drive the practitioner's attention away from the experience of illness. The system thereby contributes importantly to the alienation of the chronically ill from their professional caregivers and, paradoxically, to the relinquishment by the practitioner of that aspect of the healer's art that is most ancient, most powerful and most existentially rewarding. (1988, p.xiv)

He advocates a rediscovery of the person of the patient, of their story, of the lost art of symptom interpretation.

Frank's *The Wounded Storyteller* (1995) is an inspiration and guide to developing illness narratives. There are many examples in the literature, such as Siri Hustvedt's *The Shaking Woman or a History of my Nerves* (2010), and Havi Carel's *Illness* (2008). It's true that our symptoms have much to tell us. With the help of therapists, we can discover useful interpretations and authentic, affirming narratives as opposed to damning, blaming certainties. We can reclaim our bodies.

This is Kleinman's description of the lived experience of those with disordered bodies:

> It has been said of Mozart's music that even where all seems quiet and under control it is best regarded as a formal Italian garden built on the side of an active volcano. The undercurrent of chronic illness is like the volcano: it does not go away. It menaces. It erupts. It is out of control. One damned thing follows another. Confronting crises is only one part of the total picture. The rest is coming to grips with the mundaneness of worries over whether one can negotiate a curb, tolerate flowers without wheezing, make it to a bathroom quickly enough, eat breakfast without vomiting, keep the level of back pain low enough to get through the workday, sleep through the night, attempt sexual intercourse, make plans for a vacation, or just plain face up to the myriad of difficulties that make life feel burdened, uncomfortable, and all too often desperate. (1988, p.44)

At least in the olden days, when I was young, you had a family doctor who knew you and your health history and might even come to your home if, say, you were worried about a sick child. Nowadays you are assigned to a practice, you can't get an appointment for two weeks and, if you do manage to see a doctor, it's often a locum who you've never met before. When my then-wife was first pregnant, we were given an appointment with a midwife. We really liked her; we were glad we had been assigned someone who was clearly so warm and caring and experienced and skilled. In all our subsequent appointments, scans, complications, scares, a traumatic emergency C-section birth and some desperate hours in the ICU, we never saw her again. In fact, we never saw any midwife, nurse or doctor involved in our creation of a new human more than once. The healthcare system turns doctors and patients into robots. Body part – tests – diagnosis – pills and/or surgery. Next!

Professor Edwards' paradigm shift is a call for the return of humanity to the system.

We are not just bodies. Nor are we just minds. We are humans.

Perhaps, however, there is an even bigger picture. Perhaps the mind-body debate is but the flickering shadows on the wall of Plato's cave. If we widen the camera lens, or look down from a greater height, or push open the doors of perception a little farther, then we encounter the human soul.

Your body and your mind together might loosely be described as your ego. But this is a manifestation of your essential you-ness, that higher, wiser, more expansive and perhaps everlasting sense of self that we call the soul.

Perhaps there is a Cartesian split between ego and soul. Descartes might have said, 'I experience transcendent, numinous moments, therefore I am.'

An ego is wrapped up in minutiae; a soul sees the whole.

An ego wants to compete and win; a soul wants to collaborate and love.

Writing from the soul is good writing – it is a gift of love to the reader.

Writing from the ego is bad writing – it is a demand of love from the reader.

The same is true for all creative pursuits – singing, cooking, giving gifts, loving.

The first half of adult life is an ego trip; the second half is a soul search.

Or to put it another way: first you must find yourself. Then you must get over yourself.

A soul-informed life – a good life – is the goal of Humanity Therapy.

Uncertainty

In a letter to his brother, the English Romantic poet John Keats wrote about how Shakespeare, good artists and people of achievement had a quality he called 'negative capability'. They were capable, he said, of holding multiple viewpoints simultaneously: 'of being in uncertainties, mysteries, doubts without any irritable reaching after fact and reason' (in Rollins, 1958, p.193).

Negative capability is an acknowledgement of complexity, a mature respect of life's shades of grey, an understanding that, despite what the strident headline, indignant tweet or demanding placard says, the situation is probably not quite so simple.

Negative capability is an embrace of doubt. It is greeting the world and people in it as if for the first time, without preconceived ideas or old habits, scripts or stereotypes. It is the opposite of prejudice. It is a willingness to say you don't know.

'Doubt is not a pleasant condition,' Voltaire wrote in 1770, 'but certainty is absurd.'

The Western world, however, is defined by irritable reaching after fact, reason and certainty. In case you hadn't noticed, life is complicated and we are hungry for clarity and simplicity. We tend to be extremely doubtful as to any merits of doubt.

We like to think in black and white, left and right, good guys and bad guys, Mars and Venus, heaven and hell. We demand decisiveness from our politicians, generals and CEOs – being unsure is a much greater crime than being wrong. All the question marks must be changed to exclamation marks. We want bullet points to help us lead our lives: 10 commandments, seven habits, five ways to achieve success, fame, fortune, happiness. We want yes or no in a world of maybe.

But to live without negative capability is to be enslaved (there is, I believe, a Sanskrit word that means both 'certainty' and 'imprisonment'). It is to be closed minded, dogmatic, fanatic; to have a resolute, immutable opinion about everything or an unwavering fidelity to one or another 'ism' or 'ology'.

It is sticking rigidly to an absurd little book of rules and ignoring all the red lights on an uncompromising march to the completely wrong place: to war, ethnic cleansing, bigotry, economic collapse, physical collapse, psychological collapse.

Certainty blinds us to possibility. We're so fixated on some notion of how things are 'supposed' to be that we totally miss the gift of how things are. We march right past the treasures in the Louvre because we're on a grim, joyless box-checking mission to stand in line to see the Mona Lisa. We're so frenetic, addicted to our busy-ness, that we don't notice when someone we love needs help or is trying to tell us something important. We're so wedded to an idea of the person we think we should be with – our 'type', our 'soul mate' – that we don't even look at the amazing person sitting next to us. We are completely surrounded by beautiful opportunities, gifts and invitations, to which we are oblivious because we are not present – we are stuck in the past or marching ahead in search of some imagined, more certain future. We attempt to navigate the turbulent waters of love, too, with an out-of-date map of a different ocean.

Richard Wiseman, a magician turned popular psychologist, conducted some research on luck. He advertised for people to contact him if they considered themselves very lucky or very unlucky, and received many replies. The lucky people seemingly had led charmed, successful, happy lives. They were always in the right place at the right time, and good things inevitably just happened to fall in their lap. The unlucky people? The opposite – an extraordinary catalogue of calamities, disastrous romances, failed businesses, missed connections, lost harvests.

Wiseman conducted a series of tests on these people. One was to count the number of photos in a newspaper. The unlucky people took a few minutes to complete the task. The lucky people took just seconds. Why? Because on page 2, half the page was devoted to a notice that said, in large letters: 'Stop counting: there are 43 photographs in this newspaper.' The 'unlucky' people, blinded by the task, never saw it.

According to Wiseman, people make their own luck, and he explains how to learn to be lucky (2003). The house of uncertainty holds no fear for lucky people, only endless possibility.

The message from Wiseman is clear: we'd do well to embrace uncertainty. Our brains have two hemispheres: the intuitive, holistic, creative, transcendent 'right brain', and the more logical, rigid, pedantic, detail-focused 'left brain'. Iain McGilchrist calls the former 'the Master' and the latter 'the Emissary'. The problem, McGilchrist says, is that the Emissary is supposed to be in service to the Master, but somehow they have taken over the controls. As a result, we have been profoundly changed – as has our world. All power, says McGilchrist, now rests with the Emissary, 'who, however gifted, is effectively an ambitious regional bureaucrat with his own interests at heart. Meanwhile the Master... is led away in chains' (2010, p.14). (A simplistic binary split of the brain into left and right perhaps shows a lack of negative capability – it ignores all the shades of grey matter. But we'll stick with it.)

Instead of working together, our bird-brained inner accountant turned on our wise and thoughtful inner poet and, in a desperate ontological battle, the latter was slain. The poet, needless to say, embraced negative capability. The accountant, however, clipboard, ruler and calculator in hand, can tolerate only certainty. They have created a fragmented Western world of technology, mechanisation and bureaucracy; a world of alienation where love is hard to find, and beauty gets bulldozed; a world of spreadsheets instead of sonnets; a world where everything is measured, itemised and indexed, where the little picture matters and there is no big picture.

The Emissary's hand can be seen in every detail of our lives – in tax returns, Ofsted reports and market research; in doomed attempts to deconstruct jokes or works of art, and in the field of mental health. The Emissary wants to shoehorn your troubles into a neat, clearly labelled pigeonhole. The Emissary wants to eradicate your symptoms with a drug and, if you insist, a bit of talking – or perhaps, more accurately, telling – in the form of some short-term CBT. A little adjustment to your levels, a bit of soldering under the bonnet, and you should be good to go – back to your spreadsheets.

If it were that simple, we would not be human. On the first page of the introduction in her book *The Impossibility of Knowing*, psychotherapist Jackie Gerrard writes:

> I am sure that I, like many of my colleagues, started my training
> eager to learn and to know, and I have subsequently spent the
> years post qualification learning that I do not 'know,' cannot
> 'know,' and, indeed, should not 'know'… by saying I do not 'know,'
> I am continually endeavouring to hold a state of mind that can
> tolerate remaining open, bearing uncertainty, and avoiding,
> wherever possible, omnipotence and omniscience. (2003, p.xi)

Not 'knowing' is not the same as indecision or ignorance. In *Tales of Un-knowing*, existential therapist Ernesto Spinelli says therapists should aspire to be un-knowing – as opposed to 'unknowing': they should 'attempt to remain as open as possible to whatever presents itself in our relational experience' (2006, p.6).

The Emissary therapist reaches for theories, models, personality tests and questionnaires about your mental state and enters your score on a spreadsheet, then reaches for the manual to find a clinical diagnosis such as 'generalised anxiety disorder' or 'oppositional defiance disorder' and some techniques to make it go away. American existential therapist Irving Yalom marvels that anyone can take such a therapist seriously, adding:

> Even the most liberal system of psychiatric nomenclature does violence to the being of another. If we relate to people believing that we can categorize them, we will neither identify nor nurture the parts, the vital parts, of the other that transcend category. (2012, p.71)

The Master therapist, by contrast, sees you – all the vital parts, all of you. All their senses are alive to you and your experience of distress.

One thing that we really can't be sure of is what happens to us when we die. As a species, we are united in this uncertainty, this vulnerability that we all share. But we can't seem to handle that. Instead, we irritably reach after fact and reason where there is none. We follow a leader who claims to know The Truth; we adopt the dogmas and prejudices of this group or another. And in so doing, we turn our backs on each other and on our own curiosity too.

One Master-like analyst is Michael Eigen, who writes that a sense of 'being right' justifies many kinds of violence in the minds of the self-righteous (2018).

Another is my supervisor, Mark Gullidge, who said to me once: 'You can either be right, or you can be open.'

The hardest three words for humans to say are 'I don't know'.

Pluralism

Modern psychotherapy has its roots in the 19th-century colonial period that was marked by the rise of 'scientific racism' and hierarchical notions of difference. Indeed, as seen in Chapter 3, the justification for imperial rule and segregation depended on the subjugators' claims of racial superiority over those they subjugated (Gould, 1981, p.31). Psychotherapeutic thought is built on the white, Western patriarchy and racism of its leading early thinkers, like Freud and Jung (Lago & Moodley, 2002, pp.42–43); as a result, the major theories today only offer 'narrow, ethnocentric, and culturally encapsulated constructions of the world' (D'Andrea & Daniels, 2001, p.301). Psychotherapy remains riddled with racism; the profession is not so much 'person-centred' as white person-centered. In England, in 2019, if you were black, you were four times more likely to be sectioned than if you were white (NHS Digital, 2020a). I doubt that's changed.

Beyond such over-arching prejudices are any number of ever-branching divisions. Dogmatic schools of therapy each seek self-validation by indiscriminately forcing complex, unique clients into these tidy, reductionist models. The schools all squabble. Academic journals are filled with indignant justifications of miniscule differences between the author's supposedly revolutionary new concept and some well-established old concept. There is much tribal academic 'schoolism'. Politics in academia are so vicious, as the saying goes, because the stakes are so low.

For psychotherapeutic theory to be useful today requires eclectic, pluralistic, integrative approaches, offering the maximum scope for flexibility (Lago & Moodley, 2002, p.45). Yet in truth, for any therapist, some unhelpful social or cultural assumptions or biases or assumptions are probably inevitable.

Lago details many common hegemonic assumptions and cultural biases in traditional therapeutic approaches, such as the notion that individuals are rational and in charge of their own destiny – 'the sanctity of personal authority is not questioned, which implies that all parental and cultural values are open to question' (2006, p.94). Many members of minority groups can have a more collective, communal orientation, which 'may be perceived by Western standards as dependent, immature, and unhealthily enmeshed in the family' (Sue, 2001, p.46). Other areas of difference might include variations along the spectrums of focusing on challenging contexts rather than only on intrapsychic machinations; materialism versus spiritualism; determinism versus free will; cognitivism versus emotionalism; attitudes toward children and life-stage expectations; reactions toward therapists being directive or nondirective, and mismatches in greetings, language, personal space, eye contact and other non-verbal communication. Difference implies a need for 'cultural competence' – a synthesis of cultural awareness, knowledge and sensitivity (Papadopoulos, 2006, p.18). It would be impossible for therapists to have all information about all cultures at their fingertips; rather, cultural competence is about 'finding a way to work with similarities and differences *at the same time*' (Eleftheriadou, 2010, p.205, original italics).

Whether or not the client has a disability, disease or impairment, each has a unique context and worldview and multiple intersecting, interconnected identities (which raises the possibility of multiple oppressions at the hands of unenlightened counsellors). Constructing difference solely on black/white binary constructions tends to reinforce power inequities and ignores the complexity of how people and their psychologies are formed.

I believe in integrating different therapeutic approaches rather than building walls between them. In particular, the foundation of my way of working is an integration of existential, psychodynamic and relational approaches. Cooper (2012) makes the distinction between 'hard' and 'soft' existential practitioners. The former adopt a more interpretative, psychodynamic stance to help the client clarify and shape their story and experience of life (e.g. Frankl, 1946/2004; Boss, 1963; Yalom, 1980; Bugenthal, 1999), while the latter tend to follow a more purely phenomenological, client-led path (e.g. Laing, 1960; Spinelli, 2007; Van Deurzen, 2012).

Pure phenomenology regards experience as an essential reality that can be known and understood. Pure hermeneutics, by contrast, sees human understanding and knowledge not as fixed 'out there' realities waiting to be unearthed but instead as socially constructed and a matter of interpretation. Nietzsche wrote in 1887: 'It is precisely facts that do not exist, only *interpretations*' (quoted in Kaufmann, 1954, p.458). Truth, he said, is 'a mobile army of metaphors'.

Edmund Husserl's phenomenological approach was to attempt to 'bracket' his own experiences and seek to understand with objectivity the unique experiences offered by the world, attempting to get to the essences of those experiences – Husserl called these 'the things themselves' (Husserl, 1927; Smith et al., 2009, p.12).

For Husserl's erstwhile student Martin Heidegger, however, such bracketing was seen as impossible; indeed, for Gadamer, the very attempt is manifestly absurd (in Laverty, 2003). In Heidegger's eyes, one cannot separate one's self; one cannot be an impartial, objective 'scientific' observer. Instead, the researcher's own subjectivity and interpretations are embraced. This is the essence of hermeneutics.

I had an old, wise dog, Daisy, who often used to sit with one ear up and one ear down. She listened to the world and she listened to herself. Daisy got through life – with dignity and aplomb – by combining phenomenology and hermeneutics. I miss her.

Similarly, in my former career as a journalist, I came to appreciate that the best writers are those who harvest information from the world through extensive reporting, but who then knowingly combine it with their own experience and interpretations. The use of their subjectivity is deliberate, reflective and transparent.

Hermeneutics and phenomenology thus appear at first glance to be at odds with each other. 'Hermeneutic phenomenology' may seem like an oxymoron. But these two paths have united in the emerging research traditions of interpretative phenomenological analysis or IPA (Smith et al., 2009; McLeod, 2001) and various phenomenologically informed narrative methods (e.g. Ricoeur, 1981; Polkinghorne, 1988). Both can be viewed as 'integral, complementary aspects of any satisfactory way of knowing about human existence' (McLeod, 2001, p.59). Heidegger saw phenomenology as a 'fore-understanding' to hermeneutic enquiry.

It is a delicate dance in therapy. A hermeneutic approach that imposes a normative worldview can be oppressive and damaging. Sometimes, after a session when maybe I have been a little too directive, or too wedded to some supposedly brilliant insight that meant nothing to the client, I am haunted by Winnicott's late-career words:

> It appalls me to think how much deep change I have prevented
> or delayed in patients... by my personal need to interpret. (1971,
> p.116)

I also like Casement's metaphor of the client as a compass needle in dynamic interplay with the therapist as magnet: if the therapist's 'magnet' is too strong or too near to the client's 'needle', it will reduce the latter's 'potential for direction-seeking' (1990, p.329).

Ultimately, an embrace of uncertainty facilitates curiosity and an embrace of difference. If we accept that every therapist, client and therapeutic dyad is unique, then it makes sense to pursue a bottom-up, open-ended therapy that emerges in an organic fashion from the relationship, rather than a prescriptive, top-down imposition of dogma from expert clinician to passively accepting client. Yalom suggests a new therapy is created for each client (2002, p.33), an idea also proposed by Jung (1961/1995, p.152).

Love

There's a kind of love in the quality of a good therapeutic bond between client and therapist – an energy that comes in many flavours, nurtured in a non-judgemental, safe, boundaried space. According to Jackie Gerrard:

> Unless and until there can be felt moments of love for the patient by the therapist, the patient is not able to develop fully. (2003, p.51)

Therapeutic love is mature, giving and sustained. It is a stance, a decision that is embodied *a priori* to embrace the miraculous possibilities that exist in whatever broken person comes through the door. It is a container that allows us to work with the full spectrum of human emotions, including the less heart-shaped ones. Come what may, we will let there be love.

It is not just 'talking therapy' but 'experiencing therapy' too. To fully heal, we need to get out of our minds and into our hearts. In the language of brain science, I understand the distinction between intellect, which involves the neocortical 'human' brain, and emotion, which belongs to the more mammalian, limbic system. I think of the neocortex as a fluid, dynamic system – cognitions rapidly come and go – whereas the limbic brain is more like steel: it is hard to make an impression on it but once changes have been wrought in the form of new neural pathways, they tend to be more permanently inscribed (Lewis et al., 2001).

Mills (2005) argues that this supposed 'relational turn' in psychotherapy is nothing new and that the relational theorists (e.g. Mitchell, 1988; Benjamin, 1990; Aron, 1991; Stolorow & Atwood, 1992; Ogden, 1994; Beebe & Lachmann, 1998) sometimes infer that intersubjectivity forecloses all other considerations, as if intrapsychic factors have no place in psychotherapy.

And therapeutic love is not some utopian, uncritical veneration of the client. Ferenczi (1932/1988) wrote of a 'confusion of tongues' if there is too much love, or love of the wrong kind, from parent to child or analyst to patient. It's possible that a therapist's need to be thought of as loving could infantilise, patronise or diminish a client by fostering dependence. While Kohut speaks of the benefits of preserving the client's idealised 'selfobject transference' towards the therapist (1984), attempts to be a 'perfect mother' and provide a 'corrective emotional experience' can be both inauthentic and self-aggrandising. Winnicott (1949) writes of the importance of accepting feelings of fear and hatred for clients. Casement similarly speaks of an 'insecure kind of caring' that keeps everything cordial but avoids true engagement, which will likely include confrontation, challenge and conflict (2006, p.81).

Sometimes love means not taking everything the client says at face value. For instance, Freud (1923b/1975) argued that attending to a client's reported symptoms takes the focus away from the underlying unconscious conflicts that created them – the symptoms may serve a psychological purpose and so a client might unconsciously defend them. Ricoeur goes so far as to say that there is a need for a 'hermeneutic of suspicion' (1981, p.117). I prefer to think of Lacan's notion of interpretation 'opening up the space of desire' (in Fink, 1999, p.42), to consider other, greater possibilities. For Ogden & Gabbard, in therapy 'the patient is helped to dream himself more fully into existence' (2010, p.533).

To heal, the anxious client must face 'exposures to the kinds of *relational experiences* he has fearfully avoided' (Wachtel, 2010, p.208). There are times to be directive, to interrupt, to confront. There are times for 'optimal frustration' (Kohut, 1971), even for what Kradin calls 'analytic aggression' (2005, p.432). Such interventions are risky. They both require and further a therapeutic relationship. Like the time I was complaining to my marvellous therapist, who has helped me so much, and she shook her head and said, 'Honestly, you can be so *annoying*.'

This is undoubtedly true.

Inevitably, a willingness to challenge a client carries the risk of ruptures – 'deteriorations in the relationship between therapist and patient' (Safran & Muran, 1996, p.447). If we can withstand the emotion of the conflict and develop a mutual curiosity about what happened – what is it we are each protecting and fighting against? – then there is a chance of repair. The relationship survives. Sometimes a rupture is entirely necessary.

The illumination of our unconscious subjectivities allows for a conscious understanding of them, which can make space for newer, healthier patterns going forward. The client and I edge our way towards relational depth (Mearns & Cooper, 2005), a co-created relationship of 'reciprocal mutual influence' (Stolorow & Atwood, 1992, p.18), or an 'implicit relational knowing' (Stern et al., 1998) – a felt sense that 'I know that you know that I know'.

Often therapy starts out with a traditional doctor–patient power relationship. The therapist is presumed to know about life and health and what to do and say and recommend for your particular problem. The therapist is well, the client is not. But in fact the therapist is wounded too, and is only able to connect and identify with the client and be compassionate by drawing on their own pain, and perhaps seeing the client's pain as universal, as a part of the human condition. As the therapist connects with their inner pain, the client connects with their inner healer. The power dynamic fades away.

Any therapist who is invested in their own wellness and power will be more likely to keep the client in a place of illness and helplessness.

Rogers' core conditions (1957) are useful, as is Erskine's idea of 'involvement' (Erskine et al., 2013) and a genuine sense of appreciation for the vulnerability, beauty and worth in each person. I try to be present and available for the client, in the moment, not trying to control the session or thinking about my next interpretation. There is sometimes a rich sense of intersubjectivity; a largely unconscious, embodied process (Gallese, 2015). We are both altered by the dynamic; a dialogic attitude (Buber, 1958; Hycner, 1993). I experience it as an altered, higher state of consciousness.

Where does it hurt? 10 sources of suffering

After the formalities, the details, the terms and conditions of therapy, the first thing a therapist might say to a new client is: 'So, what brings you here?'

Some clients want things to change. They've had it with the status quo, with feeling bad all the time, with aspects of their life that have become worn out or problematic. They're tired of being stuck. They have faith that better days lie ahead.

Sometimes the problem a client presents turns out not to be the real problem, just a way in. Sometimes the source of their suffering is a complete mystery. They might be struggling somewhere among the existential challenges of death, freedom, isolation and meaninglessness (Yalom, 2002). Perhaps their roadmap of life, their 'provisional personality' (Hollis, 1993, p.9), doesn't work anymore.

Into each life some rain shall fall. For many, it's a torrential downpour from birth. Others seem to escape with the occasional light shower.

Whatever the weather, there are always choices to be made. Faced with suffering, there are many different reactions, including, in various ways, avoidance. Others turn to face the strange, and are changed; somehow they manage to thrive despite all the hard knocks, and sometimes because of them. Oftentimes the bar is simply set too high, even for the finest of high jumpers. At such times it is hard to hold onto one's soul. One way or another, sooner or later, everyone faces the Humanity Test.

The rain is indiscriminate. It falls on the just and the unjust.

What kinds of stormy weather have you lived through?

The thing about psychological distress is that it feeds on itself. Often we don't know what is cause and what is effect. Here are 10 possible origins of suffering that a client might find meaningful. Each can produce symptoms – depression, anxiety, anger, addiction, suicidality, for instance – and then these symptoms in turn can produce more suffering. They are identified as the problem. They are pathologised, labelled and 'treated' – usually with little consideration of or enquiry into the root cause. Some clinical psychiatric diagnoses are little more than adjectives dressed up and repackaged as nouns.

Good therapy goes deep into the ventricles and dark chambers of meaning and possibility. It gets to the heart of the matter.

We will return to the subject of suffering in Chapter 5. And so, to the list – some possible origins of suffering:

1. Because of your body

Making peace, accepting and loving yourself includes tending to the body you were born with. You're not getting another. But many people dislike their body and abuse it, or starve it, or punish it too hard in the gym, or attempt to change it, or have as little to do with it as possible. It's hard to love a body whose owner doesn't.

Bodies can do amazing, extraordinary things. They can also be a storehouse of trauma, a reservoir of shame. The body remembers (Rothschild, 2000); the body keeps the score (van der Kolk, 2014). Bodies have much to tell if we're prepared to listen.

Some have bodies that get injured, impaired, ill, create excruciating pain or are otherwise classified as disabled.

Perhaps asking why we got this body is asking the wrong question. Better questions might be: What are you going to do about it? How will you care for this body? What help do you need? What are you going to learn? And, above all, how are you going to live?

There are, of course, some people with brain impairments, intellectual disabilities that may make it a bit harder to make conscious decisions and have agency in this life on earth. But the size of a soul is completely uncorrelated to size of intellect or level of educational attainment. Perhaps a reduced ability to interact with this life on earth affords a soul the possibility of shining more, not less.

2. Because of your mind

So much of the human experience is a story of war, violence, oppression, poverty, natural disasters. For the 'antipsychiatrists' like R.D. Laing and Thomas Szasz, asylums were full of people who were completely sane and guilty only of expressing sane responses in and to an insane world. They regarded 'mental illness' as a myth, a social construction, a form of political control.

The sane view is that we're all at least a little bit mad. Even in the absence of external hardships, we are conflicted. We are perpetually at war with ourselves. We poleaxe ourselves with negative thoughts, imagined catastrophes, a barrage of self-criticism.

The central internal dispute, as old as humankind, is this: Do we do what we like, following our desires, our id, or do we do what we should, guided by the super-ego's demands of what's best for others – the family, group, or society? Freud likened this internal war between id and superego – with our ego in the middle, caught in the crossfire – to the fabled ferocity of the 5th-century battle between Attila and the Romans and the Visigoths. The demands of the superego, says Lacan, 'grow increasingly fastidious and cruel' (in Fink, 1999, p.176). It 'rages against the ego with merciless violence' (Freud, 1923a/1961, p.53). That violence can be a cause of much psychological and somatic distress.

Plato, the Stoics, the Ascetics, Aquinas, Hobbes, Descartes, Locke, Mill, Kant and Schopenhauer tend to be on the side of the superego, generally favouring restraint imposed by society and/or religion. Rousseau, Machiavelli, Kierkegaard, Nietzsche, Lacan, Sartre and the existentialists, and hippies are advocates of more of a free expression of the id.

(An aside: It's ironic that a book arguing for a greater appreciation of diversity must rely so heavily on the views of a bunch of old white men. And is written by one. Proof, as if any were needed, that there is a great need for a greater appreciation of diversity.)

We all have multiple identities born of our developmental, familial, intergenerational, genetic, cultural, socioeconomic, personal and relational histories (e.g. Sen, 2006). Earlier in the chapter, I wrote that it can be useful to think of humans as being made up of multiple 'selves', a tapestry made up of lots of disparate strands (e.g. Sullivan, 1953; Laing, 1960; Winnicott, 1971; Rowan, 1990). They all inhabit our being, in a loose confederacy. I likened it to a raucous committee meeting. Perhaps it is like a rather unruly football team. The id, ego and superego are the three most important members of the team – similar to Berne's child, adult and parent ego states (1964) and corresponding perhaps to the centre forward, the manager and the goalkeeper. But there are many other players, including representatives from the other three dimensions of existence (Binswanger, 1963): a physical self, an emotional self and a spiritual self. We are able to 'feel like one self while being many', as Bromberg writes: 'Health is the ability to stand in the spaces between realities without losing any of them' (2001, p.274). Perhaps the soul is what unites our various selves – like the chairperson emeritus whose portrait hangs in the committee room.

Or perhaps we are each Mount Olympus and carry within us all the gods of Greek mythology. We need to pay attention to them all, and not worship any of them too much. The Ancient Greeks believed the gods weren't that bothered about human morality; the one thing they couldn't stand in a human was hubris. Ignore any of the gods – or worse, think you are one – and you will quickly be cut down to size.

Jung interpreted and adapted the wisdom of Greek mythology to create his ideas about archetypes – universal patterns of behaviour that form part of our collective subconscious.

We all have our times of being Zeus-like, but equally, we are all quite capable of being Koalemos, the god of stupidity, or Oizys, the goddess of misery (her Roman name is Miseria). Oizys was a terrible worrier. Worry has little faith in the worrier. Worry is a tyrant, a bully, an addiction. Worry has no sense of humour. Worry is fear. Worry needs to lighten up.

Today, in the Western world, are we free-thinking postmodern me-generation individualists who can be whoever we want to be? Or are we ever-more enslaved to a rapacious, introjected capitalist machine?

3. Because you're unloved

We've all felt the bitter sting of loneliness. You're definitely not alone – we're all in it together. This has been called the 'Age of Loneliness'.

We've become an alien-nation, isolated from each other – and our own selves. The cup of human kindness is empty these days.

We are social animals. We seek connection; it is through what Cozolino calls the 'social synapse' (2014, p.xv) that we develop and grow, certainly as babies but throughout our lifespan, too. As Sue Gerhardt writes in the excellent *Why Love Matters*:

> My understanding is that human beings are open systems,
> permeated by other people as well as by plants and air and
> water. We are shaped not only by what we breathe and eat but
> by our interactions with other people. (2004/2015, p.10)

Sullivan wrote: 'There is no way that I know of by which one can, all by oneself, satisfy the need for intimacy' (1953, p.270).

Loneliness, then, could be thought of as useful information akin to hunger or thirst. It is a call to arms, a warning, a klaxon in the dark night. We can tolerate it for a while and carry on, but the more socially starved and weakened we become, the harder it's going to be to rectify. And we do need to address it. Because loneliness can be a toxic companion. It is bad for your health. Ever since Émile Durkheim's book *Suicide* (1897/2005), we've understood the dramatic negative impact of social isolation. 'We know that loneliness shaves about eight years off your life expectancy,' writes Dan Buettner in *The Blue Zones* (2010), which is about those places around the world known for their inhabitants' extraordinary longevity. What promotes longevity is, of course, the opposites of loneliness: love, connectedness, belonging. Love is not all you need, nor does it make the world go round, but it is certainly a vital part of being human.

Loneliness might be as old as humankind, an inextricable part of the human condition. Loneliness – a dread of being alone – has always served an evolutionary purpose, ensuring that we humans seek out other humans and create baby humans. It's thanks to loneliness that you and I are here, today.

In his classic, slim volume *Loneliness*, Moustakas writes:

> Man's inevitable and infinite loneliness is not solely an awful
> condition of human existence… it is also the instrument
> through which man experiences new compassion and new
> beauty. (1961, p.x).

In the womb, we are alone. At death, we make a journey to something else, and again, we travel solo. In the part in between, our hour upon the stage, loneliness is a call to love. But the love starts with you. If you don't love you, why should anyone else?

Krishnamurti writes:

> The entity who tries to fill or run away from emptiness, incompleteness, loneliness, is not different from that which he is avoiding; he is it. He cannot run away from himself; all that he can do is to understand himself. He is his loneliness, his emptiness; and as long as he regards it as something separate from himself, he will be in illusion and endless conflict. When he directly experiences that he is his own loneliness, then only can there be freedom from fear. (1956, p.112)

One possible cure for loneliness starts with solitude.

4. Because of poverty

It's very hard to live well when you're hungry, homeless or in danger. To a great extent, the possibility of living a soulful life depends on what country you were born into. It is easier in prosperous, well-run, egalitarian nations. Maslow proposed a 'hierarchy of needs' – not until the basic physiological demands of survival have been met (food, water, sleep, safety) can we find love, self-esteem and, finally, 'self-actualisation', which might be searching for knowledge, understanding, meaning or spirituality in life: a connection to the soul.

You would think that, with so many governments around the world struggling to find solutions to similar issues – 200-plus giant petri dishes – there would be more consensus over the best way to run a country. What system seems to work best? Where are people happiest? The latest annual World Happiness Report ranks Finland as the happiest country in the world (WHR, 2020), with Iceland, Denmark, Switzerland, Netherlands, Sweden, Germany, Norway, New Zealand and Austria rounding out the top 10.

If you were born into any of these prosperous, well run, generally egalitarian nations, you should be thankful – it could have been so much worse. It could have been Syria, Burundi or Togo for you. The US is 14th on the list; the UK 18th.

The report highlights the corrosive effect of inequality.

Rousseau's dictum is that people are born free yet are 'everywhere found in chains' (1762/1998). Like Fromm (1955/2001) and other social environment psychologists (e.g. Horney, 1950/1991; Sullivan, 1953), I believe that much human distress and suffering is the result of powerlessness born of a deeply unfair, unequal social order. Depression can be viewed as an embodiment of social inequality (Cromby, 2014). Smail argues that, rather than looking for insight into clients' psychological distress, therapists should look for 'outsight' – an awareness of a person's environment. He claims that, in the face of corporate power, people have little agency. 'There is no such thing as an autonomous individual,' he writes (2005, p.46). Sartre, by contrast, states: 'Man is nothing else but what he makes of himself' (1957/2002, p.7). While there are limits, I believe in human agency. However dire one's circumstances, we still retain the freedom to choose how to respond. The caged bird can still sing.

But therapy's tendency to blame the victims of oppression for their suffering can make it an instrument of oppression as opposed to emancipation (Foucault, 1964).

5. Because of loss

To live is to experience loss. We know people die but it's still shocking when it happens. Where did they go? Each loss reminds us of the pain of all the previous ones. They pile up. Every day we die a thousand deaths. In the end everything will be taken from you.

We mourn the losses. As discussed in the previous chapter, Elizabeth Kübler-Ross's 1969 model sets out five stages of mourning (for loss of our life, or the lives of others) – denial, anger, bargaining, depression, acceptance, not necessarily followed in that order – but real life is much more complicated, unpredictable and idiosyncratic. We mourn lost loves and lost loved ones, we mourn the childhood we had or the one we didn't. We mourn all the dreams that didn't come true, we mourn the passing of time, we mourn our youth.

Or we choose not to. Instead, we stay frozen in grief. We're unable to accept the loss and move on. We're alive but we have killed ourselves off. Like Queen Victoria, we are permanently funereal. One client has a letter from his beloved that she wrote on her deathbed 20 years previously. It remains unopened.

Among the tens of millions of deaths resulting from the last great 'flu pandemic 100 years ago – the so-called Spanish 'flu – was

Sophie Halberstadt, the fifth of Sigmund Freud's six children. She died on 25 January, 1920. There was no comfort in religion for Freud – famously atheistic, he regarded a belief in God as an infantile need for a father figure. Writing of Sophie's passing to fellow psychoanalyst Sandor Ferenczi, Freud said: 'As a confirmed unbeliever, I have no one to accuse and realize that there is no place where I could lodge a complaint.'

Sophie left behind two sons. The younger one, Heinele, was just a baby. He was, wrote Freud, 'physically very fragile, truly a child of the war, but especially intelligent and endearing'. When he too died, three years later, of tuberculosis, Freud was undone.

Freud's landmark paper on mourning and melancholia (1917/2001) distinguished between the former as a healthy, temporary depression following a loss that, when completed, successfully allows the bereaved person to live and love again, and the latter, which he believed was more self-defeating, enduring and, with no apparent conscious cause, more problematic. It was, he said, 'an open wound'.

But, rather than lessening in intensity, the losses can sometimes be felt more keenly over time, and the distinction between mourning and melancholia can become blurred by all the tears and the fog of remembrance.

Freud suffered in his life. A perpetual cigar smoker, he had more than 30 surgical operations on a mouth cancer that caused him excruciating pain. He and his youngest daughter, Anna – a famous psychologist in her own right – fled the Nazis in 1938 and came to London. Freud died by doctor-assisted suicide the following year, three weeks after the start of the World War II – a war in which his four sisters, who did not escape Austria, were murdered in the Nazi death camps.

The death of Sophie, however, and of little Heinele were defining moments in the landscape of his 83 years on earth.

There is loss. There is grieving. There is life after loss. But the loss remains. In a sense, we never get over it.

6. Because of your past

Attachment theory – which in essence claims that children need strong, nurturing early relationships with caregivers for optimal social and emotional development – was formulated by John Bowlby in the 1950s, following a world war in which so many attachments were violated. His ideas on the impact of the early environment on adult life were strenuously resisted by the psychoanalysts and drive theorists of the day, partly because, perhaps, they explored the kind of early traumas, separations and losses that the likes of Freud and Melanie Klein had experienced and which they themselves had repressed and dissociated (Marrone & Cortina, 2003, p.11). But gradually his ideas became accepted as more child studies revealed the impacts of early maltreatment.

Largely thanks to Bowlby, many of the old parenting norms, such as limiting newborns' contact with their parents in maternity wards, rationing the attention parents paid to babies, and even subjecting babies to prolonged periods of isolation outdoors, fell out of vogue in the 1950s and 1960s (Hinde & Stevenson-Hinde, 1991, p.53). (These anachronistic attitudes live on in spirit still, however, with notions of 'controlled crying' and bestselling parenting guides that reject 'baby-led parenting' in favour of the imposition of strict, one-size-fits-all routines for feeding, bathing and sleeping.)

Fortunate babies are delivered into a favourable situation that includes parents who love them. Insecurely attached children have parents who are less sensitive to their needs. Such parents may be consistently unresponsive or rejecting, in which case the child learns to detach and shut down, or else they respond inconsistently – unresponsive at times, smothering at others. This inconsistency leaves the child ill-equipped to manage difficult emotional states. The seeds of adult personality are planted in childhood. As Larkin noted: 'They fuck you up, your mum and dad' (Larkin, 2003). (He added, more kindly, 'They may not mean to, but they do.')

Sometimes the early environment not only is not 'good enough', to use paediatrician and psychoanalyst D.W. Winnicott's well-used phrase (1971), but is actually abusive. Van der Kolk describes this as a 'hidden epidemic', citing shocking statistics: one in five Americans has been sexually molested as a child, and one in four beaten by a parent (2014, p.1). The statistics in the UK are comparable (Radford et al., 2011).

Trauma isn't necessarily only caused by major abuse or harm – it can emerge from a consistently sub-optimal, hostile environment. The child adapts as best they can, but the wounds run deep, especially when they are inflicted in the early years, in the small window of opportunity when most brain growth occurs, creating Balint's 'basic fault' (Balint & Ornstein, 1992). Early relational trauma can cause the brain and nervous system to be flooded with stress hormones that can lead to a 'developmental overpruning' of the corticolimbic system (Siegel, 1999, p.85), compromising the ability to cope with stress throughout the person's life (Gerhardt, 2004/2015).

Parts of the self that are not responded to by a loving parent are dissociated or split off; the child becomes a 'divided self' (Laing, 1960). To survive and find love, a 'false self' is developed (Winnicott, 1960). A large part of therapy is reclaiming the shadow side, those disowned, 'not-me' parts of the self (Bromberg, 2011).

Survivors often emerge into adulthood with 'a debased and an exalted self', which cannot integrate (Herman, 1992, p.106); a fragmentation of self that permits only fragmented relationships with others. Early trauma, too, makes people especially susceptible to pathologically adverse reactions to traumatic events in later life, with an over-vigilant nervous system easily triggered into a state of high alert (van der Kolk, 2014). The therapeutic task in such cases is to complete the blocked response, discharging the high arousal levels by carefully revisiting the precipitating event, avoiding retraumatisation by hitting the 'brakes' when necessary (Rothschild, 2000), and working throughout with the client's bodily experience (Levine, 1997).

In extreme cases, the psychic injury can be simply too hard to bear. Greatly traumatised children, victims of abusive, hostile or disorienting parenting, cannot resolve the double bind of fearing those who are supposed to love you (Fonagy, 2001, p.36). The result can be a kind of disintegration, or what Janet called 'psychological disaggregation' (1889/2010). Dissociation provides a means of escape when there is no escape (Schore, 2012, p.159); symptoms include amnesia, fragmentation of identity and feelings of detachment and unreality about one's self, body and environment. Such a start in life, coupled with predisposing genetic factors, may induce an array of possible psychiatric disorders, including psychosis, which for Verhaeghe is characterised by 'the impossibility of entering a dialectical exchange' (2003, p.432) – a total alienation from self and from others.

The good news is that we are highly adaptable creatures. We grow, we overcome, we transcend. Our brains are highly plastic. We can spend the rest of our lives repairing and strengthening our shaky foundations.

7. Because you're excluded

It is depressingly easy to manufacture 'in-groups' and 'out-groups' based on the most meaningless of differences, and the fear, loathing and hostility directed towards the out-group can quickly intensify. Using the power of projection, the out-group is demonised: 'we' are good; 'they' are bad – deviant, dangerous, dirty, lazy (and any number of other aspersions). The more unknown 'they' are, the easier it is to imagine them as barbarians. Racism – and fervent identification with a national identity – are strongest in areas with least diversity of population.

This crude scapegoating of people from foreign parts, or 'othering', is vigorously and cynically exploited by rightist politicians, the media, apartheid regimes (e.g. South Africa), dictators inciting genocide (e.g. Somalia, Rwanda, Myanmar, Serbia…), and Western governments seeking to justify illegal overseas interventions (e.g. the UK and the US in Iraq and Afghanistan most recently, but the historic list is endless).

The message used to be that the Russians were the primitive barbarians who wanted to take over the world – a view that has been revived by President Putin's ambitions in Eastern Europe. In recent decades, it is Muslims who have been demonised. The idea that 1.6 billion people – more than a fifth of humanity – speak with one violent voice and think with one murderous mind is patently ludicrous.

Members of an out-group might understandably join forces to campaign for better treatment. And so identity politics is born and, paradoxically, the divisions are reinforced.

Can't we all just get along?

8. Because you're frightened

Did you hear the news today? Be very afraid. The world is a scary place these days. Perhaps it's not surprising that many people – housebound 'shut-ins' in the US or young men lured by the growing trend of *hikikomiri* in Japan – choose to have as little to do with it as possible. We live in an age of anxiety.

But we always have. Evolution favours the anxious. As a species, we have survived by being hypervigilant to danger. Early humans who weren't worried about the rustle in the undergrowth got eaten by bears.

We are sophisticated creatures, but part of us remains indelibly primitive. Running through each life, like the lettering in a stick of rock, is an ever-present vigilance, an unerring fidelity to the overriding question: 'Is it safe?'

The human brain is really a ramshackle structure of three brains in one – a 'triune brain' (Cozolino, 2010, p.5). At the base is the brainstem – the reptilian, physiological brain responsible for basic animal survival functions. Above that is the limbic system, the mammalian brain responsible for learning, memory and emotions, including the orbitofrontal cortex, anterior cingulate and amygdala, which coordinate the higher and lower brain functions such as the regulation of emotion (Siegel, 1999, p.10).

And at the top is the human, thinking brain, the large cerebral cortex, to do with conscious thought, reason, problem-solving and self-awareness (Gerhardt, (2004/2015, p.34).

The lizard brain is an ancient structure, hardwired and never at rest. It doesn't care about your quality of life. It doesn't care about your poetry, your appreciation of sunsets, your love of the way your partner laughs. It's just trying to keep you alive.

Anxiety and its sidekick, worry, are meant to keep us safe, but they can feed on themselves and become addictive, aided and abetted by news media that inflict a daily diet of things we should supposedly worry about: Ebola, SARS, swine flu, Zika, the flesh-eating virus, killer food bugs, MMR, HPV, Y2K, AI, benefit cheats, hoodies, paedophiles, new age travellers, criminals, terrorists and a litany of other 'moral panics', the consistently leading one being, of course, foreigners. Governments, too, understand, that fear is a vote winner. Sometimes the fearmongering is justified. At the time of writing, the world is emerging from a devastating global pandemic. And we resolutely didn't see that coming.

But generally, it's best to avoid the fearmongers. Watching the news right before bed – horrific things from around the world that you have no control over – is a seriously bad idea. And fear, like any emotion, is just information, not an imperative. You can choose what you do with that information. You might decide, for example, despite the endless array of flashing warning lights, to 'feel the fear and do it anyway'.

You want to live, don't you?

You might also decide it's a good idea to calm the inner lizard. Breathe. Soothe your senses. Relax. When fear takes to the stage, enjoyment heads for the exit.

9. Because you're stressed

George, a client, had a busy, demanding job. He didn't delegate because he was a perfectionist and he preferred things done his way. He had a reputation as a doer, a fix-it kind of a person; he didn't want to let anyone down and he hated confrontation, so he ended up doing a lot of other people's work. He took work home with him. He would often wake in the night worrying about a project, grab his laptop and get to work. He used to socialise with people from the office after hours. He used to be involved in amateur theatre. But he gave all that up years ago. He came for therapy because, a couple of weeks earlier, he'd been putting on his tie in front of the mirror, getting ready to leave the house at 6am as usual, and he burst into tears and couldn't stop crying. He was a year away from retirement. He took to his bed.

George was under an enormous amount of stress, yet his conscious mind was completely oblivious. And it wasn't just his job that was causing problems – it was prospect of leaving it, too, and not being needed or useful any longer.

The hamster's wheel spins faster and faster. More is demanded of us. We are on call 24/7. Our inner meerkat is on permanent red alert. We are overstimulated, oversaturated. We can buy anything anywhere any time. The horror of the news will always find us. We didn't choose the soundtrack, and the music is too loud. Our bodies are stressed.

We are experiencing a kind of psychic global warming.

We are anxious. Or we turn away, we shut down: we are depressed. Or we turn to something else: we are addicts. We need to learn to chill, regulate, self-soothe.

George, by the way, never did go back to work. The tie, for decades a noose around his neck, was never tied again.

10. Because it all seems pointless

Life is short and then you die.

Tolstoy experienced a crisis at 50, when life seemed meaningless. 'Why should I live?' he wrote. Camus maintained that the only serious philosophical question was whether to live or die. I see lots of clients in midlife – successes on paper – who can't see the point of their existence.

Some people find meaning in their work, in the use and interaction of their unique combination of skills and talents with the world, which is one reason why unemployment and unrewarding, degrading occupation are so crushing to the human spirit. Others find meaning in love, in relationships, in their children. Hovering above these earthly concerns is a yearning for communion with some kind of higher meaning.

We humans want answers. We tell stories. We believe. Research shows religious believers are happier than atheists. A conviction that you've been pencilled in for a good karmic afterlife or a place in heaven probably does make a lot of people quite happy. Atheists might regard such believers as deluded, cocooned in blissful ignorance. In the film *The Truman Show*, Jim Carrey would have stayed blissfully happy if he'd never discovered he was living in an entirely artificial town – an unwitting pawn in a reality TV show.

But the truth is, we don't know. We humans do our best, but we each have a particular and highly circumscribed apparatus with which to understand our lives. Our 'doors of perception' (Huxley, 1954) are only partially open. We cannot be expected to know the truth of the universe any more than an ant can be expected to read the open page of the book upon which it walks.

There are greater truths that we cannot know, only glimpse in transcendent moments of mystery and magic. The word 'god' is a question mark, an absence, an empty frame, a blank page – or just a word.

The dubious 'evidence' for CBT

There is no better example of bias, political pressure, public relations, marketing and the seductive use of numbers than the National Health Service's provision of cognitive behavioural therapy (CBT), which is now pretty much the only psychological treatment it offers.

CBT itself is not all bad, and I sometimes use elements of it with clients. It started in the 1950s, when the prevailing approaches to psychological treatment were either psychoanalysis, which suggested clients were at the mercy of their unconscious processes, or behaviourism, which suggested they were at the mercy of their external environments. Aaron Beck felt little consideration was given to people's power as conscious beings with the ability to make good choices.

It was an innovative 'third way' at the time, and it has evolved since then. But it is generally offered as an absurdly simplistic, quick-fix, one-size-fits-all approach that only targets symptoms rather than underlying causes. It busies itself with strategies and tactics, as opposed to meaning and understanding. The 'blame-the-victim' ethos that's inherent to CBT – all your problems are the result of your faulty thinking and behaviour – only makes people feel even worse when the treatment fails to make any lasting difference.

Here is how it works. Let's say you have a medical condition – Parkinson's, for example – and you think it might help to talk to someone. You go to see your GP and they refer you to your local psychological therapy service (in England, known as IAPT, or Improving Access to Psychological Therapies). There will likely be a long waiting list, but eventually – if you're determined to get talking therapy with a live human being, rather than a self-help book, some photocopied sheets of advice, a website, or a voice on the telephone – you'll be offered six sessions of CBT.

The CBT therapist may not have had therapy themselves, and they may not necessarily have much knowledge or experience of what life is like with Parkinson's. They will likely assume you are suffering from depression and/or anxiety because that is what the algorithm and the research into Parkinson's says. The therapist might listen to you for a bit, but soon will start to discuss your negative thought patterns and the ways that you could improve your behaviour so you cope better and spend your time more productively. There might be some more handouts with bullet points and diagrams and charts that detail how you 'should' be thinking and living, the way 'normal' people do it, and worksheets to fill out.

You will be asked to complete some forms each week, such as depression and anxiety and quality of life questionnaires for example, and these will give you numerical scores that reveal the extent of the error of your ways and, ideally, your progress towards improving them. The therapist will be highly motivated to get your scores lower each week, because this is considered 'evidence' that you are better, that the CBT worked and the therapist did a good job. You might feel pressured or coerced or just morally obliged to play along, if only because the therapist is harmless enough and you like to please. And if you don't play along, the blame for you not feeling better will be placed squarely with you.

Further 'evidence' that people with Parkinson's are depressed and anxious and that CBT makes them better comes from 'research' conducted by people who don't have Parkinson's but who are invested in maintaining this charade. There is for example a document called *Psychological Interventions for People with Huntington's Disease,*

Parkinson's Disease, Motor Neurone Disease, and Multiple Sclerosis, published by the British Psychological Society (BPS, 2021). It is subtitled 'Evidenced-based guidance', which means the authors conducted a 'systematic review of the current literature'. And what did they find? Amazingly, the evidence all pointed towards CBT!

Such a myopic, self-fulfilling prophecy is like letting someone set their own homework, make up their own answers, and mark it themselves.

Obviously, some CBT therapists and practices are much better than the rather cartoonish image I have presented here, and services vary across the land, but the truth is that the real evidence for the effectiveness for CBT is poor (e.g. Bolsover, 2002; Orlans & Van Scoyoc, 2009; Holmes, 2002; Leichsenring & Steinert 2017). Yet it continues to be the one talking therapy recommended wholeheartedly by the agencies that set out what the NHS can offer across all four nations of the UK.

CBT reveals an extraordinarily impoverished view of the human condition. CBT is what you get when you put an economist in charge.

CBT is therapy stripped of its vital ingredient, the thing that heals: love and care for the human soul.

EMDR: In the eye of the beholder

Francine Shapiro was a high school teacher in New York. In her spare time, she was pursuing a PhD on the poetry of Thomas Hardy. But then illness came a-calling: she got breast cancer, recovered, sold all her possessions and headed for California in a camper van. She wound up in a small coastal community north of San Francisco.

One day, in May 1987, she went for a walk. She had a lot on her mind. But she noticed that if she looked to the left, then right, then back again, the troublesome thoughts became less intrusive and her mind cleared. It wasn't communing with nature that soothed her, or the California sea air, or the joyous, healthy privilege of walking. No, Shapiro decided the thing that made the difference was moving her eyes from side to side.

Thus was born something called eye movement desensitisation reprocessing (EMDR). Or so the story goes.

Shapiro devised a rigorous, standardised, manualised, eight-phase treatment protocol, at the heart of which are sessions where the client goes over upsetting or traumatic memories while the EMDR therapist moves a finger from side-to-side in front of their face like some vaudeville hypnotist, or clicks their fingers on either side of the client's head, or alternately taps the client's knees. It is EMDR's founding belief that this bilateral eye movement helps the brain process past traumas. Giving the brain something else to do while reliving a painful memory sort of dilutes the weight attached to it, supposedly. EMDR disciples also point out that it is a bit like a simulation of the rapid eye movement (REM) phase of sleep, which is known to be important to the consolidation of memory.

EMDR's claims of scientific legitimacy have been met by much eye-rolling from critics (e.g. Sikes & Sikes, 2003). Yet what was a simple idea, discovered and self-administered by Shapiro in a moment during a walk in the park, has proliferated into an empire. There are ever-more demanding training requirements and certification procedures. To become an EMDR Accredited Practitioner, a therapist will minimally need to complete a four-part training course, have conducted 50 hours of EMDR therapy with 25 clients and have received 20 hours of supervision from an EMDR-accredited consultant/supervisor. Thousands of therapists have spent thousands jumping through all of these hoops. EMDR has been widely accepted. In 2013, the World Health Organization approved its use in treating PTSD and other mental health disorders. Since so much of the experience of disability involves traumatic aggressions and discrimination at the hands of a cruel social order, EMDR is often used in treating clients with disabilities. Prince Harry reportedly had EMDR to process the trauma of growing up in the madhouse of Windsor.

There is much research in favour of EMDR's efficacy. And much against. An arm's-length review by *Scientific American* concluded that, while it was effective, 'researchers have found scant evidence that the eye movements of EMDR are contributing anything to its effectiveness' and 'not a shred of good evidence exists that EMDR is superior to exposure-based treatments that behaviour and cognitive-behaviour therapists have been administering routinely for decades' (Arkowitz & Lilienfeld, 2012). One piece of research discovered one effect of the eye movements was to increase the likelihood of false memories (Houben et al., 2018).

With or without the eye movements, the *trompe-l'œil*, the processing of difficult material in the presence of a compassionate other is a cornerstone of any therapy. The client tells their story, often for the first time, in the safe, non-judgemental, confidential context of a well-established therapeutic relationship. A shameful or hurtful aspect of a life is exposed to the light. They are met with acceptance, understanding and love. And often, all the hurt and frozen emotion and excess baggage that had been adhering to the underbelly of that time melts and then evaporates, never to burden the soul again.

EMDR has helped many people. But personally speaking, as a client, when I have talked about hard times with a therapist, what has mattered the most is their warmth and humanity in responding and understanding. I have been grateful that they have not felt the need to wave their fingers in front of my face. In Chapter 2, I quoted Wilfred Bion, who said the best therapy is conducted 'without memory and without desire' (1970). I imagine he would have added 'without gesticulation', too.

Therapy for people with disabilities

We now turn to the specifics of therapy for people with disabilities. It could be argued that such an effort is doomed. First, the social model of disability locates the problem not in the person who is disabled but in society – surely, it is the architects of society, the politicians, who need their heads examined? Second, people with disabilities are people too, and as such subject to the same range of human sufferings as anyone else – why do we assume that all, or indeed any of their suffering comes from their disability? Third, people with disabilities are such a large and diverse group of people, one in seven humans, each unique in our combinations of impairments, contexts and individual psychologies – surely any generalisations about 'how to work with us' are almost meaningless?

Yet the social model hinges on defining people with disabilities as a minority group whose members share similar experiences of discrimination and prejudice in society. And, as with any minority group, the challenge is to be armed with knowledge about this population, but without that knowledge becoming reified, dogmatic or stereotypical. Therapists working with clients with disabilities would do well to have an understanding of the disability experience and culture, but at the same time there should be no assumption that any of it will necessarily apply to your next client.

The challenge of disability

The fact is, however, that life is generally harder with a disability.

There's an assessment tool in therapy called the 'five aspects of life,' otherwise known as the 'hot-cross bun' (Greenberger & Padesky, 1995). Four of the aspects of life – thoughts, behaviour, emotions, body – make up the quadrants of the hot-cross bun. Each is connected to the other three by a double-sided arrow, meaning energy can flow in either direction. The whole thing sits in a big circle – a plate perhaps? – which represents a person's environment.

Here's how it works. Let's suppose deep down, you don't feel very smart or talented or attractive or interesting. That thought will influence your behaviour. Perhaps you avoid social situations. You fly below the radar at work. The thought and the behaviour keep you isolated. Your energy is invested in keeping safe, avoiding life rather than engaging with it. This affects your mood. You feel flat, shut down, invisible. This just further amplifies your original thoughts about yourself. All of this has an effect on your body. You feel heavy, slow, dull. Everything seems stagnant.

Maybe something happens to interrupt this downward spiral. Something good, perhaps – you notice an opportunity and go for it, or someone notices you, or believes in you, or you have some therapy and decide that you actually quite like yourself after all. Or something bad – you get fired, ill, dumped, cheated, or someone dies. The whole system falls apart, you crash. And then, somehow, out of the wreckage, you emerge. Your breakdown precipitates a breakthrough. You find some strength you didn't know you had. You interact with the world and get feedback from it. You share more of yourself with others, and some of them reciprocate, and you feel more connected. A vital energy floods through your body – and the whole system. You walk tall, engage, and take up your rightful place in the world.

Even a minor change in one part of the system affects the whole system. If you're happy, you smile. But each arrow is bidirectional: smile and you will feel happier.

So the body plays a huge role in how we experience life. And an impaired, broken or ill body will inevitably have a major impact on our thoughts, behaviour and emotions. Merleau-Ponty was right; Descartes was wrong.

It's not like disability or illness get added on top of a conventional, healthy life. Your suboptimal body becomes an integral part of your life, contributing to everything you think, feel and do.

People with disabilities have a great deal of experience with all the 10 forms of suffering I outlined above. They don't just get rain, they get a permanent perfect storm.

They suffer because of their bodies (No. 1), and in turn their thoughts – endlessly reinforced by a brutally cruel, ableist world – can become disabling too (No. 2). And this in turn can affect behaviour. It might already be physically hard, or painful, to go out, and when you do, you are met with prejudice on top of the physical obstacles. So it's understandable you might decide to stay at home, forego a social life, and end up feeling lonely (No. 3). Dating with a disability is hard. According to one survey, 44% of British people would not consider having sex with someone who had a physical disability (Mann, 2014). There again, I can't imagine anyone would consider having sex with someone who is so crippled by prejudice.

Poverty and disability often go hand in hand (No. 4). Disability can be both a cause and a consequence of poverty. Disabled people are almost twice as likely to be unemployed as non-disabled people; yet life costs you £583 more on average a month if you're disabled (Scope, 2019). The vast majority of people with disabilities live in developing countries.

Losses, of course, abound for anyone with a disability – especially an acquired progressive disability (No. 5).

Children with disabilities often have a rough ride – a difficult start in life (No. 6). It can be harder for secure attachments to develop between the child and their caregivers (e.g. Howe, 2006); children with disabilities face a disproportionally high risk of neglect, abuse, violence and trauma (Flynn, 2020; Thomas-Skaf & Jenney, 2021).

The discrimination, exclusion and bullying start early and continue right through into adulthood. People with disabilities are perhaps the most marginalised, generally not made to feel welcome in 'non-disabled world' (No. 7), and understandably there is a great deal of fear (No. 8), stress (No. 9) and hopelessness (No. 10).

When the body is whole, fully functioning and healthy, you can take it for granted. You are on automatic pilot. When your body stops operating the way it used to, or isn't able to operate the way most other people's bodies operate, you have to switch to manual. You have to work much harder. You have to pay great attention to your body. You have to live purposefully.

Is it possible to weather the storm? Yes, it is. Maybe it's much more difficult to get around, have a social life, work, travel. Maybe impossible. But millions of people have a disability or chronic illness and live well, and they are healthy and happy. They think beautiful thoughts, do beautiful things, feel beautiful feelings. But it's not easy. They have to contend not only with their own unreliable, broken body but with other people too, and a healthcare system and a world that only sees them in one way – lacking, limited, lamentable.

This is the Advanced Humanity Test.

Those that pass have had to learn to do things their way, and listen to their soul. But we all need a little help sometimes.

My research identified four themes, four fundamental pillars that create and shape the psychological experience of living with a disabling physical health condition (and, by extension, potentially any disability): bodily loss, discrimination, identity, growth. I used this as the basis of a therapeutic framework (Barton, 2020), one that can be used to help clients with disabilities to:

- develop a good relationship with their body and themselves
- mourn any actual or perceived losses in their life resulting from disability
- develop effective coping strategies, adaptations and support systems
- reject the stereotypical, prejudiced, negative views of disability and instead foster an authentic and empowering sense of identity; an identity and a story that instil pride
- cultivate resilience in the face of discrimination and develop the motivation to protest and become an advocate for change.

The nature of the response to the first three themes dictates the extent to which the fourth, growth, can happen – it can inhibit growth or sometimes accelerate it. However painful and traumatic the loss, however acute the level of discrimination, however impacted the identity, there is always the possibility of choice – of choosing growth over safety; of choosing life over a kind of death. Of choosing ability over disability.

Clinical directions

1. Don't make any assumptions about the client's relationship with their condition, illness or disability. One of the worst things is dealing with other people's reactions. The assumption that it must be terrible, that life must surely be hardly worth living, is bad enough; the opposite – the demand to be relentlessly cheerful and upbeat – isn't much better. Two of the commonest countertransference issues with clients with disability revolve around pity, leading to unhelpful expressions of sympathy and curiosity, and to unwanted, insensitive interrogation. Other unhelpful therapist assumptions include believing that all the client's problems stem from their disability; thinking that they know better than the client about what treatments and procedures the client should undergo, and the sometimes unconscious belief that the client is lucky and should be grateful for the therapist's supposed beneficence and munificence in treating them.

While there may be similarities in the problems they face in a disabling world, every client is (dis)abled in their own unique way. Each therapeutic dyad is unique, dictating a bottom-up psychology that emerges from the relationship rather than a modernist, top-down imposition of theories, techniques and methods from expert clinician to grateful client. Your job is to try to be alongside your client, to 'be with,' not 'do unto'.

2. Consider where you are coming from. How have you and people close to you been impacted by health issues, and how might that impact the work? What are your attitudes and assumptions? Notice and reflect on your transferential reactions, but try to keep things real. Your job is to be a solid, steady, secure base. From that place, you can offer emotional support and embark on a strong working alliance, a co-created venture, a joint exploration. The work may be all about the client's physical condition, or it may not be about that at all.

3. Invite the client to acknowledge what has been lost, to connect with all the emotion surrounding that, to mourn. There are no short cuts. People with health conditions or disabilities are often regarded as objects of shame; inevitably shame can be internalised, where, by definition, it often remains hidden because it's so shameful. Be alert to clues to shame and endeavour to cultivate a relationship in which it is safe for shame to be explored. The overall goal is to enable change where change is possible and acceptance where it isn't. Says the rather

brilliant Serenity Prayer: 'May you find the serenity to accept the things you cannot change, the courage to change the things you can, and the wisdom to know the difference between the two.'

4. On an ongoing basis but especially around diagnosis, explore with the client their relationship with their physical self. Bodywork should be conducted cautiously, respectfully (and generally without physical contact). What would their body say if it could speak? What are the body's abilities, inabilities and capabilities? How does the client experience and respond to emotions? How do they see their identity as a diseased or disabled person – and where do those ideas come from? What is introjected; what is projected? Take a 'community of selves' approach – how do they conceptualise all their other identities and how do they all intersect and integrate and work together? The 'crip', the minority, the gender, the sexual orientation, the class, the community, the nationality, the age bracket, the religion, the political party, the professional role, the social media page, the dating profile, the CV, the letters after your name, the victim, the angry self, the withdrawn self, the army of younger selves, the rapturous, the suicidal. All are welcome.

5. Invite the client to tell their whole story. How does being ill or disabled fit in their life story and their sense of self? What other competing and conflicting identities are influencing the client? What sense or meaning is to be made? What is their narrative identity? The therapist is not obligated to collude in the client's self-blaming or self-critical moralistic interpretations.

6. Introduce Judith Butler's idea of 'queering' (1990, 1993) – rejecting the bleak identity assigned to you by the medical establishment, friends and family and instead wearing your cloak of disease and disability in your own unique way. Role models can help the client see what is possible; they in turn can become role models to others.

7. Introduce the client to the idea of disability apartheid and explore their relationship to the 'non-disabled' and 'disabled' world. What has been the effect of ableism on the client; what traumas have been experienced – at school, at work, in families, socially, from healthcare services? What do they believe, say or do that sustains the two-world status quo? And what do they do to subvert the mainstream and promote 'one world'?

8. Does the client feel isolated? Take a systemic approach. Who is around – family, friends, colleagues, carers, service providers? Explore with the client what support they have in their life, and what they need – a good support network can make such a difference. Respect boundaries; be on the side of client agency and autonomy. Are they good at asking for help? Who has power? A life audit can be helpful – who are the people (and what are the activities, places and things) that are life affirming? And what brings them down? Who or what is discriminatory? And what can be changed? What promotes resilience? Above all, be hypervigilant for any signs of unhelpful power dynamics or unwitting ableism or discrimination from you in the consulting room. Working through ruptures together can be enormously therapeutic for both client and therapist.

9. Join the client in solidarity in understanding and empathising with the daily insult of hassles, discriminations and challenges they may face as a disabled person. Become an advocate for disability rights. Utsey et al. (2001, p.334) suggest that counsellors should become activists, seeking to deconstruct the oppressive social order in their own worlds. In this way, 'the psychologist is invited to conjoin the personal, the professional and the political' (Gergen, 1990, p.27). Both the therapist and client thus strive for emancipation. 'There is no such thing as an unpolitical therapy' (Olkin, 1999, p.307).

10. As the therapeutic relationship develops, you might like to invite the client to explore whether there are any good things to come from their condition or disability. What are they grateful for? Where is the growth – what are their progressive abilities? Where is the love? Introduce the concepts of hormesis, advantageous disadvantage and post-traumatic growth.

11. Health conditions can be an opportunity to care for yourself, finally, after perhaps years of neglect. And I believe caring for yourself slows the progression of symptoms. I have found it useful to be reminded about the importance of the basics: healthy eating, drinking, sleeping, exercising. In a very direct, CBT way, the therapist may take on the role of a coach. Or parent.

12. In searching for meaning in disease and disability, a way to live, a purpose, *ikigai*, the client may be supported in accessing and

developing greater meditative, spiritual, numinous, religious or transcendent aspects of themselves and life.

Some further clinical considerations for therapists

- **Be prepared**: Do your homework. Disability is a minority group with its own culture and, as with any transcultural therapy, competence requires at least these three elements:

  - attendance to the client's intrapsychic, cultural and sociopolitical context

  - an appreciation of issues of power, structural oppression and discrimination in society

  - a self-exploration of the counsellor's own assumptions, values, biases, prejudices and cultural frames of reference (e.g. Lago & Moodley, 2002, p.3; Tuckwell, 2006, p.211).

  Arm yourself with knowledge of disability culture, the medical and social models, and the client's condition. Find some disability-related CPD days. Familiarise yourself too with the 2010 Equality Act and the legal rights of people with disabilities in the UK. There's no excuse for ignorance, warns Olkin; it 'can be expected to have the predictable problems inherent in cross-cultural counseling, such as premature termination, insufficient rapport, or negative outcomes' (1999, p.153).

  The flip side of an appreciation of difference is an awareness of similarity. I try to remain hypervigilant to the danger of seeing or responding to my own material, rather than the client's, and making unhelpful assumptions. It's important for me to adopt a habitual attitude of reflexivity (Aron, 2000).

- **Access**: The first obvious question is: Does your consulting room present any obstacles to easy access for anyone with a disability? This obviously includes bathroom facilities. You might think that the normalisation of online therapy thanks to the Covid-19 pandemic has resolved such problems. But clients with disabilities have the same right as anyone else to see a therapist face to face, and perhaps a greater need, since isolation is so often a part of the disability experience. Access might usefully be considered more broadly. Do you use inclusive language in your marketing materials, for example? Do you provide access information on your website and in your directory entries and publicity? Do you make it clear how you welcome all comers into your counselling room, not just your aspiration to do so? Who might you be unconsciously (or knowingly) excluding by the kind of premises you use? Do you raise concerns with other organisations you know that wittingly or otherwise practice in an exclusionary manner?

- *Etiquette*: A few obvious, general rules:
  1. Don't stare, but do look your client in the eye and see the person first, not the disability.
  2. Don't tell clients about all the other people with disabilities you've met or you know.
  3. Don't assume the person needs your help, and don't help without asking.
  4. Don't touch – not the client or any of their equipment – without consent.
  5. Don't assume you know how a client feels about their disability; similarly don't assume you know how they should feel – remember that the client is the expert.
  6. Check what terminology the client prefers to use. As I explained earlier, I am happy to be labelled as a person with a disability (person first); others prefer 'disabled person' (society as disabling). Depending on the client's preferred term, you could use 'personal assistant' rather than 'carer'.
  7. Invite the client to share their preferences and to tell you when you are being unwittingly ableist. Apologise when you get it wrong. And relax, for goodness sake; you're just connecting with another human being, and it's human to make mistakes.

- *Boundaries*: Your usual rules may not apply. Clients with disabilities may need more time to arrive at a session and leave at the end. They may bring with them third parties or a service dog or assistive equipment, requiring modifications to your room and your usual way of working. Clients with disabilities may or may not have communication difficulties that make it difficult for you to fully hear them. If you didn't quite hear them or understand them, don't pretend that you did. A client with a disability may become fatigued more easily, in which case you might consider offering shorter sessions (at a reduced rate, of course). Or they may be more likely to have to cancel at short notice because they are feeling unwell or have an urgent medical appointment. If you charge for late cancellations, make this an exception to your standard terms and conditions, and make it explicit in your introductory session. Flexibility is key, though boundaries remain important, of course. Halacre and Jalil (2017) helpfully outline ways in which therapy with clients with disabilities can be both flexible and holistic while remaining safe and empowering.

- *Touch*: Unless you are a body-oriented psychotherapist, you probably have a rule that there is to be no physical contact with a client. The consulting room must be a safe space and physical touch can be experienced as invasive, oppressive and even abusive. Given the historic power dynamics in an ableist world, a non-disabled therapist should be extremely aware of this issue when working with a client with a disability. On the other hand, on a pragmatic level, clients with disabilities sometimes need assistance to get around. For example, I have a non-sighted client, and we have agreed that after our sessions I will escort her to the underground station, and she takes my arm. Such arrangements need to be carefully negotiated, thought about, and talked about. However, touch is a basic human need and some clients with disabilities may be starved of such human contact. In the eyes of some, they are untouchable. They might ask for a hug at the end of a difficult session, and to refuse would likely be experienced as rejecting. Exploring how the client can meet this and other needs is a good topic for discussion in therapy.

- *Third parties*: A client with a disability might want or need to attend their therapy appointments with their PA, partner, friend, family member or interpreter. Sessions like these can become quite complicated, especially when the third party is one of the things that is making life difficult for the client. Always put the client first; always address the client. Even in the absence of third parties, the consulting room can feel quite busy when the client is discussing the constellation of friends, family and healthcare professionals in their orbit. An exploration of the strengths and weaknesses of the family system and the broader medical and societal system in which the client is situated is an important part of the work.

- *Referring on*: Given all the potential pitfalls, challenges and complexities presented by a new client who has a disability, you might be tempted to conclude you are outside your comfort zone and outside your area of expertise, and to refer the client on to another therapist. There are times, of course, when that is the right thing to do. The client wants a specific kind of therapy that you don't offer, for example. Or the client's material is just a bit too close to the bone of your own material, which might impact your ability to remain clear-headed and wholehearted. Or your caseload and your life are so full that you don't have the capacity to give this client the attention they deserve. But if you are referring on for no good reason other than the client's disability, perhaps you are guilty of ableism, and so part of the problem, not the solution. Under these circumstances, especially if the referral is handled clumsily and felt by the client as a rejection, then you have failed the Humanity Test.

- *Supervision*: Supervision is a vital part of the work for any therapist. It's also something I find extremely enjoyable and rewarding. I take a broad view of supervision, sharing Van Deurzen and Adams' view of it as 'a joint search for the truth of human existence' (2011, p.37).

  Good supervision is especially essential when working with clients with disabilities, and it's important that your supervisor has knowledge, experience and expertise of disability and disability culture.

  In the guidance *Working with Disability across the Counselling Professions* (2020), published for its members by BACP, Mel Halacre lists some of the typical issues for supervision evoked by this client group, including:

  - our own thoughts and experiences around disability, difference and oppression
  - anxieties about complex impairments
  - reliability of life-sustaining equipment
  - existential fears about deteriorating conditions

- fear of 'getting it wrong'
- 'survivor guilt' for non-disabled therapists
- overwhelm from the client's story
- urges to create distance from the client or creating a 'them' and 'us'
- hopelessness stemming from a belief that a client's problems are insurmountable
- 'rescuer' versus 'wounded healer'. The tragedy model positions the non-disabled helper as saviour or rescuer.

- *Support and self-care*: The work of a psychotherapist can be extremely rewarding, but also demanding. Over the years it can take its toll. It's vital that the therapist takes responsibility for their own support and self-care. Therapists are very good at talking about this kind of thing; a lot aren't quite so brilliant at actually doing it. It's vital to have some kind of meaningful, soulful life outside of the counselling room.

  Working with clients with disabilities can sometimes be challenging, provocative even, to the relationship that the therapist has with their own body. My clients are a constant reminder to be grateful for the body I have, however broken, and to look after it, at the very least committing to the basics: sleep, diet, exercise, meditation. This is in keeping with the ethical principle of self-respect. I want the best for my clients. This requires that I, too, want the best for me.

5. Spirituality –
The transcendental turn

'As far as we can discern, the sole purpose of human existence is
to kindle a light in the darkness of mere being.'
Carl Jung

Freud argued the point of therapy was to turn 'hysterical misery
into ordinary unhappiness' through the restoration of a healthy ego
and a strong sense of self (Breuer & Freud, 1895/1995, p.305). Thus
equipped, the patient can better accept and endure the vicissitudes of
life. Jung parted company with his old mentor when he transcended
that view. For Jung, the development of a healthy ego was an important
stage in the first half of life, a precursor to the goal of the second half of
life: to let go of it and submit to the idea that we are part of something
larger, something infinite, something Rudolf Otto a century ago called
the *mysterium tremendum* – the numinous, the idea of the holy.

For some people, that means surrendering to a particular god
and a particular religion that comes with its own dogmas, peculiar
texts, places, vestments, incantations, rituals, art, music and stories.
Grasping after such mutually exclusive 'certainties' inevitably brings
large swathes of humanity into conflict with each other. It's possible
to reject organised religion as blind faith, misguided, deluded even,
yet wholeheartedly embrace the idea of the numinous, the eternal, the
magical, the transcendental. (But not for Freud. Throughout his life,
he dismissed any such sentiments as 'infantile'.)

There is such a thing as 'religious atheism'. For Dworkin (2013),
this entails an understanding that human life has meaning and
importance and comes with an 'innate and inescapable responsibility'
to live it as well as possible, and also that the universe 'is itself sublime:
something of intrinsic value and wonder' (2013, p.10). Einstein

rejected organised faiths yet considered himself a deeply religious man. He said:

> A human being is a part of the whole, called by us the 'Universe', a part limited in time and space. He experiences himself, his thoughts and feelings, as something separate from the rest – a kind of optical illusion of his consciousness. This delusion is a kind of prison… Our task must be to free ourselves. (1977)

Where therapy ends, often spirituality starts, although the lines are increasingly blurred. Perhaps most therapists eventually make some kind of turn towards the spiritual in their lives, and their work, too, then inevitably takes on a more transpersonal flavour.

Jung wrote:

> The main interest of my work is not concerned with the treatment of neurosis but rather with the approach to the numinous. But the fact is that the approach to the numinous is the real therapy and inasmuch as you attain to the numinous experiences, you are released from the curse of pathology. Even the very disease takes on a numinous character. (1973, p.377)

This is an astonishing, audacious thing to say, and would have had Freud choking on his wiener schnitzel. Imagine not just being released from the curse of your disability, your disease, even in your death; imagine coming to see those things in themselves as sacred.

I believe people who are challenged daily by disease or disability have a head start in seeking this kind of transcendence. Our bodies are cracked, and the cracks, as Rumi, Leonard Cohen and others have observed, are where the light gets in. Writes Thomas Moore: 'Illness offers us a path into the kind of religion that rises directly from participation in the deepest levels of fate and existence' (1992, p.167).

Finding 'religion'

You are not your body. You are not your mind. You are not your emotions. You are not your thoughts. These things are manifestations of your essential you-ness – that higher, wiser, more expansive and perhaps everlasting sense of self that we might call the soul.

Soul is a-theistic yet deeply religious. Soul is the divine within and without. To be in communion with the soul is a lasting cure for loneliness.

Soul is your North Star, a guiding light, both the compass and the treasure map. It is a spirit level; the nondenominational ghost in the machine.

Soul is hard to define. Like quicksilver, writes Jungian analyst Donald Kalsched, it 'slips away as soon as we try to grasp it with language'. Nevertheless, he has a go: for him soul is 'a vital animating core of our embodied selves – a certain essential something that links us (through love) to the divine, to each other, and to the exquisite beauties of the natural and cultural world' (2013, p.22).

Soul is your teacher, your friend, your parent, your guide, your carer, your guru. It is the whisper of your ancestors.

Soul is the poetry of your life, the melody, the amazing grace.

Soul is wild, undomesticated, limitless, free.

If you only let it, the soul will breathe life into your life, and you, by acting on its inspirations, will in turn enhance your soul. Every time you turn away, however, you die a little, and such expirations diminish the soul. Access to the soul does not require any special robes, instructions or advanced knowledge. It is always there if you pay attention. It can be found in many ways, but most easily in stillness, silence, in our breathing, in our present. Meditation is but a silent prayer to the soul.

Soul is the fierce intelligence and ancient wisdom that you see in the eyes of a newborn baby. It is the warming, illuminating light that shines from the eyes of the profoundly autistic child who does not speak and the person with dementia who has forgotten your name and that you are their child.

Soul is there to return to for those who have turned away from it, or who have been so traumatised by life that their connection to it has been temporarily closed through dissociation or other defences. Soul, eventually, is a refuge.

Soul vitalises the most mundane of tasks; its absence renders any experience hollow.

Soul is not something you do only at weekends or on vacation. It is your life's work.

Soul is perhaps your connection to the vast mystery of the cosmos, to all other souls, to whatever it is that came before and whatever it is that comes after.

Soul gives you a sense of perspective and relativity about the supposedly crucial daily dramas and decisions that preoccupy your ego.

Soul is what you love with. It is the source of humanity; the fountainhead of all that is you. Souls are gregarious. They like to mingle with other souls. They congregate, they aggregate, they disseminate. In this way, souls are perhaps the constituent ingredients of Jung's idea of the 'collective unconscious'.

Soul cannot be defined, measured, weighed or photographed. It has no shape, colour or language. It cannot be bottled, downloaded or streamed. It cannot be counted, but it counts. It does not easily submit to the pedantries of scientific method.

In school we learn Pythagoras' fairly useless maths theory that 'the square of the hypotenuse of a triangle is equal to the sum of the squares of the other two sides'. Much more interesting is his theory of the 'transmigration of souls': every soul is immortal; upon death, it enters a new body.

But of course, we don't know.

Plato spoke of 'the turning about of the eye of the soul', rising up above the quotidian tedium towards something greater. Soul is what Kierkegaard described as 'infinite inwardness'. Soul is akin to the Hindu-Buddhist idea of the 'third eye' in the centre of the forehead that serves as a portal to higher states of consciousness.

People who come for therapy are usually, in one way or another, feeling soul-less. I try to use my imperfect soul to help clients find theirs, as others have done for me over the years. Once the lost soul has been found, once we come to our senses and connect, the self-healing can begin.

Soul is especially what people with addictions turn to in order to truly heal. It is an integral part of the third step of the Alcoholics Anonymous 12-step programme, when you pledge to surrender to a 'higher power' or a 'power greater than ourselves'. This is a step too far for some people. The wording is thought to come from William James' classic, gently perambulatory *The Varieties of Religious Experience* (1902/2003), based on a series of lectures he delivered in Edinburgh in 1901 and 1902. James was an American naturalist turned psychologist-philosopher. His brother was the novelist Henry James. His writing – lyrical, personal explorations of inner worlds – is important to psychology, which at the time, in stark contrast, was strictly behaviourist and mechanistic.

'Religion' for James does not necessarily mean a belief in a god, although it did for him personally. Instead, it is an inner phenomenon; a subjective experience of awe and wonder and gratitude for life, the universe and everything in it; the humbling sense that we are 'continuous with Something More' (James, 1896/1956, p.12). So many Romantic artists, writers, poets and thinkers found inspiration in such experiences. These 'religious atheists', soulful men like William Blake, John Keats, D.H. Lawrence and, across the Atlantic, Walt Whitman, Ralph Waldo Emerson and Henry David Thoreau, rejected not only Enlightenment ideas of science and logic as being the only truth but also the dogmas of organised religion. Instead, they beheld the beauty of the world with passion and intensity. You don't need the homilies and interlocutions of Reverends to open your eyes and experience the world with reverence.

Irreligious people, according to James, were indifferent to such sentiments. They are akin to people who cannot love.

As Rumi wrote, back in the 13th century (1995):

Those who don't feel this love
Pulling them like a river
Those who don't drink dawn
Like a cup of spring water
Or take sunset like supper
Those who don't want to change
Let them sleep

Suffering and soul-searching

A billion people struggle daily with disability. Almost seven hundred million people in the world live in extreme poverty. There are currently some 80 million refugees, forcibly displaced from their homes. Nine million people are incarcerated. All around the world, families and friends are grieving the six million people who died in the 2020/21 coronavirus pandemic, many in great distress and alone.

Life is suffering, as Buddhists say – a perpetual samsara of highs and lows.

Mostly lows, according to the rather gloomy 19th century German philosopher Arthur Schopenhauer. 'If the immediate and direct purpose of our life is not suffering then our existence is the most ill-adapted to its purpose in the world,' he wrote in his marvellously doleful essay 'On the Suffering of the World':

> For it is absurd to suppose that the endless affliction of which
> the world is everywhere full, and which arises out of the need
> and distress pertaining essentially to life, should be purposeless
> and purely accidental. Each individual misfortune, to be sure,
> seems an exceptional occurrence; but misfortune in general is
> the rule. (1850/2005, p.3)

All philosophy is rooted in biography.

When Schopenhauer was 17, his father drowned in a canal near their home in Hamburg – a suspected suicide. A decade later, his mother told him in a letter: 'You are unbearable and burdensome, and very hard to live with; all your good qualities are overshadowed by your conceit, and made useless to the world simply because you cannot restrain your propensity to pick holes in other people' (Durant, 1961, p.229). His mother lived for another 24 years, but never saw her son again. Famously misogynistic, Schopenhauer wrote that women were 'the second sex, inferior in every respect to the first'. He never married.

For Schopenhauer, there was no escape. The only response to suffering was to be longsuffering, the sole consolation being the realisation that we all suffer, we're all in this together. Accepting that pain is inherent to the human experience invites something like compassion (literally to 'suffer with'). He wrote:

> He only becomes truly awe-inspiring when he lifts his gaze
> from the particular to the universal, when he views his own
> suffering as a mere example of the whole and becoming a
> genius in the ethical sense, treats it as one case in a thousand, so
> that the whole of life, seen essentially as suffering, brings him to
> the point of resignation. (Wicks, 2020, p.559)

Friedrich Nietzsche was a contemporary of Schopenhauer, a fellow atheist, and initially a follower, but he came to reject the older man's submission and notions of compassion or pity as weak. Life was to be experienced, its hardships embraced. His famous assertion was, 'That which does not kill us, makes us stronger.' Yet in his life he was considerably weakened by his own sufferings, including ill health from childhood, a psychotic breakdown, two crippling strokes and syphilis.

If we find scant appeal in either Schopenhauer's dour pessimism or Nietzsche's obnoxious hubris, are there other approaches? How are we to respond to such a traumatic, dangerous, riven existence? Should we strive to be Epicureans – or better yet, Hedonists – and seek out what pleasure we can? Or should we be Stoics and, like Kipling, treat those two imposters, triumph and disaster, just the same? Do we accept the Buddhist idea that suffering is born of desire, and so surrender our attachment to our own ego and its demands? Or are we to regard our sufferings in the manner of the Christian tradition, enduring whatever life throws at us as a test of faith we must pass in order to enter the kingdom of heaven?

The latter, of course, necessitates a belief in an all-mighty god who would allow such suffering in the first place. In a memorable interview with Gay Byrne on RTÉ One, actor, author and humanist philosopher Stephen Fry said he would address such a god thusly:

> How dare you? How dare you create a world to which there is such misery that is not our fault. It's not right, it's utterly, utterly evil. Why should I respect a capricious, mean-minded, stupid god who creates a world that is so full of injustice and pain… the god that created this universe, if it was created by god, is quite clearly a maniac… utter maniac, totally selfish… We have to spend our life on our knees thanking him? What kind of god would do that? (Fry, 2015)

Perhaps, as with psychotherapy and knowledge in general, we'd do better to take a pluralist approach. Do we believe in the Greek gods, ancient Pagan gods, deities that were worshipped long before organised religion? Writes Bernie Neville:

> We may wish to take them more seriously, to acknowledge that the Greeks, like other polytheistic cultures, knew something about cosmology and psychology which we have forgotten. We may as readily approach ultimate reality through a fantasy of the Many as through a fantasy of One. Whatever our religious beliefs, it can be argued that psychologically we are polytheistic. Whether we summon them or not, the gods are present. (2020, p.58)

The most soulful approach to this vexing, confounding business of living is to accept that we don't know, that we cannot know, and that we are united as a species in not knowing. Then we can simply be, enjoy the show without forever trying to look behind the curtain. We can follow the example offered by the Romantics, those 'religious atheists' who cherished the highs and lows of existence with courage, humility, love. Life provided the ingredients for great art, but their true art was in their art of living.

The English poet John Keats provides perhaps the best example. He suffered greatly too and, like Schopenhauer, was a critic of religion. 'Love is my religion,' he wrote in a letter. 'I could die for that' (Rollins, 1958).

But while Schopenhauer described the world as a 'playground of tortured and anguish-ridden beings that endure only by eating one another' (Wicks, 2020, p.560), Keats rather more romantically suggested it should be thought of as a 'Vale of Soul Making'. 'Do you not see how necessary a world of pains and troubles is to school an intelligence and make it a soul?' he wrote in a letter to his brother, George, in 1819; 'A place where the heart must feel and suffer in a thousand diverse ways!' (Strachan, 2003, p.20).

The idea that humans are forged in the searing heat of suffering is, of course, far from new. But Keats saw his 'system of Spirit-creation' as something different: 'A system of Salvation which does not affront our reason and humanity.' It wasn't about accepting Schopenhauer's dismal, resigned nihilism, passively withstanding the slings and arrows of existence; nor was it about being cowed into a longsuffering life of dull rectitude by religious fears of eternal damnation and hellfire. It was about living! If you accept your suffering, engage with the process of its education, embrace it even, there is a kind of alchemy that opens the human heart to transcendent truth and sensuous beauty.

The word 'suffering' comes from the Latin *subferre*, which means to 'bear under'. But another Latin word for suffering is *passionem*, from the past-participle stem of the Latin *pati*, which means 'to endure, undergo, experience' – a word of uncertain origin. *Passionem* gave rise to the word passion. There is a sense that 'suffering' and 'passion' are thus intimately linked, the one potentially precipitating the other.

Writes Walt Whitman:

O joy of suffering! To struggle against great odds! To meet
enemies undaunted! To be entirely alone with them! To find
how much one can stand! To look strife, torture, prison,
popular odium, death, face to face! To mount the scaffold! To
advance to the muzzles of guns with perfect nonchalance! To be
indeed a God! (1871, p.51)

In the book *Philosophy of Suffering: Metaphysics, value and normativity*
(2020), Carel and Kidd (pp.165–179) argue that suffering can be
transformative – it can change your worldview, your identity, what
matters to you. It can enhance your empathy, compassion, creativity,
love. But, in addition, in the same volume, Scrutton (2020. pp.211–
226) provides plenty of examples to support her contention that
suffering commonly leads to a greater appreciation of aesthetics,
beauty, wildness too.

In the first of his famous odes, *Ode to Psyche* – the goddess of
soul – Keats writes that he will be her priest, and build a temple to her:

In some untrodden region of my mind
Where branched thoughts, new grown with pleasant pain
Instead of pines shall murmur in the wind. (2007, p.188)

Keats suffered greatly in his short life. When he was eight, his father
died falling off his horse and fracturing his skull on his way home from
visiting Keats and his younger brother, George, at boarding school.
An infant brother died, as did a favourite uncle, and then, when he
was 14, his mother died too, of tuberculosis. When his grandparents
were gone, Keats looked after his even more sickly youngest brother,
Tom, who also was stricken by tuberculosis. Returning home from
a wretched, wind-tossed tour of Scotland, in August 1818, Keats
discovered that Tom's condition had worsened. Tom did not see the
year out.

The following year, Keats got engaged to his muse, the source of
his infatuations, his neighbour's daughter, Fanny Brawne. And he
wrote most of his famous poems, including, after a summer of love,
'To Autumn' ('Season of mists and mellow fruitfulness…').

But, so soon, it was already autumn for Keats. He, too, showed
signs of tuberculosis. His health deteriorated fast, accelerated by grief,
depression, money worries, and perhaps by some snooty reviews of
his poetry. His friend and fellow Romantic poet, Percy Bysshe Shelley,

invited him to Italy. Keats wrote back: 'There is no doubt that an English winter would put an end to me, and do so in a lingering hateful manner' (Rollins, 1958). He spent his final weeks in an apartment beside the Spanish Steps in Rome, the eternal city. He died there on 23 February, 1821. He was 25.

Keats' poetry was born of hardship; a fierce lust for life came from the ever-present spectre of death.

Anyone can be similarly spiritualised through their suffering.

T.S. Eliot was not a well man. His childhood was accented by a congenital double hernia, for which he had to wear a truss; he couldn't take part in sports, which isolated him from his peers. As an adult, he often teetered on the edges of physical and mental collapse. He wrote much of his masterpiece, *The Waste Land*, during a breakdown in 1921, convalescing first in Margate and then at a Swiss sanatorium. He wrote: 'It is commonplace that some forms of illness are extremely favourable, not only to religious illuminations, but to artistic and literary composition,' and cited A.E. Housman, who said 'I have seldom written poetry unless I was rather out of health' (Bloom, 2007, p.171).

Eliot also wrote to Virginia Woolf: 'We know what constant illness is, and I think very few people do' (Fifield, 2020, p.111). Woolf also had a lifetime of poor health and suffered repeated breakdowns and suicide attempts. She regarded these hardships as vital catalysts to creativity, an integral voice in her writing. Her essay 'On Being Ill' opens with this long, marvellous sentence:

Considering how common illness is, how tremendous the spiritual change that it brings, how astonishing, when the lights of health go down, the undiscovered countries that are then disclosed, what wastes and deserts of the soul a slight attack of influenza brings to view, what precipices and lawns sprinkled with bright flowers a little rise of temperature reveals, what ancient and obdurate oaks are uprooted in us by the act of sickness, how we go down into the pit of death and feel the waters of annihilation close above our heads and wake thinking to find ourselves in the presence of the angels and the harpers when we have a tooth out and come to the surface in the dentist's arm-chair and confuse his 'Rinse the mouth—rinse the mouth' with the greeting of the Deity stooping from the floor of Heaven to welcome us—when we think of this, as we are so frequently forced to think of it, it becomes strange indeed that illness has not taken its place with love and battle and jealousy among the prime themes of literature. (1930/2012, p.3)

As a World War II fighter pilot, author Roald Dahl survived a crash-landing in the desert in Egypt that fractured his skull, smashed his nose and temporarily rendered him blind. He pulled himself from the wreckage before he lost consciousness. The life that followed was full of pain and tragedy that fuelled his craft as a writer.

Dahl's friend and mentor Charles Marsh contracted cerebral malaria from a mosquito bite in Jamaica and suffered a series of small strokes that left him permanently physically damaged. Dahl wrote to him:

I just want to tell you this: I am an expert on being very ill and having to lie in bed. You are not. Even after you get up and get well after this, you still will be only an amateur at the game compared with us pros. Like any other business, or any unusual occupation, it's a hell of a tough one to learn. But you know I'm convinced that it has its compensations—for someone like me it does anyway.

I doubt I would have written a line, or would have had the ability to write a line, unless some minor tragedy had sort of twisted my mind out of the normal rut. You of course were already a philosopher before you became ill. But I predict that you will emerge a double philosopher, and a super philosopher after all this is over. I emerged a tiny-philosopher, a fractional philosopher from nothing, so it stands to reason that you will advance from straight philosopher to super philosopher.

I mean this. I know that serious illness is a good thing for the mind. It is always worth it afterwards. There's something of the yogi about it, with all its self-disciplines and horrors. And it's one of the few experiences that you'd never had up to now. So take my view and be kind of thankful that it came. (Sturrock, 2016, p.36).

Everyone is potentially a poet. In the 2018 documentary *To Stay Alive – Method*, with Iggy Pop, French author Michel Houellebecq advises:

> The first step for the poet is to return to the origin; that is, to
> suffering… All suffering is good. All suffering is useful. All
> suffering bears fruit. All suffering is a universe.

Maya Angelou grew up in the Great Depression. When she was eight, her mother's boyfriend raped her. He was found guilty, served all of one day in jail, and was murdered four days later. Angelou, deeply traumatised, fell silent. She was mute for almost five years. She was tested, tormented, but from that place, somehow, she triumphed, and rose to become a poet, singer, filmmaker, groundbreaking writer and civil rights activist.

How wondrously she passed the Humanity Test. How soulfully she lived.

This verse is from her famous poem 'Still I Rise' (Angelou, 1978):

> You may shoot me with your words,
> You may cut me with your eyes,
> You may kill me with your hatefulness,
> But still, like air, I'll rise.

Life is not about the pursuit of happiness – and the denial or avoidance of pain – it is about living more authentically and meaningfully. This includes being in touch with our suffering and with our madness, the richness of which gets lost in the push for 'superficial sanity' (Phillips, 2006). Winnicott says: 'We are poor indeed if we are only sane' (1958/1992, p.190). There is more to life than being merely happy.

The lure of soullessness

'For the secret of life is suffering,' wrote Oscar Wilde from his jail cell.

> It is what is hidden behind everything… I was no longer the
> captain of my soul, and did not know it. I allowed pleasure to
> dominate me. I ended in horrible disgrace. There is only one
> thing for me now, absolute humility. (1905, p.3)

Because of the inherent unknowability of the soul, people often become estranged from it. They doubt it, fear it, deny it, preferring to cling to false selves, false idols and other supposed certainties of the material world – even the certainties that are harsh and self-limiting. They avoid their soul with the relentless busyness of the mind and the body. They create a to-do list and keep adding things such that they know it will never all be done, to ensure that the soul will never need to be addressed.

Or, like Wilde, they attempt to avoid suffering through the pursuit of pleasure. They numb the soul with addictions, work, alcohol, pornography, trash TV. Some have almost completely forgotten about it, perhaps only catching fleeting glimpses in dreams, sunsets, love, memories.

Keats hung onto his soul for dear life. But it's not easy. The Enlightenment, the Industrial Revolution, the growth of reductionist, positivist science, the inexorable rise of capitalism and a materialist, consumer society, the internet and the advent of social media, the relentless Promethean march towards ever more progress, development, efficiency and economic growth – all of these things have eroded the importance of soul, alienating us from ourselves and from each other and robbing us of our humanity.

Writes Hafiz, the 14th century Persian poet (2011):

I know the way you can get
When you have not had a
drink of Love:
Your face hardens,
Your sweet muscles cramp.
Children become concerned
About a strange look that appears in your eyes
Which even begins to worry
Your own mirror
And nose.

In Goethe's famous play *Faust*, the principal character goes out for a walk and is followed home by a poodle. The dog turns into the Devil's messenger, Mephistopheles, and makes Faust an offer: he can do whatever he wants in his life without consequence if he agrees that, upon his death, he will work for the Devil in Hell. A trail of destruction ensues. (*Faust* was Jung's favourite book. Incidentally Goethe, a contemporary of Schopenhauer and Nietzsche, was yet another 'religious atheist'; he described the history of Christianity as a 'hodgepodge of fallacy and violence'.)

Those who take a Faustian bargain – turning their back on their soul, selling it off for some imagined material gain – are exchanging something priceless for something worthless. Without soul, the wealthy tycoon lives an impoverished, bankrupt life; a dead man walking. We are living in Faustian times, and it is crippling us and our planet.

Mephistopheles appears in many guises. Do not trust a talking poodle. Do not become one.

The choice of a soulful life

Viktor Frankl, the Austrian Jewish psychiatrist, a contemporary of Freud and Alfred Adler, was in 1944 sent with his wife first to Auschwitz, then to other concentration camps. Frankl survived the Holocaust. His wife, mother and brother did not. They were all murdered by the Nazis.

Unimaginable horror, suffering and loss. Yet in this most desolate and despairing of settings, in this most monstrous, shameful manifestation of the human propensity for evil, Frankl chose not to abandon hope. He hung onto his soul. After World War II, he wrote *Trotzdem ja zum leben sagen: Ein psychologe erlebt das konzentrationslager* ('Saying yes to life in spite of everything: A psychologist experiences the concentration camp'). Today the slim volume, part-memoir, part-philosophy of life, part-inspirational self-help book, is called *Man's Search for Meaning* (1946/2004). It is also a manifesto for Frankl's brand of existential psychotherapy that he developed after the war and called logotherapy.

Frankl argued that it is the absence of meaning that makes life unbearable – if you can find the 'why' of your existence, he wrote, you will be able to bear almost any 'how'. Even in the most inhumane of circumstances, a person can choose not to abandon their soul, their humanity.

Wrote Frankl:

> Everything can be taken from a man but one thing: the last of
> the human freedoms – to choose one's attitude in any given set
> of circumstances, to choose one's own way. (1946/2004, p.86)

Anyone can choose a life of passion and compassion.

People with disabilities – people who have been selected for the Advanced Humanity Test – similarly can choose their attitude. We can accept all the projections of others. We can take the shame and see ourself as deficient and downtrodden – a victim. Or we can choose to live.

You don't need to buy anything or join anything. You don't need to go anywhere, or study. There is no hierarchy. You are the guru. All you have to do is turn to face your soul and start a conversation. Befriend your soul, nurture your soul and listen to your soul. You can start right now. Epicurus wrote: 'It is never too early or too late to care for the well-being of the soul.'[1]

Ten aspects of a soulful life

'My soul, where are you? Do you hear me? I speak, I call you – are you there?'

This is how Jung began his 'self experiment' – an extended exploration of his inner world. By using 'active imagination', he conjured up conversations, encounters, imagery and dreams, then recorded rather florid, fanciful accounts of these experiences in his 'Black Books', which were then aggregated into his famous *Red Book* (2009). To Jungians, this work is a sacred scripture, but it has something of the flavour of a midlife version of a teenage diary.

It would be easy to construct a list of commandments that must be followed in order to lead a soulful life, but such a one-size-fits-all prescription of dos and don'ts would be an affront to everything a soul represents. It would be offering reductive, quick-fix certainties for a lifelong process of discovery that is inherently mysterious and personal.

How you find your soul, cultivate it and integrate it into your daily life – these are things for you decide. You may find your feelings of soulfullness wax and wane. A soul can be elusive. Under the full-beam searchlight of your demands and beseechings, it can evaporate. Even those who have a strong connection to their soul can sometimes temporarily misplace it. You might have been feeling out of sorts for a while – disconnected, alienated – and you realise you have been neglecting your soul, and you pay attention anew. Or, if you fly to a far-flung country many time zones away, you may find it can take a couple of days for the soul to catch up with you.

How to live a soulful life? In *Care of the Soul*, Thomas Moore highlights 'good food, satisfying conversations, genuine friends, and

---

1. www.the-philosophy.com/epicurus-letter-menoeceus-summary

experiences that stay in that memory and touch the heart' (1992, p.ix).

Keats favoured 'books, fruit, French wine, fine weather and a little music out of doors played by someone I do not know' (1819).[2]

I am by no means an expert in the practice of soulful living – far from it. I am a student at it, a beginner, a dilettante. I love spending time doing soulful things that are so engaging that I forget that I have Parkinson's.

I offer, with respect and humility, the following aspects of soulfulness you might like to consider.

Fidelity

A soulful life is one that honours its present manifestation. We are 'thrown' into existence, said Heidegger. Do you accept the body and the mind that you were handed on day one? Or are they both a constant source of disappointment for you? Will you love, honour and obey this mysterious 'me' that you are, in sickness and in health, forsaking all others, as long as ye both shall live?

Me, myself, I – we're stuck with each other, so we might as well be friends rather than enemies.

Fidelity is faithfulness. There are many ways of being unfaithful. It's hard to have faith in others and for others to have faith in you if you don't.

'Self-acceptance' sounds a little begrudging; maybe 'self-love' is a little too narcissistic. But self-care – yes, that's important. Pay attention to the basics. Hydrate. Exercise. Relax. Food activist Michael Pollan says we should avoid 'food-like substances' and instead offers these seven words to resolve the whole conundrum of nutrition and diet: 'Eat food. Not too much. Mostly plants' (2007). I once did a story on a 111-year-old golfer. The secret, he said, was something a teacher told his class 100 years earlier: eat slowly, enjoy your food and chew it well.

Simplify. As you get older, you realise that regular prunings are important to foster continued growth. Edit your life. Get rid of the dead wood, the bad stuff.

The longest-living men on the planet are shepherds who live in the highlands of the Nuoro province of Sardinia. They walk several

---

2. http://keats-poems.com/to-fanny-keats-winchester-august-28-1819/

miles on an average day. They sometimes take an afternoon nap. They meet their friends in the taverna and eat a Mediterranean diet in the actual Mediterranean.

Slow down, you move too fast.

A friend goes on holiday and in a small town in southern France notices something really weird: everybody walks everywhere slowly.

If you're always racing, you might reach the finish line sooner than you intended.

Try to get enough sleep.

To thine own self be true. Find out what you need, what you like. There might be elements of you that are different or unusual – these things that make you stand out can also make you outstanding. There is a wild, abundant energy within you that the world sometimes conspires to restrain. Let your soul guide you.

Movement

'We clearly know that movement over time equals health,' says Dr David Agus, author of *The End of Illness* (2012) and *A Short Guide to a Long Life* (2014).

One early study, from 1953, compared the health of London bus conductors, who spent all day on their feet selling tickets, with the bus drivers, who sat behind the wheel. There were dramatically lower rates of heart disease and cancer in the ticket sellers.

It is not always clear in studies like these what is cause and what is the effect. But it is probably true that the problem today is that metaphorically we've become a society of bus drivers.

Agus says our bodies were designed to move, and that if you sit for five hours a day, it's the equivalent of smoking a pack of cigarettes.

Mindlessly pumping iron for hours in the gym can become self-punishing. It might be better to incorporate into your daily routine periods of *bodyfulness* – fully inhabiting and enjoying your physical self in a loving, playful way through things like walking, swimming, dancing, sex, yoga, tai chi, *fartlek* running, and leaping about to loud trance music. Our psychology affects our body – the reverse can also be true: putting your body into unfamiliar, freeing positions can also free your mind.

We order online. We telecommute. In the pandemic lockdowns, we got used to catching up with family and friends on social media and video-conferencing platforms. Technology has robbed us of the use of our legs. Fitness – and cardiovascular health – is now something to be worked at, rather than a part of living.

James Hillman wrote:

My heart is my love, my feelings, the locus of my soul and sense of person. It is a place of intimate interiority, where sin and shame and desire, and the unfathomable divine too, inhabit. (1992, p.13)

Look after it.

Perhaps your mobility is compromised by illness or disability. So you move what you can. And on a broader level, anyone can allow themselves to be moved. The word 'emotion' comes from the Latin 'emovere', meaning 'to move out'. It's possible to be moving a lot, leading a busy life, but to feel like you are going nowhere. The opposite is also true: in stillness you can travel all the way to your soul.

Presence

A new day starts with an inward breath, an inspiration that enlightens and empowers the senses. Then you breathe out, an expiration. The moment dies, replaced by another. Presence is to be fully alive and present in this moment. And this moment. And this moment. It's only ever now.

There are many things clamouring for your attention that will impede your presence. Top of that list are your thoughts. How many times have you sat with a delicious plate of food before you, then suddenly the plate is empty, as was your experience of eating it because you weren't there – your thoughts hijacked the moment. How much of your life are you missing?

In *The Power of Now*, Eckhart Tolle writes: 'So the single most vital step on your journey toward enlightenment is this: learn to disidentify from your mind' (1999, p.17). Our thoughts are a constant monologue that demands to be heard. They are often horrible thoughts. Your thoughts are not you. Nor are your emotions you. Nor is your body you. You are your soul, that amorphous, indefinable entity that experiences these things. A soulful life is one lived with awareness and presence of the soul.

Presence is an energy. Says Patsy Rodenberg: 'I began to know that presence is a universal quality that we all have but is somehow flattened out of us' (2007, p.xiii). You can find it in your body, in your breath, in your interactions with others and with the world. Rodenberg's book tells you how.

Mindfulness – focusing on your breath, noticing your thoughts, letting them pass and experiencing the you when you are not thinking – helps. You can do it with a regular practice of meditation. But you can go further, into soulfulness. Setting some time aside each day for some sort of communion between your human self and your soul can be very integrating, insightful and enlightening. Finding your soul is like heading back up river, back towards the source, to the pure, unpolluted waters where everything is clear.

Experience

When we are not mired in the disappointments of yesterday, or the fears of tomorrow, we at last experience the rich fullness of ourselves and our world. This allows us to be open, empathic and spontaneous.

One time I was walking in the countryside with my daughter.

'Look!' she said.

I couldn't see what she was pointing at. On much closer inspection, it was a tiny, camouflaged praying mantis on a leaf in the middle of a bush we were walking by – a miracle of engineering, design, life. I was astonished. Children see everything, but then learn not to.

Keats never lost the ability to experience his life fully, with all the senses, often with childlike delight. The average person might not go for a walk on a chilly winter's morning, and even if they did, they might not notice the world around them. They might be distracted by their preoccupations. They might be worried about a future commitment. They might be scrolling through pages of vacuous messages on their phone, searching for that elusive golden nugget. Perhaps they don't even notice the rabbits in the field up ahead. Keats, however, would take it all in. He would go home and write this: 'The hare limp'd trembling through the frozen grass' (2007, p.165).

In his sweet, personal homage, *How to Make a Soul: The wisdom of John Keats* (2015), the American professor of English Eric Wilson begins with an account of Keats in 1819, writing a miserable letter, full of complaints. Keats was despondent: 'Lax, unemployed, unmeridian'd, and objectless.' Writes Wilson: 'He is self-absorbed, confused, bitter.' Then suddenly, Keats announces: 'I was writing with one hand, and with the other holding in my Mouth a Nectarine – good God how fine – it went down soft, pulpy, slushy, oozy – all its delicious embonpoint melted down my throat like a large beatified Strawberry.'

Experience beauty. Keats saw beauty everywhere. He wrote to a friend: 'With a great poet the sense of Beauty overcomes every other consideration.'

His poem *Endymion* (2007, p.38) begins:

A thing of beauty is a joy for ever:
Its loveliness increases; it will never
Pass into nothingness; but still will keep
A bower quiet for us, and a sleep
Full of sweet dreams, and health, and quiet breathing.

And his *Ode to a Grecian Urn* (2007, p.192) ends:

Beauty is truth, truth beauty—that is all
Ye know on earth, and all ye need to know.

Beauty does not exist as an external, physical phenomenon. It requires the participation of a beholder. The poet David Whyte calls it 'the harvest of presence' (2014, p.17). You must open not just your eyes but your heart, too.

Oliver Sacks, the brilliant British neurologist, prolific author and drug-taker, became famous for his work in 1966 with patients who for years, decades in some cases, had been living in a catatonic state brought on by a form of encephalitis. He injected them with a new wonder drug that had just been invented and that ever since has been the standard treatment for Parkinson's: synthetic dopamine. After years in a coma-like state, the patients came back to life. It was an overwhelming experience. They all went a bit mad, trying to make up for lost time; then wrote Sacks, they 'became poets'. He recalls coming across one patient in a park near the hospital, shortly after treatment had started. She was sitting in the grass, stroking a leaf, with tears running down her cheeks. She told him: 'I've never seen anything so beautiful.'

We see the world not as it is but as we are. Beauty depends on finding something within that is beautiful. It also means that beauty can be found almost anywhere. Writes James Hillman:

How is it possible that beauty has played such a central and obvious part in the history of the soul and its thought, and yet is absent in modern psychology?... If beauty is not given full place in our work with psyche, then the soul's essential realization cannot occur. (1992, p.34)

Sign up for that retreat, workshop, event. Do things that you've always wanted to do but haven't because they scare you a little. Try different flavours.

Nature

Sometimes, I get out of London and head down to the coast. When I get out of the car, I always notice something is different. Immediately I feel the crisp, perfumed caress of something strange, something that city-dwellers have long had to live without: fresh air. I fill my lungs with this exotic elixir and instantly feel stronger, happier, fitter. I sleep better. I become more alive, more human. I am restored.

When you're feeling loveless, writes Hafiz (2011):

Squirrels and birds sense your sadness
And call an important conference in a tall tree.
They decide which secret code to chant
To help your mind and soul.

Even though we may not understand all the reasons, it makes intuitive sense that metropolitan living can be detrimental not only to our physical health but to our very psyches, too. The research findings are not a huge surprise: urbanites have higher rates of anxiety and depression (Peen et al., 2010), although the World Happiness Report found that city and urban happiness levels were 'essentially identical' when comparing like with like (2020, p.12). We city types are more frazzled, more sensitive to criticism (Lederbogen et al., 2011). Schizophrenia, too, is much more common in cities (Krabbendam & Van Os, 2005). And since 2009, more than half the world's population lives in cities, according to the United Nations (2009). That's almost four billion souls potentially denied the oxygen of a healthy environment, one free of pollution, car alarms and armies of sharp-elbowed, impatient people rushing to the next meeting – or away from themselves. The Hopi call it *Koyaanisqatsi* or 'life out of balance' (and if you haven't seen the mind-blowing 1982 film of that name, please stop reading this or whatever else you are doing and order it now).

So what to do if, like me, you're one of the stressed majority living in a state of such un-nature? How to combat the growing global scourge of 'nature deficit disorder'? How to reconnect with our natural state, the one out there and the one within?

Walk out the front door. Gaze at trees, clouds, thunderstorms. Waste time. You don't have to hike through Yosemite National Park to awaken your spirit, or even move to Scotland (although both sound appealing) – a stroll around your local city park works just fine. Check out city farms, nature reserves and wildlife centres, too; even a trip to your local natural history museum will soothe the soul.

Gardening, too, has been shown to relieve stress and is enormously therapeutic for all kinds of people. There's something so elemental about the ancient satisfaction of getting your hands into the earth and making things grow. Especially in the company of others. Johann Hari (2018) describes a novel approach to treating depression undertaken in the 1990s by an East London doctor, Sam Everington. He invited 20 of his depressed patients to meet for an afternoon twice a week to work on a patch of scrubland behind the clinic. One of the participants said: 'As the garden began to bloom, the people in it began to bloom too' (Hari, 2018). We are nurtured by nurturing. If you don't have a garden, go and help a neighbour who does, apply for an allotment, support community gardens, volunteer with a gardening charity or join a Green Gym.

Fill your living space with greenery and photographs or artwork depicting the great outdoors. Research shows that just having a pot plant or looking at pictures of nature can significantly improve your mental health. Don't just get plants, commune with them, too. Buddha once gave a famous wordless sermon to his disciples: he simply held up a white flower. By saying nothing, the disciples were free to experience the flower fully and appreciate its *tathātā*, which might loosely be translated as 'suchness'.

Join or get involved with local wildlife organisations. Take regular daytrips beyond the city limits (and beyond your comfort zone). Hopefully this will be more successful and uplifting than the legendary, foul-mouthed scene from the movie *Trainspotting*, when Tommy drags his sceptical city pals to the beautiful, desolate Rannoch Moor ('This is not natural, man,' says one.)

Use your vacations, too, to get back to basics. Head for the hills: camp in the Lake District for instance, and 'walk in blessedness' there, as Wordsworth did all those years ago. As the wandering, wondering wordsmith said: 'Nature never did betray the heart that loved her.'

It's good to experience yourself within a vast, majestic landscape from time to time. To learn a sense of perspective – in these mountains, you are insignificant. All your daily worries and plans and strivings melt away. You can let go of the fantasy that you are in control. You surrender your petty human desires and into that space you are flooded instead by soulful feelings – wonder, gratitude, awe, humility.

Creativity

Picasso said we are all born artists. Then we go to school and we are told we are not. Creativity is not some kind of special gift bestowed on the chosen few. It is instead like love – a good, healthy and universal part of being human. You don't need to be tortured or a genius – or to take class A drugs – to see with kaleidoscope eyes.

> No matter what your age or your life path, whether making art is your career or your hobby or your dream, it is not too late or too egotistical or too selfish or too silly to work on your creativity.

So writes Julia Cameron in *The Artist's Way* (1995, p.xiii), which argues that accessing creativity is akin to a spiritual awakening: anyone can plug into some kind of cosmic or divine grid of 'spiritual electricity'.

For Betty Edwards, author of *Drawing on the Right Side of the Brain*, becoming creative is simply learning how to see:

> You may feel that you are seeing things just fine and that it's the drawing that is hard. But the opposite is true... By learning to draw you will learn to see differently and, as the artist Rodin lyrically states, to become a confidant of the natural world, to awaken your eye to the lovely language of forms. (2008, p.4)

Suffering can provide the raw materials and the motivation for art. Creative pursuits can be enormously healing for dissatisfied, distressed or damaged souls. As the saying goes, good art comforts the disturbed and disturbs the comfortable.

Maybe you have a disability that makes it hard to be creative. Maybe you can still find a way. Chuck Close is a well-known portrait artist who, at age 48, suffered paralysis after the collapse of a spinal artery. But he found a way to clamp his hands onto a super-long paintbrush and continued to produce extraordinary giant portraits from a wheelchair.

In 1995, the French journalist Jean-Dominique Bauby, editor of *Elle*, suffered a massive stroke that left him with locked-in syndrome. The only thing he could move was his left eye. He wrote his memoir, *The Diving-Bell and the Butterfly* (1997/2002), entirely by the painstaking process of choosing letters by blinking his eye. Two days after publication, he died of pneumonia. He was 44. The book sold millions.

There are many different ways of being creative. Improvise. Now and again, put away the instruction manual, or the sheet music, or the cookbook, and just do it.

Get lost. Take a different route to work, take your watch off, travel without a map, go somewhere new on holiday, camp in the wilderness, explore a very different country, travel alone.

Play

Creativity, at heart, is play. The late great British psychoanalyst D.W. Winnicott said creativity and play are essential parts of being fully human, and should be nurtured and encouraged in people of all ages, starting in childhood:

> It is in playing and only in playing that the individual child or
> adult is able to be creative and to use the whole personality, and
> it is only in being creative that the individual discovers the self.
> (1971, p.73)

If you don't, won't or can't play, if access to your 'child' self has been cut off, you will turn into a drone, a worker bee, an automaton – serious, lacking in passion, colourless. The 'Person Who Cannot Play,' writes Thomas Harris in *I'm OK—You're OK*, is 'duty-dominated, always working late at the office, all business, impatient with family members who want to plan a skiing trip or a picnic in the woods' (1995, p.97).

Michael Rosen has written a book that tells grown-ups how to play, so there's no excuse. He says:

> Our concept of play in the West is often bound up with the
> idea that play is inseparably connected to childhood, while
> adulthood is connected to seriousness and responsibility... In
> fact, I believe play is key to helping us develop and reach our
> full potential. (2020, p.21)

Spend time with children. Learn from their streams of consciousness and ability to be spontaneous, joyful and unselfconscious.

Work

If you're lucky, you can work to live, rather than live to work. If you're doing the latter, but can afford to do the former, it's time to get a life.

American mythologist Joseph Campbell advises us to 'follow your bliss'. But I believe many people choose a career – an occupation in which you will spend the majority of your waking life – by following their fear. Some people go into business because they fear they might not be good enough, or they have no sense of their own worth; teachers choose teaching because they fear they might be stupid; actors choose acting because they fear they might not be liked; nurses opt for nursing because they fear no one will care for them; models model because they fear they might be ugly; preachers preach because they fear they might be damned; psychologists opt for working with mental health because they fear they might be mad (and a lot of them are quite magnificently mad). Fear can be a great motivator. Love is a better one.

Many young clients have complained to me that they don't have a passion to follow. If that's true for you, give yourself another childhood and try out a bunch of things. Passion and skill take time. Fred Astaire's first screen test review was: 'Can't act, can't sing, can dance a little.'

Whether in work or play, it's important to have some activity in your life that you care about; something that engages you. The Japanese have a word for it: *ikigai*, roughly translated as the thing that gets you out of bed in the morning, a sense of purpose. A soulful life is a meaningful life.

What do you like doing? If you were a dog, what would make you wag your tail?

Do you know the number one regret of people on their deathbed? According to palliative care nurse Bronnie Ware, who spent years listening to those final thoughts, it is: 'I wish I'd had the courage to live a life true to myself' (2011, p.37).

Writes Kahlil Gibran:

> You work that you may keep pace with the earth and the soul of
>   the earth.

> For to be idle is to become a stranger unto the seasons, and to
>   step out of life's procession, that marches in majesty and
>   proud submission towards the infinite.
> When you work you are a flute through whose heart the
>   whispering of the hours turns to music.
> Which of you would be a reed, dumb and silent, when all else
>   sings together in unison? (1926/1992, p.35)

Maybe loving your work is a privilege afforded to very few. Most people are not fortunate enough to do what they love. But some of them find ways, people, moments of the day or aspects of their work that are acceptable, where gratitude and even love might be possible.

There is soulfulness to be found in spreadsheets.

And however menial or mundane the job, however miserly the pay, it can always be done well or badly. It can be done with soul – fully present, with care and love and commitment (but not enslavement), or without – with resentment.

And your job is not static. You can change it. You can explore from the inside how and where it passes the Humanity Test – and where if fails. You can appoint yourself as the unofficial Humanity Officer and tell your bosses what the firm needs to do to be better.

In the myth of Sisyphus, the gods punish the deposed king by making him see out his days pushing a boulder to the top of a hill, only to have to watch it roll all the way back down, and start it all over, again and again. But he accepted his fate. We can imagine, perhaps, the respite of the joyous, restorative walk back down the hill, and therefore, writes Camus, 'One must imagine Sisyphus happy' (1942/2013, p.89).

Love

Does this curious word mean anything anymore?

Is it true that it is all you need, or it makes the world go round?

Love is the lifeblood of humanity. We give it and we seek it from family and friends, lovers and strangers, from within and from above. To love and be loved is to be human.

Platonic love is what we connect with, and connection is a prime, ancient human need. It allows us to belong – to a relationship, a friend, a family, a community, a club, a tribe, a society.

Relationship love comes in three varieties, honed by evolution for the furtherance of our peculiar species: sex/lust, romance/attraction and attachment/commitment. Each involves a different part of the brain (Fisher et al., 2006). Each can stand alone, or in different combinations, and these can change over time. It's just not possible to have all three, all of the time, in one life-long relationship.

Don't believe anyone who offers you that. As the proverb says, don't trust the naked person who promises to clothe you.

When we fall in love with someone, writes Jungian analyst James Hollis (1992), we do them a great disservice because we don't see them really. We see a projection, a fantasy, an idealised perfect other.

Better to stand in love than fall in love, writes Eric Fromm in *The Art of Loving* (1957/1995). Love is not some fleeting feeling, he says. It is an action, a decision, a choice.

We get it wrong, over and over.

'We all make mistakes,' says Helen Fisher, a biological anthropologist specialising in the science of romantic partnerships. In an interview I did for *Psychologies* magazine (Barton, 2017), she told me:

> There's a part of the brain, in the ventromedial prefrontal
> cortex, whose job is to be sceptical – in charge of what scientists
> call 'negativity bias'. This is the part that always says, Oh, no,
> this isn't going to work. And when you begin to fall in love,
> activity in that brain region actually goes down.

Neuroscientific proof that love is indeed blind. If it weren't, our species would have died out eons ago.

'The heart was made to be broken,' according to Oscar Wilde. Love is not need. Love is not perfection. In Tolle's words:

> Love is a state of Being. Your love is not outside; it is deep
> within you. You can never lose it, and it cannot leave you. It is
> not dependent on some other body, some external form. (1999,
> p.128)

Don't expect anyone to fix you or accept you or love you if you can't. Why should they? Says Fromm: 'Paradoxically, the ability to be alone is the condition for the ability to love' (1957/1995, p.88).

Writes Hollis in *The Eden Project*:

> If I am expecting the other to be the good parent and take care
> of me, then I have not grown up. If I am expecting the other to
> spare me the rigor and terror of living my own journey, then I

have abdicated from the chief task and most worthy reason for my incarnation on this earth. (1992, p.57)

Love your friends and family. Meet new people. Hurl yourself into unfamiliar social situations. Interact with a wide range of people. Richard Wiseman wrote of how some of the success stories in his research on luck were people who often sought out ways to force them to meet different people. One of them noticed that, whenever he went to a party, he tended to talk to the same type of people. To disrupt this routine, he now thinks of a colour before a social event and then speaks to people wearing that colour of clothing.

Death

There comes a point in every child's life when they realise there is such a thing as death.

'Daddy, what happens when you die?'

You might tell them that there are three main ideas: 1. It's like you go to sleep forever. 2. If you've been good, you go to heaven, and if you've been bad, you go to hell. 3. You come back as someone else or an animal or some other life form.

My daughter thought 3 was the most likely.

Death is not something that comes at the end of life as a definitive and permanent replacement. Death is an ever-present part of a soulful life. There's a café in the crypt of St. Martin-in-the-Fields, a church just off Trafalgar Square in central London, where you can drink a latté and eat a piece of cake while, beneath you, lie the remains of those who have gone before. If you listen, you can almost hear their spirits whispering the lines of that old song: 'Enjoy yourself, it's later than you think.'

In David Eagleman's marvellous slim volume *Sum* (2010), one of the afterlife scenarios he imagines is that you die and meet the 'Technicians', who congratulate you on your life and ask if you'd like to participate in a piece of research. You get to do your life all over again, but you're allowed to change one thing. (I would choose no illness or disability.) And you have the brilliant idea of living your life again but with no death. The Technicians frown—they've seen this before. They try to discourage you, but you are insistent. And so you find yourself back on Planet Earth, and everybody lives forever, and it is awful, like one long Sunday afternoon, and nobody bothers to do anything because what's the point? An unlimited supply of life means there is no demand for it.

I have never liked the imperative to 'seize the day' because it sounds so aggressive and demanding. But maybe death helps us to have a more soulful day, a day of gratitude and appreciation and love. Ama Diem.

No one actually know what happens when we die. We know that something lives on, if only in the memory of others.

Jung lost his father, a pastor, when he was 21. And that's when his relationship with him took off. He said he learned more from his father in death than he ever did in life. Rituals that allow you to commune with other souls, remembering and honouring and relating to the dead, can be very healing.

We know that we lose our body and our mind when we die. Ashes to ashes, dust to dust.

Some atheists claim with certainty that it's the end of the story: there is no meaning or point to life, and there never was. They congratulate themselves for being unsentimental, rational, clear-eyed and unafraid. But maybe their devotion to nihilism, to nothingness, is just another blind faith.

Does the soul live on?

We don't know.

Our subjective, felt sense of ourselves in the world, our human disposition, was something Heidegger called *Befindlichkeit*.

The last word of Jung's *Red Book*, all on its own on an otherwise blank page, is *Möglichkeit*.

It means 'possibility'.

6. Society –
Uncivilization and its discontents

'A good and just society is neither the thesis of capitalism
nor the antithesis of communism, but a socially conscious
democracy which reconciles the truths of individualism and
collectivism.'
Martin Luther King, Jr.

The current situation: 'A human catastrophe'

The word was invented in 1990, but the practice of 'ableism' is as old
as humans. It would be nice to think that the history of disability I
outlined in Chapter 3 illustrates some kind of progress, leading to
justice, to a new world order of fairness, respect and empowerment
for the physically impaired. It would be nice to think, too, that human
societies have long ago left behind primitive ways of relating to each
other. But alas, the inhumanity lives on. Its differently coloured
historical, cultural and religious strands are deeply woven into the
fabric of how disease and disability are viewed and experienced today.

The law of the jungle from prehistory remains very much a factor
in the lives of those with disabilities. The most vulnerable members of
the human herd are often singled out for abuse and attack. Research
shows that children with disabilities are almost four times more likely
to experience violence than non-disabled children (Jones et al., 2012).
Even in a prosperous, industrialised nations (Australia, in the case of
this research), people with disabilities are significantly more likely to
experience all types of violence (Kavanagh et al., 2015).

The ancient Greco-Roman practice of infanticide, or killing
unwanted babies, has continued since antiquity, and prenatal
screening techniques mean that, increasingly, disabled foetuses are
aborted, too. Mostly it is female babies that are killed, especially in

parts of north Africa, India and China, resulting in more than 100 million 'missing women' (Sen, 2003). But disabled babies are killed too. A 2018 report found widespread instances of neglect and killing of disabled children in Kenya, for example (DRI, 2018); the children were considered 'cursed, bewitched, and possessed'.

Philosophers Michael Tooley, Steven Pinker and vegetarian evangelist Peter Singer have all argued in favour of the option to euthanise infants with severe disabilities, which, wrote Singer (2011, p.160), 'cannot be equated with killing normal human beings, or any other self-conscious beings'.

In 2014, Belgium became the first country to allow voluntary child euthanasia without any age restriction.

Old religious prejudices endure. There are plenty of contemporary fundamentalists and evangelicals who regard abnormalities as an abomination; who approve of excluding people with disabilities, or 'treating' them with exorcisms or 'prayer camps'; or who still believe that Aids was a divine punishment for gay men's 'sinful' ways.

In Pentecostal settings, a person with an illness or disability is likely to be regarded as someone who simply hasn't prayed enough – there will be no shortage of people wanting to lay hands upon them and pray. There are plenty of people who, on hearing of your illness, let you know that it's part of 'God's plan', or that you will be in their prayers. At best, religion largely still regards people with disabilities as objects of pity – 'charity cases' who survive at the mercy of donors, fundraisers and volunteers. The givers assume the recipients are very grateful for their beneficence.

Karma, too, lives on, in the form of the assumption that anyone who is suffering must have behaved poorly at some point and is thus the cause of their own suffering. This sheer prejudice has real-life consequences in the way individuals and societies respond to the injustices and gross inequality experienced by those with disabilities – with complacency, passivity and diminished empathy. Or worse. Much worse.

This malevolent version of karma is frequently used to justify an unfair social order and to further empower the powerful. It emboldens authoritarian right-wing politics; it is invoked to justify the caste system in India, and ethnic cleansing in the supposed Buddhist paradise of Bhutan, and racism in America (Prashad, 2000), and the exclusion and mistreatment of people with disabilities everywhere.

In 1999, the then-manager of the England football team, Glenn Hoddle, said people are born with disabilities 'for a reason' – namely karma, 'working from another lifetime'. (A barrage of criticism forced him to resign.)

Eugenics in various guises has proved enormously popular and fuels many cruel current practices and state policies: discriminatory immigration rules, withholding medical care, human testing, electroconvulsive therapy, institutionalisation, forced sterilisation, euthanasia, genocide. Sophisticated technological advances are heralding a new eugenic era – the new non-invasive prenatal test for Down's syndrome, for instance, puts more pressure on mothers to have an abortion when the results appear to be less than optimal. ('Didn't you know?' people said to actor Sally Phillips while her son Olly, who has Down's syndrome, happily played on the swings nearby. Phillips, incidentally, reports that Olly has taught her a great deal about happiness (Phillips, 2016).)

A gene-sequencing company in Shenzhen, China called BGI – the largest such facility in the world – has been scrutinising the DNA of 1,600 high-IQ high-fliers around the world. This work, coupled with possibilities offered by pre-implantation genetic screening of embryos, raises the prospect of a brave new elite of disability-free and disease-free geniuses, with no regard for the moral, ethical and practical issues this raises and the unintended consequences of such a path.

§

All of these old attitudes, along with a prevailing medical model that diminishes and disempowers people with disabilities and societies that fail to accommodate their needs, conspire to keep these human beings as far from the non-disabled as possible.

Today, in supposedly fair-minded Britain, disabled people are suffering after having been deliberately targeted in a decade of austerity that dismantled public services, decimated local council budgets and destroyed any meaningful sense of welfare. The basic provisions many needed to live were withdrawn, while at the same time disabled people have been scapegoated as benefit cheats and scroungers in media, government and cultural discourse. A 2017 United Nations report concluded that the UK government has 'totally neglected' disabled people, precipitating a 'human catastrophe' (Disability Rights UK,

2017). The European Union afforded British people with disabilities some basic human and social rights and protections; the UK's departure from the European Union has eliminated them.

Meanwhile, the Covid-19 pandemic was disproportionally deadly to those with disabilities. They comprised 60% of Covid fatalities in England, and the shocking practice of imposing 'do not resuscitate' orders on patients with learning disabilities was widespread.

In the US, in a one-term, two-impeachment presidency jam-packed with low moments, one of the most shocking was when, in 2015, Donald Trump openly mocked and impersonated a *New York Times* reporter with a disability – 'You gotta see this guy,' he said.

The White House hosted a ceremony to celebrate US Paralympic athletes. Asked about his interest in the Paralympics in South Korea, Trump said he watched as much as he could but it was 'a little tough to watch too much'.

Trump also liked to impersonate the arm movements of fellow Republican John McCain, a former Navy pilot who spent five-plus years of the war in Vietnam in the notorious prison known as the 'Hanoi Hilton', where he was held much of the time in solitary confinement and was repeatedly tortured. McCain's arms were permanently damaged by his experiences in Vietnam.

'He's not a war hero,' said Trump. 'He was a war hero because he was captured? I like people who weren't captured.'

Trump repeatedly avoided military service in the 1960s, citing a bone spur in his foot. When later asked by reporters which was the problem foot, Trump could not say.

In his four years in office, Trump consistently chipped away and demonised the Affordable Care Act, and in the closing convulsions of his presidency proposed adding another layer of complications to the Social Security Disability Insurance system, requiring that beneficiaries 're-prove' their disability every two years. This was described by opponents as a 'brutal and vile attack' on disabled America.

The inhumanities

Corrosive capitalism

One Bank Holiday Monday in 2022, when the shops were reopened. I was lost in a mall in a sizeable city on the south coast of England. Bright, disharmonious colours, throbbing music and swooping escalators assaulted the senses from all angles, inside a vast building of ungeometrical design, engorged with strident, fleshy, non-social distancing hordes, determined, after much delayed gratification, to exercise their democratic right to shop. At a time when life is increasingly atomised, conducted on tiny hand-held devices, the congregations at malls, these Faustian shopping temples, are ever swelling.

Disoriented, thirsty and robbed of any daylight, direction and sense of identity, I did what was expected of anyone in such circumstances: I bought a lurid, flamingo-patterned, green-and-pink shirt.

In the new religion of materialism, appearance replaces substance.

Whatever soulful human urges exist will be commodified, marketed and sold back to humans as soul substitutes.

Even the countercultural, anti-materialist ideals of the 1960s (and every New Age quasi-spiritual fad that followed) are seized by corporate psychopaths, forced into the capitalist machine, and repackaged as merchandise. To show your individuality, authenticity and desirability, all you need to do is buy a T-shirt made by Third-World sweatshop child labourers for pennies. As long as it's the right brand. You wouldn't want to be so foolish as to wear the wrong brand, would you?

There were groups of cool kids hanging out at the mall, and a lot of them were wearing clothes emblazoned with the word 'Hollister'. What does this word mean to them? California? Surfing? Why are they declaring their allegiance to this city whose name was expropriated by a marketing executive in a nondescript Ohio office in the 1990s, presumably because it outperformed other alternatives in midwestern focus groups and suburban product testing?

'Yes, we are all individuals,' chants the crowd of followers in Monty Python's excellent film, *Life of Brian*. (Except for one who turns around and says: 'I'm not.')

In 2013, incidentally, a US federal judge ruled that the Hollister chain of stores was in violation of the Americans with Disabilities Act for having such poor wheelchair access.

Humans are biddable, eager to be manipulated, readily inveigled to part with hard-earned cash, follow a crooked leader, or behave in abominable ways. We get cheated, swindled, conned, and we vow not to be so gullible next time. Our scepticism grows – along with our fervent desire to believe in something. And the marketing methods designed to disarm the former and exploit the latter become ever-more sophisticated and deceitful. There is no soul in negative advertising, lobbying, bribery, coercion, misinformation, corporate-funded 'news', internet trolls or 'think tanks', fraud, propaganda, the utterly cynical manipulation of elections at home and in foreign lands, or violence. The money flows upriver to the modern-day proto-Satans at the top, but there are vast armies of well-paid, smooth-talking Mephistophelian-poodle lieutenants doing their bidding.

We buy things we don't need or have space for, with money we have not yet earned, to impress people we don't know or even like, and in the process we are ravaging this very earth.

We are all complicit in this Faustian game.

And the more someone plays it, the more alienated they become from their soul, their fellow humans, their planet.

Alien nation.

We imagine alienation to be a modern malaise, and to an extent, it is. In the olden days, we suppose, people would spend their sepia-coloured evenings together, gathered round the hearth, the repast or the piano, at the beating heart of the home, family and town where they grew up, where they would live, work, marry, procreate, recreate, retire and die. Then television came along and conversation petered out, and when central heating was invented, we withdrew into our bedrooms and into ourselves. Electronic devices and headphones – we retreated further still. Then aeroplanes – we could get even further away from each other. Then came the Apollo rockets, and the aching prospect of an infinite outer space, and the terrifying idea that, when it comes to life, our planet is all alone – or the terrifying idea that it isn't.

We used to work to live; ever since what Polanyi called the 'Great Transformation' (1944/2002), we tend to live to work, enslaved to a rapacious, introjected Faustian machine. Ever since – unless you're lucky enough to be French – we've been working longer hours, moving to the ever-sprawling suburbs, and spending an awful lot of time commuting. In 2018, 55% of Americans did not use all of their paid vacation time – that's a record 768 million days voluntarily donated to their employer, instead of devoted to family and friends (USTA, 2019).

Even a generation ago, Erich Fromm argued that we are now mere robots, compliant economic units, stripped of soul, concluding: 'In the twentieth century the problem is that *man is dead*' (1955/2001, p.352, original italics).

With society already on its knees, along comes email, the internet, mobile phones, virtual reality, and Kafkaesque scenes of humans avoiding real contact with each other and their environment, even at social gatherings, family meals, weddings, vacations. We commune instead with tiny little screens. The lure of texts, emails and what is laughingly called 'social' media. Alfred J. Prufrock measured out his life with coffee spoons. Ours are measured out in 'likes'. 'Did you have a good life?' the nurse will ask us on our deathbed. 'I don't know,' we will answer, 'I missed most of it. I was too busy checking my messages.'

Facebook and Instagram feed you misinformation and hate. Silicon Valley pioneer Jaron Lanier says social media 'hates your soul'; your accounts have killed your empathy, made you more gullible, afraid, sad and 'You're probably becoming more of an asshole' (2018, p.125).

Love thy neighbour? Or just make sure yours is the better car on the driveway.

None of it seems to be making us happy. A pre-pandemic YouGov survey showed that 74% of UK adults had felt so stressed that at times they felt overwhelmed or unable to cope; 32% said they had experienced suicidal feelings and 16% said they had self-harmed (Mental Health Foundation, 2018).

Tim Kasser, an American psychologist who has done a lot of research into the psychological effects of materialism, writes:

> Substantial evidence shows that people who place a relatively
> high priority on materialistic values/goals consume more
> products and incur more debt, have lower-quality interpersonal
> relationships, act in more ecologically destructive ways, have
> adverse work and educational motivation, and report lower
> personal and physical well-being. (2016, p.489)

Writes Sue Gerhardt in *The Selfish Society*:

> The hidden source of both selfishness and materialism, those
> unholy twins, is a feeling of deprivation. This is rooted in the
> actual experiences that people have had, and the way that they
> have been treated in their childhoods, particularly their infancy.
> With a poor experience of early dependence, children grow
> up longing to feel emotionally secure and accepted, yet lack

the understanding of how to achieve satisfying relationships with others. Instead, they turn to materialism, status or power, because these are the values endorsed by our culture. (2010, p.46)

Psychopathy

Growing up during the Russian Civil War, Ayn Rand saw how unfairly her parents were treated by the communists – her father's business was seized and the family fled to Crimea. So, as an adult, she went to the other extreme: to America, the far right, to writing novels and academic works extolling the virtues of greed and selfishness. She regarded those with wealth and privilege as heroic, the rest as slothful parasites. Government should be 'small'; she saw taxation as theft.

Her law-of-the-jungle message has been embraced by American conservatives, especially people who like to attribute their wealth and power to themselves and their 'hard work', rather than the sheer fluke of having been born into a fortunate situation that facilitated a good education and a pathway to the levers of power. It's a self-aggrandising, guilt-relieving credo: whether you're rich or poor, you get what you deserve.

Perhaps that is one key difference between Europeans and Americans. Europeans tend to believe one's socioeconomic status is largely down to chance; Americans, by contrast, tend to believe it is down to oneself.

The American Dream suggests that anybody can be successful at anything, as long as they want it enough and work hard enough. But it's not true. It's a very unlevel playing field, and those with power – often largely unearned – devote a lot of it to ensuring it stays that way. Social mobility is lower in the US than in some European countries, and, if anything, is declining.

Capitalism rewards greedy, heartless psychopaths. Robert Hare, who started his career as a psychologist at a maximum-security prison in Vancouver, has spent a lifetime studying psychopaths. Not the murderous, chainsaw-wielding, Hannibal Lecter types, but driven, high-functioning, succeed-at-any-cost characters who live among us, at loose in the wild. They can be found in all walks of life. They love power. They love to win. In his 1993 book *Without Conscience: The disturbing world of the psychopaths among us*, Hare estimated there were at least two million psychopaths in North America, with 100,000 in New York City alone – psychopaths like the bright lights, apparently.

And the bright lights, seemingly, like them. Society applauds them. They are celebrated. They are idolised. They stalk the corridors of power, finance, culture. They are our sporting heroes. The higher you climb in any field, the more of them you will encounter. Poor psychopaths go to jail, as they say; rich ones go to business school.

Psychopaths have a profound effect on society. They are the high priests of capitalism. Jon Ronson, author of *The Psychopath Test: A journey through the madness industry* (2012), explains in an interview in Forbes:

> Capitalism, at its most ruthless, is a physical manifestation of psychopathy. Theirs is the brain anomaly that shapes our world. (Bercovici, 2011)

So what exactly is their brain anomaly? What makes a psychopath? Hare has identified 20 characteristics of psychopaths, including superficial charm; grandiose sense of self-worth; pathological lying; cunning/manipulative; lack of remorse or guilt; shallow emotions, and callousness/lack of empathy. Psychopaths are generally considered to have been born that way. They are the bad seeds of our species. By contrast, the psychopath's less charming counterpart, the 'sociopath', is someone whose unpleasant habits supposedly derive more from bad nurture than bad nature.

Psychopaths of course have no conception of compassion or consideration for anybody with a disability. Ayn Rand, who incidentally spent the last eight years of her life living off benefits, was asked about special education programmes. This is what she said:

> I think it's monstrous, as is everything they're doing to feature or favor the incompetent, the retarded, the handicapped… at an impossible expense. I do not think that the retarded should be allowed to come near children. Children cannot deal, and should not have to deal, with the very tragic spectacle of a handicapped human being. (Smith & Polloway, 2013)

Michael Eigen describes the current period as the 'Age of Psychopathy'. 'There have been worse times in history,' he writes, 'yet I am not sure I have ever lived through a crazier moment of abrasive fragility' (2018, p.22).

Toxic masculinity

'What is it with men?' a client said to me recently. Another relationship had ended in disappointment; she was being 'ghosted'. Her father vanished years ago. She'd had no contact with him at all since childhood.

Three-quarters of American men are circumcised – subjected as babies to a barbaric mutilation that belongs in another, more primitive century. The emotional circumcision follows swiftly thereafter. Writes feminist author bel hooks:

> The first act of violence that patriarchy demands of males is
> not violence toward women. Instead patriarchy demands of all
> males that they engage in acts of psychic self-mutilation, that
> they kill off the emotional parts of themselves. (2004, p.66)

We tell our sons to man up – or, in the absence of fathers, father figures or modern-day tribal elders, they are told nothing at all; they feel nothing, say little. We create numb, inarticulate loners; we idolise flinty, monosyllabic killers played by John Wayne, Charles Bronson, Clint Eastwood, Sylvester Stallone.

Men are taught to be tough; to win, not love. We don't know how we feel. We certainly don't know how others feel.

We are raised to be expendable cogs in a loveless machine. In the UK, men make up 97% of workplace fatalities (HSE, 2021); in the US, the figure is 93%. Men make up 99% of American combat fatalities. The wheels of capitalism spirit fathers away from their sons and daughters.

In many families, the father (if there is one) is like a shy, mythic woodland creature: sightings are rare, and fleeting; vocal utterances few. Perhaps he becomes the hapless chump of the household, the doofus dad who just doesn't get it and can't do DIY; the lovable loser who is part of the furniture. He is neutered, like the family pet. He dreams of making his own declaration of independence, of kicking over the saloon tables and riding off into the sunset, leaving women to clear up the mess. Sometimes, he actually does it.

More than three-quarters of suicides are by men (ONS, 2021a); men are three times more likely than women to become alcohol dependent (NHS Digital, 2020b), and men are much less likely to access psychological therapies (Mental Health Foundation, 2021).

For all their supposed dominance and patriarchal oppression, 43% of British men regularly feel worried or low (Mind, 2020). And men live shorter lives than women – on average a whopping four years shorter (ONS, 2021b). Equal pay – of course. But what about equal lifespan?

Many men who have done everything they were supposed to do wind up on the therapist's couch in midlife because they feel like dead men walking. I see plenty of male clients who never met their fathers, or never really knew them, or had fathers or stepfathers who they wished had been absent rather than violent, excessively demanding or abusive in other ways. These men in my counselling room are often success stories on paper; in person they are ghosts. Cupid's arrow passes right through.

The Austrian psychologist Alfred Adler argued that men will often overcompensate for their fear of vulnerability, with a lurch towards stereotypical male aggression and competition. What Jung called the anima, the feminine, is denied; the animus is embraced. (To be whole, said Jung, both must be integrated.) The boy-man is pure animus – animosity – shorn of anything that might be considered anima – the animating effects of emotion, creativity, compassion, collaboration. The most macho are the most afraid.

Adler called this the 'masculine protest' and regarded it as an evil force in history: 'the arch evil of our culture' (in Connell, 2005, p.16), underlying, for instance, the rise in fascism in the 20th century. To be taken seriously as a leader, one must appear devoutly unempathic, unfeeling, uncompromising, unflinching. And, above all, 'strong' – ready to go to war at the slightest provocation. This is perhaps especially true of women leaders, the 'Iron Lady' Margaret Thatcher being the obvious, almost cartoonish example. Ayn Rand is another. Ambitious women take part in the masculine protest too. This perhaps explains why an analysis by the University of Chicago of European leaders from 1480 to 1913 found that queens were 27% more likely to go to war than kings (Dube & Harish, 2020).

In *Under Saturn's Shadow: The wounding and healing of men* (1994), Jungian analyst James Hollis writes that men's lives are essentially governed by fear, and their lives are violent because their souls have been violated.

Fearful and violent people make dystopian, dog-eat-dog societies, shorn of human decency, kindness and compassion, inevitably trending towards gross inequality and fascism – where, as recent history shows us, people with disabilities are the first to be executed.

Othering

A century ago, American journalist Walter Lippmann wrote that society consists of two groups: a small, powerful, educated elite, and the rest, which he called the 'bewildered herd' (1922/2012). And to keep democracy ticking over, in Lippmann's view, the bewildered herd must be kept complacent, pliant and distracted by things like sports, soap operas and the fantasy of salvation through material goods. Occasionally, the bewildered herd needs to be persuaded to swallow an unpopular action, such as austerity or war. Writes Noam Chomsky: 'Propaganda is to a democracy what the bludgeon is to a totalitarian state' (2008, p.20).

So much of what we hold dear about Britain, including much of its relative prosperity, originated overseas, brought here over the centuries by intrepid, industrious and determined people from afar. But politicians know that pandering to people's fears keeps them in power. The British Empire was built on a strategy of 'divide and rule'; today's politicians know that, if the 'bewildered herd' turn on one another, or 'the Other', they're less likely to turn on their government.

As mentioned at other points in this book, it is very easy to manufacture and exploit division and difference; to kindle and foment racism. It's frightening how easily people can buy into loud, simplistic, aggressive, finger-pointing explanations as to why life is hard, especially when the finger points down, to the powerless, rather than up, to the powerful.

Sections of the British media are skilled at fabricating ridiculous, cartoonish straw men that they can then mercilessly malign, blame and destroy.

Among their many political piñatas is the European Union. On Brexit referendum day, the *Daily Mail* ran a lead article that lamented 'a campaign characterised by mendacity'. It had little to say about its own mendacity – *The Economist* reported that the *Daily Mail* was the clear leader in publishing endless stories about the EU that simply weren't true, such as Euro banknotes being responsible for impotence; or the EU demanding that cows wear nappies; or that the Latin name be used for 'cod' instead of fish and chips; or that corgis be banned. This of course is just a very small sample. All the tabloids tell tall tales of asylum seekers stealing royal swans or donkeys from London parks and barbecuing them, or councils banning hot-cross buns from being served at Easter in favour of naan bread.

A lot of the lies about the EU came from Boris Johnson. He got fired from his first job in journalism for making up a quote, and was then hired by Max Hastings at age 24 to be Brussels correspondent for *The Daily Telegraph*, whence he dispatched a steady stream of ranting, racist anti-European hysteria – facts be damned. The basic message was: Loathe thy neighbour. Martin Fletcher wrote in *The New Statesman*:

> He made his name by mocking, lampooning and ridiculing the EU. He wrote stories headlined 'Brussels recruits sniffers to ensure that Euro-manure smells the same', 'Threat to British pink sausages' and 'Snails are fish, says EU'. He wrote about plans to standardise condom sizes and ban prawn cocktail flavour crisps. (Fletcher, 2016)

Years later, Johnson told the BBC he was 'sort of chucking these rocks over the garden wall and I listened to this amazing crash from the greenhouse next door over in England as everything I wrote from Brussels was having this amazing, explosive effect on the Tory party, and it really gave me this, I suppose, rather weird sense of power' (BBC, 2005).

Hastings today describes Johnson as 'a tasteless joke' who is 'utterly unfit to be Prime Minister' (Hastings, 2019).

The cosy relationship between media and government has a long history. In the 1930s, the *Daily Mail* was owned by Harold Sidney Harmsworth, First Viscount Rothermere, reportedly a keen pre-war admirer and supporter of Adolf Hitler and his annexation of Czechoslovakia; he wrote in the newspaper in praise of fascism, Oswald Mosley and the British Union of Fascists, too. How much of the discriminatory editorial content, politics and tone of today's *Mail* is a reflection of the beliefs of the current owner, great-grandson of Harold, Jonathan Harold Esmond Vere Harmsworth, Fourth Viscount Rothermere? We don't know, but wealthy press barons – those 'patriots' who often live and bank offshore – have long favoured explaining away the problem of gross inequality with a simple message: blame not the perpetrators of cruel, discriminatory, steal-from-the-poor-and-give-to-the-rich government policies that further empowers the powerful, blame the victims! Blame the poorest, most desperate – asylum seekers, refugees, travellers, rough sleepers, people on benefits – with relentless, endlessly repetitive, disparaging, stereotyped negative characterisations using words like 'criminals', 'scroungers', 'dirty', 'barbaric', 'violent', 'cruel' and 'deviant'.

And of course, people with disabilities do not escape government othering or the tabloids' concocted wrath. The age of austerity was sold to the public on a tide of propaganda and rhetoric against those it hit the hardest – often coming directly from the Department of Work and Pensions, led by bully-in-chief Iain Duncan-Smith. The DWP was also caught pressuring people with disabilities into accepting 'deals' that would cheat them out of what they were entitled to (Ryan, 2020).

Writes the group Disabled People Against Cuts:

> Time and time again, the *Daily Mail* has published stories about disability benefit claimants who supposedly did not deserve their benefits because they were either fit for work, or because it was too easy to claim benefits.
>
> Time and time again, the Work and Pensions Committee and/or the UK Statistics Authority which has investigated complaints about the media treatment of disability benefit claimants, have found DWP guilty of giving 'direct quotations from Ministers [which] can give undue credence to inaccurate or misleading reports'. (DPAC, 2015)

In one typical story, in 2016 the *Daily Mail* accused 'benefit cheats' of a scam in which 'thousands are driving off in brand new vehicles paid for by YOU – by pretending they're disabled' (Tweedie, 2016).

The tiny correction, two months later, admitted that there was no data on people claiming cars by pretending to be disabled.

Imperialism

When Christopher Columbus arrived in the New World in 1492, he brought with him the promise of a better life for the indigenous Taíno people. They welcomed the arrival of the Europeans. Columbus noted their generosity, friendliness, strength. He concluded that they would make excellent servants – he and his men quickly turned from rescuers to persecutors. They subjugated the Taíno. They were put to work and prevented from growing the crops that had fed them for centuries. Many were killed, many starved, a huge number died from European diseases for which they had no immunity. After a few decades, the Taíno had been all but wiped out.

A few centuries later, the British colonial project was presented to the British people as 'trusteeship'; a humanistic, paternalistic, 'civilising mission'. Giving a helping hand to people who were portrayed as a lesser 'race' was promoted, in Kipling's words, as the 'white man's burden' – Britain thus as both the rescuer and the victim. But these flimsy disguises cannot conceal the horrors of persecution. By the end of 1914, European control had expanded over 84% of the earth's surface. London was the capital of the world's biggest empire in 1945 – a quarter of the Earth's land. This was achieved with all the usual tools of imperialism – slavery, division, rape, incarceration, exploitation, appropriation, brutality, famine. Colossal amounts of violence, bloodshed, killing.

Adolf Hitler, one of the most unequivocally vile persecutors in history, exploited the power of a victim mentality: he sold himself to the German people as a rescuer of their nation, defending Germany against supposed Allied and Jewish aggression. Many disturbed, power-hungry men, often overcompensating for some sense of deep deficiency, have emulated Hitler's methods. You tell your nation that life is hard, and that it used to be great but is now on its knees; in fist-pounding rallies and speeches, you place the blame for that squarely on some imagined enemy within or without – the Russians, blacks, Jews, Kurds, Tutsis, Croatians, Mexicans, Muslims, the EU, Democrats. You pull all the levers of propaganda to portray this enemy as evil, sick, weird, subhuman, different from you and hell-bent on your extinction. You invoke wars from ancient history as proof that you have always been enemies. You incite violence and hatred, which you blame on the enemy. And you present yourself as the saviour. Persecutor-victim-rescuer: the classic 'drama triangle' (Karpman, 1968).

Can't we give these childish you're-the-evildoer-no-you-are arguments the contempt they deserve? Can't we see through these schoolyard posturings and just play nicely? Are the Scots and the English suddenly to remember – I don't know – the Battle of Flodden, and rebuild Hadrian's Wall and take up arms again?

As for the more recent example of Afghanistan, it's easy to see the Taliban as persecutors, and they are, but it is now widely known that the American government played a major role in creating them. Using the logic of 'the enemy of my enemy is my friend', the White House recruited and funded the most extreme and violent Islamic fundamentalists in Afghanistan in CIA covert operations started in 1979, as a deliberate provocation to the USSR. The aim was to precipitate a Russian invasion and a long, drawn-out war that would bring the Russian empire to its knees and end the Cold War. President Jimmy Carter's National Security Advisor Zbigniew Brzezinski was asked in 1998 if he regretted this intervention:

> Brzezinski: 'Regret what? That secret operation was an excellent idea. It had the effect of drawing the Russians into the Afghan trap and you want me to regret it? The day that the Soviets officially crossed the border, I wrote to President Carter, essentially: "We now have the opportunity of giving to the USSR its Vietnam war." Indeed, for almost 10 years, Moscow had to carry on a war that was unsustainable for the regime, a conflict that bought about the demoralization and finally the breakup of the Soviet empire.'
>
> Interviewer: 'And neither do you regret having supported Islamic fundamentalism, which has given arms and advice to future terrorists?'
>
> Brzezinski: 'What is more important in world history? The Taliban or the collapse of the Soviet empire? Some agitated Moslems or the liberation of Central Europe and the end of the Cold War?' (*Le Nouvel Observateur*, 1998)

Nine days after the horrific terrorist attacks of September 11, 2001, in which 2,986 people were killed, George Bush declared war. 'Tonight we are a country awakened to danger and called to defend freedom,' the US president told the nation from the Capitol building. He declared a 'War on Terror,' adding: 'It will not end until every terrorist group of global reach has been found, stopped and defeated… Every nation, in every region, now has a decision to make. Either you are with us, or you are with the terrorists.'

The 'War on Terror' – accompanied by much racist rhetoric about Muslims, the supposedly new monolithic evil empire – gave the US government free reign to pursue its own imperial interests with impunity. And indefinitely, since, as Gore Vidal pointed out (2002), it's not possible to win a war against an abstract noun.

'Operation Enduring Freedom' began on 7 October, 2001 and the high-altitude bombs began to fall on a country already ravaged by its decade-long war with the USSR. By 10 December, at least 3,767 civilians had been killed (Zunes, 2003, p.206).

The Taliban – formerly funded by the US taxpayer (Napoleoni, 2003) – was defeated and Afghanistan was won. The US then turned its attention to Iraq, starting with a pre-emptive attack in March 2003, in violation of international law. Saddam Hussein was a ruthless dictator who committed crimes against humanity. Like the Taliban, however, he was once a friend of Washington as a useful buffer against Iran. In 1988, when he was committing genocide against the Kurds, the US government provided him with $500 million in subsidies, which was doubled to $1 billion the following year (Chomsky, 2003, p.67).

The USSR broke up into pieces, but Russian imperialism, of course, did not go away. The Cold War continues to get very hot periodically, usually on other peoples' lands – in Chechnya, Georgia, Crimea and, as of February 2022, Ukraine. By mid-April 2022, almost two months after Russia's invasion of Ukraine, nearly 2,000 Ukrainian citizens had been killed, and 2.7 million refugees had fled their nation. Their towns and cities lie in ruins.

Vladimir Putin's leadership is brutal, authoritarian and corrupt. But it's not as if there's much humanity or morality or soul in US foreign policy, which the UK has blindly followed (with the notable exception of the Vietnam War – thank you, Harold Wilson).

Report Benjamin and Davies:

The US and its allies have dropped more than 326,000 bombs and missiles on people in other countries since 2001, including more than 152,000 in Iraq and Syria.

That's an average of 46 bombs and missiles per day, day in day out, year in year out, for nearly 20 years. In 2019, the last year for which we have fairly complete records, the average was 42 bombs and missiles per day, including 20 per day in Afghanistan alone. (2021)

Writes author and director of World Beyond War, David Swanson:

> Since World War II, during a supposed golden age of peace, the United States military has killed or helped kill some 20 million people, overthrown at least 36 governments, interfered in at least 85 foreign elections, attempted to assassinate over 50 foreign leaders, and dropped bombs on people in over 30 countries... The U.S. government provides weapons, military training, and/or military funding to almost every dictatorship and oppressive government on earth... US weapons are used on both sides of many wars.

What kind of perversion of democracy is this? What suffering has been wrought by the scale of American persecution?

For every child killed in warfare, three are injured and acquire a permanent form of disability. In some countries, up to a quarter of disabilities result from injuries and violence.

Afghanistan, once a crossroads of civilisation and culture, where women got the vote in 1919 – a year before the US – has been used, abused and abandoned. Four decades of war have left a great deal of damage. One study reported that a whopping 80% of adults in Afghanistan live with some form of disability (Shinwari et al., 2020). Iraq, too, has one of the largest populations of people with disabilities, most of whom 'have little to no income' (IOM, 2021).

If America ever was the 'world's policeman' – echoes of the 'white man's burden' – he's a cop whose gone rogue and needs to be relieved of his badge and his gun.

Violence

There used to be a little platform at London Zoo where you could see 'The Most Dangerous Animal in the World'. You read the sign and then realise you are standing in front of a mirror.

The most dangerous animal in the world is us.

We humans do an awful lot of killing. The death toll of Native Americans at our hands might be as high as 130 million. The Holocaust – millions of people, brothers and sisters, parents and children, friends and lovers, most of the Jewish population of Europe – murdered. So many genocides, mass murders, purges, famines, war deaths, bombing raids.

We kill each other but we also enslave, torture, rape, imprison and persecute each other on a monstrous scale.

We kill ourselves – hundreds of thousands every year.

We kill billions of animals every year for food, fashion, medical experiments, sport. As America's colonisers moved westward across the great plains, they slaughtered tens of millions of bison, sometimes shooting them from the train windows just for fun. By 1884, there were just 324 bison left.

Now a million species are on the brink of extinction.

We might well be one of them.

In the book *Demonic Men*, Wrangham and Peterson argue that violence is favoured by evolution because the violent are more likely to survive. Power reproduces itself. It has no interest in morality. They write, we are 'the dazed survivors of a continuous 5-million-year habit of lethal aggression' (1996).

Is this who we are?

Is this who we want to be?

We can choose.

Nietzsche called humans 'clever animals'. But if we carry on like this, allowing damaged, demonic egos, crippled by fear and loathing and an inability to love, to lead us to our inevitable grotesque self-destruction as a species, we are very stupid indeed.

Environmental neglect

Not only have we surrendered our minds, bodies and souls to the higher power of capitalism; we have co-opted our planet into service, too. We have blithely fed the Earth's natural resources into the cavernous furnace of the hungry machine, and we have not cared what kind of choking mess the belching machine spews out in return. The British scientist James Lovelock – 102 at the time of writing – suggested that the Earth and all things in it are not the playthings of humans to use and abuse as they wish. With his 'Gaia hypothesis', he proposed that the Earth is a self-regulating system that our species should respect. Gaia is a primordial goddess of Greek mythology, mother of all the gods, Mother Earth. We mess with her at our peril.

Lovelock was hired by NASA in the 1960s to develop space monitoring equipment to help them in their quest to determine if there was life on Mars. Lovelock understands what a planet needs to sustain life. He says Gaia is interested in life, not necessarily human life.

He writes:

Gaia, as I see her, is no doting mother tolerant of
misdemeanours, nor is she some fragile and delicate damsel
in danger from brutal mankind. She is stern and tough, always
keeping the world warm and comfortable for those who
obey the rules, but ruthless in her destruction of those who
transgress. (1988, p.212)

The issue of our potential for self-destruction as a species makes any
contentions about disability, therapy, society completely irrelevant.
Writes Neville in *The Life of Things: Therapy and the soul of the world*:

There are plenty of people prepared to argue that the care of the
worried well and even the mentally suffering is an indulgence
and an irrelevance in the current ecological emergency. If we do
not do something quickly we are doomed. Our efforts should
be spent on saving the planet. After that we can worry about
whether we are happy or not. (2012, p.45)

Many regard the forest fires, devastating floods, rising temperatures,
melting ice caps and even Covid-19 as examples of Gaia's fury as she
lashes out at her ungrateful children who have so comprehensively
defiled her and despoiled her precious gifts.

Who said this, in September 2021?

It is time for humanity to grow up.

It is time for us to listen to the warnings of the scientists –
and look at Covid, if you want an example of gloomy scientists
being proved right – and to understand who we are and what
we are doing.

The world – this precious blue sphere with its eggshell
crust and wisp of an atmosphere – is not some indestructible
toy, some bouncy plastic romper room against which we can
hurl ourselves to our heart's content.

Daily, weekly, we are doing such irreversible damage
that long before a million years are up, we will have made this
beautiful planet effectively uninhabitable – not just for us but
for many other species.

Was this some 'woke' Green Party activist? Some fringe spokesman of the loony Left? No, it was Britain's Conservative Prime Minister Boris Johnson.

He seemed to be partly 'mansplaining' and partly talking to his own reflection when he told the 76th session of the UN General Assembly in New York:

> We still cling with part of our minds to the infantile belief that the world was made for our gratification and pleasure and we combine this narcissism with an assumption of our own immortality.
>
> We believe that someone else will clear up the mess we make, because that is what someone else has always done.
>
> We trash our habitats again and again with the inductive reasoning that we have got away with it so far, and therefore we will get away with it again.
>
> My friends, the adolescence of humanity is coming to an end. (Johnson, 2021)

The road to humanity

The problems of the world seem overwhelming, insurmountable, impossible.

Are we doomed?

Is change possible?

It begins with you. And your humanity.

For starters, how do you respond to people who are different from you?

Do you pass the Humanity Test?

How ableist are you?

At the state level, do you support a philosophy of exclusion with respect to disability? You might vote and argue for strict border controls, infanticide, sterilisation and genocide. The goal is the complete eradication of disability from the land, as was attempted in Nazi Germany in the 1930s and 1940s. Such a philosophy would be rooted in the evolutionary model and/or the moral model of disability.

Or perhaps you prefer something a little less brutal – segregation? If so, you would favour a system where the disadvantaged group are corralled into their own areas that are separated from the mainstream society where power and status lie – presumably only if you belong to the latter group though. You might live in a gated community of privilege, regard the rest with disdain, and look back with admiration at apartheid South Africa.

No? How about integration, where the minority group is brought within the borders of the state but they remain clustered in ghettoes of disadvantage with prejudice and economic circumstance often keeping them there?

Doesn't really seem fair, does it?

An inclusive society, by contrast, is one where all citizens have equal rights and opportunities for growth and development and the pursuit of a soulful life.

Do the organisations you are associated with pass the Humanity Test? Where are they on the evolutionary scale from our origins as feral creatures toward becoming intelligent, caring beings invested in a fair, aspirational, utopian society? What can you do to change things?

Look around. Where do you see exclusion? Segregation? Integration? Inclusion?

All four modes of existence are in operation today for people with disabilities in the Western world. Taking education as an example, for instance: the school that takes no students who have a disability practises exclusion. The special education school might be part of a regional government policy of segregation. Schools that accept special education students but make provisions for them within the school, such as having them in a separate unit, or in separate classrooms, practise integration. Schools where kids with disabilities are in class with all the other kids, perhaps supported by dedicated teaching assistants, practise inclusion.

Research in different countries often shows a preference among parents and students – both those who experience disability and those who do not – for segregated schools, but other reviews reveal mostly positive attitudes toward inclusive education (de Boer et al., 2010). Florian & Spratt (2013) promote 'inclusive pedagogy', which they define as:

> an approach to teaching and learning that supports teachers to
> respond to individual differences between learners but avoids
> the marginalisation that can occur when some students are
> treated differently.

A similarly enlightened report on education in Australia states:

> All children in Australia have the right to an inclusive
> education. However, there are many barriers to the realisation
> of this right in the lived experience of children and families.
> Current efforts towards upholding the rights of all children
> are impeded by a lack of understanding of inclusive education
> and misappropriation of the term. Additional barriers include
> negative and discriminatory attitudes and practices, lack
> of support to facilitate inclusive education, and inadequate
> education and professional development for teachers and other
> professionals. Critical to addressing all of these barriers is
> recognising and disestablishing ableism in Australia. (Cologon,
> 2013).

Anything other than inclusion perpetuates ableism in society. Only inclusion brings an end to disability apartheid.

As for education, so for government, employment, sports, the arts, media, your town, community, family.

Are you an advocate for humanity?

Much progress has been made. But we will never all live together in one world, where individual abilities and capabilities are enabled and vulnerabilities are supported and catered for, until the disabling internal psychological barriers are removed and we meet, greet and get to know each other.

7. Humanity –
Passing the test

'Either we heal now, as a team, or we will die as individuals.'
Al Pacino, in Any Given Sunday

The lockdowns during the coronavirus pandemic in 2020 and 2021 turned my central London neighbourhood into a ghost town. At night, the silence from the deserted streets and boarded-up bars felt ominous and dangerous. Out there in the darkness, unseen, the virus continued its hideous invasion. With astonishing speed, it took over our hospitals, our conversations, our news feeds. It closed our schools and factories, bankrupted businesses, ruined lives. It made a mockery of our sophisticated systems, our plans, our hopes and dreams. It dominated, controlled and threatened our very existence. At the time of writing, in April 2022, it has killed more than six million humans worldwide.

Never before has something so large – human civilisation – been felled by something so small. The coronavirus is a mini-vampire, sub-microscopic, a life-form a hundred times tinier even than bacteria.

The crisis brought out the best in many people. Our doctors and nurses faced the daily apocalypse with selfless care, kindness and good cheer. We clapped for the NHS, that slightly battered but still beautiful beacon of care that shines its light into every corner of this increasingly sharp-elbowed, ambitious, ruthless land. People around the world were volunteering, donating, checking up on the vulnerable, doing what they could. Captain Tom did a sponsored walk in advance of his 100th birthday and raised £32 million.

I've listened to clients talk a lot about how the pandemic has affected them, and what they have realised is important in life, and what would be different about their lives when the lockdowns ended and the opening up began. Some said that everything would change. Others said nothing would change. Maybe both beliefs are true for all of us.

We were completely alone, quarantined, forced into self-isolation and social distance. The coronavirus wasn't interested in your country's borders, its reputation, history or your culture. It didn't carry a passport or respect yours. We were all vulnerable. No one was safe. In the absence of celestial salvation, we turned to each other.

Covid-19 was a wake-up call. It's time for humanity to rediscover itself.

§

When I looked into the eyes of my newborn daughter, I saw not a blank slate but an astonishing intensity; a kind of universe of ancient wisdom and intelligence.

There is much nature within us. More than 20 involuntary reflexes have been identified in newborn babies (Cozolino, 2010, p.183). We already have plenty of subjective and intersubjective skills at birth.

But there is also much nurture. The brain more than doubles in weight in the first year of life – if the baby is loved and cared for. Says Sue Gerhardt:

> What needs to be written in neon letters lit up against a night
> sky is that the orbitofrontal cortex, which is so much about
> being human, develops almost entirely post-natally. (2004/2015,
> p.35)

The development of the architecture of the infant brain is like an ongoing process of downloading software from the environment, especially via social interaction with primary caregivers. Even a simple smile can set off a biochemical chain reaction of physiological pleasure and the creation of new neural pathways in the young brain.

Vivian Gussin Paley's book *The Kindness of Children* (2000) opens with an account of Teddy, a boy with profound special needs, who uses a wheelchair, visiting a London school. The children are kind to Teddy. Teddy says 'Car' and they help him play with a toy car. They include him. They play together. 'I love Teddy,' one of the children says later.

Children as young as six months have a sense of morality, preferring, for instance, to choose a good puppet rather than one that has behaved badly. From an early age, writes Rutger Bregman in his extraordinary book *Humankind: A hopeful history*, young children 'are only too eager to help others' (2020, p.213).

Of course, children are equally capable of being cruel and malicious. They learn this from grown-ups. We are all capable of being manipulated and turned against others. We learn how to be human from other humans. We attune; we hear, adapt and pass along the songs of life. We know how to love because we have been loved. We can be kind because others have offered us a drink from the cup of kindness. We feel for others because we, too, feel. Hate, cruelty and blame can also be taught.

One of the casualties of the Enlightenment, of the Industrial Revolution – an ever-more rapacious capitalist machine – is basic human kindness. Write Phillips and Taylor:

> Kindness was steadily downgraded from a universal imperative to the prerogative of specific social constituencies: romantic poets, clergymen, charity-workers and, above all, women, whose presumed tender-heartedness survived the egoist onslaught. By the end of the Victorian period, kindness had been largely feminised, ghetto-ized into a womanly sphere of feeling and behaviour where it has remained, with some notable exceptions, ever since. (2009, p.40)

There is a wealth of evidence that acts of kindness bring joy both to the giver and the recipient. In one landmark study (Ford et al., 2015), people in different countries were asked to pursue happiness. In America, they tried to please themselves, and this did not make them happy. In countries where they tended to try to help others, lo and behold, they were happier. 'In collectivistic (vs individualistic) cultures, pursuing happiness may be more successful because happiness is viewed – and thus pursued – in relatively socially engaged ways,' says the report.

Maybe kindness is making a comeback. We saw in Chapter 4 how attachment theory, first formulated by John Bowlby in the 1950s, has ushered in kinder, more nurturing parenting norms, very different from the old, harsh, tame-the-beast, spare-the-rod-spoil-the-child ideology.

What children most need isn't a big house, strict teachers or even necessarily a traditional nuclear family. Writes Gerhardt:

> My own experiences – as a parent and as a psychotherapist – lead me to think that what matters for a child's emotional health is not the particular form of family life, but above all for a child to have at least one permanent relationship with a loving, available adult who really listens and cares... The developing child then feels safe to explore the world and learn how to relate effectively to the others – by listening to others, valuing them and restoring relationships when conflict occurs. (2010, p.219)

No one really tells new parents this. You leave a department store with a new toaster that comes with a manual on how to look after it. You leave hospital with a baby.

We need people around who love us and make us feel safe. That never goes away. The brain – with a hundred billion neurons that together form a million billion connections (Siegel, 1999, p.13) – retains a degree of plasticity, an ability to develop and grow, like a muscle, throughout life. Software upgrades – and learning – are always available through good experiences, which can come from education, practising skills, overcoming challenges or through relationships – including a psychotherapeutic working alliance. Indeed, the brain 'continually changes in response to environmental challenges' (Cozolino, 2010, p.19). You can teach an old dog new tricks – if the old dog wants to learn them.

An important aspect of humanity is having some sense of how others are feeling. Empathy is an important ingredient for a soulful life, a life of love. Empathy is part of what makes humans humane.

Keats was a man of great feeling. He was steeped in his own experience but was highly attuned to others and could readily step into their shoes. He would watch sparrows from his window and imagine being one of them, pecking at the gravel. He would imagine being a billiard ball, delighting in 'its own roundness, smoothness and rapidity of its motion'. In a room full of people, he would be keenly aware of the identities and emotional states of others.

Empathy is not enough, however; it is biased, fickle, easily deceived, exploited. Acts of kindness can be misconstrued, ill-conceived, potentially manipulative or intrusive. A wasted opportunity to connect. People with disabilities are forever experiencing people trying to be kind but just being weird instead.

We hear a well-told story of someone who is attractive, from a similar background to us, bravely going through some form of palatable – bearable – suffering, all set to a dramatic musical score, and we are moved; the floodgates of empathy open. Meanwhile, across town, on the other side of the tracks, a similar but darker-skinned story goes untold. Writes Bregman: 'The sad truth is that empathy and xenophobia go hand in hand' (2020, p.219). As psychologist Paul Bloom points out in his book *Against Empathy*, we need rational compassion (2016). We need information.

We need to learn more about each other. We need to get to know our human family. Instead of being afraid, we should develop a sense of *xenophilia*.

§

In *Civilization and its Discontents* (1930/1961), Freud took a pretty dim view of human nature. He said civilisation is necessary to protect us from our violent, destructive drives and desires. But going against what he considered our true nature isn't going to make us happy.

The top 10 happiest countries in the world, according to the 2020 World Happiness Report (WHR, 2020) are Finland, Iceland, Denmark, Switzerland, Netherlands, Sweden, Germany, Norway, New Zealand and Austria. Besides prosperity, low levels of inequality and relatively trustworthy politicians, a crucial ingredient common to these countries, the X-factor, is the concept of 'social capital', which is defined as 'the networks of relationships among people who live and work in a particular society, enabling that society to function effectively'.

Social capital describes the extent of trust and social support and cohesion that exists. When social capital is high, people are less selfish, more communal, kinder.

There's a kind of *togethering*, rather than an *othering*.

Social capital is the soul of a nation.

Almost no one can keep a straight face when old Etonian politicians like David Cameron or Boris Johnson utter the party line: 'We're all in this together.' We live in a deeply divided world – a world where the richest 42 individuals have the same amount of wealth as the poorest half of the global population – 3.7 billion people. But in egalitarian, truly democratic nations with high levels of social capital, such words spoken by leaders are slightly easier to swallow.

It's not a straightforward picture. It's true, for instance, that Finland has higher than average rates of suicide. Depression is quite common among young Finns, who feel the added burden of being unhappy in a nation that has such a reputation for its opposite (Savage, 2019). But in general, the happiest nations are awash with social capital.

The Scandinavian system or 'Nordic model' of government features high taxes, a large, well-run welfare state, a high standard of free education and healthcare, and low levels of inequality. The machine works for betterment of the people, not the other way round.

Ayn Rand/Donald Trump-style capitalism creates casualties. The richest Americans now live 10 to 15 years longer than the poorest, and the gap is growing (Misra, 2016). Inequality has grown in most countries in the past three decades (UN, 2020). A ranking of 39 Organisation for Economic Co-operation and Development countries by income inequality lists the UK in 33rd position and the USA at 34th (OECD, 2021). Books like *The Spirit Level* (Wilkinson & Pickett, 2010), *23 Things They Don't Tell You About Capitalism* (Chang, 2012), *Capital in the Twenty-First Century* (Piketty, 2014) and *In it Together* (OECD, 2015) clearly show how higher levels of inequality are ultimately bad for everyone. In *A Theory of Justice*, John Rawls demonstrates through his 'original-position' thought experiment that, if people meet to create an ideal imaginary society – one where they don't have any prior knowledge about the circumstances they would be born into – they will generally opt for a fair, redistributive political and economic system that treats all fairly, maximising the prospects of the least well-off (1971/1999, p.15). Grown-up countries have moved beyond tribal capitalism-versus-socialism arguments and recognise that, for optimum functioning, a blend of both is required. Is it so difficult to hold two ideas at the same time? Why go to extremes?

Immanuel Kant argued for the principle of fairness: a distributive justice. The likes of David Hume and Adam Smith believed in impartial benevolence. If you're disabled, disturbed, destitute or dangerous, the state still supports you, invests in you, believes in you. Not just because morally this is the right thing to do, but because it builds a better society.

When the OECD countries are ranked in terms of what they spend on incapacity – benefits for those impacted by sickness, disability and occupational injury – the leaders are Denmark (4.9% of GDP), Norway, Sweden, Finland and Iceland. These are governments that pass the Humanity Test. The UK (1.9%) and the US (1%) are far down the list.

The Nordic model is a system that appears to make people happy. People are invested in each other and in society. Scandinavian cities tend to do well in the famous 'lost wallet' experiments in which full wallets are left lying around to see how many get returned to their owner or handed in to the authorities. Prisons are focused on rehabilitation, introducing criminals to their humanity rather than merely continuing the pattern of abuse and brutality that has been the story of so many offenders' lives. There are high levels of atheism in these countries – the Scandinavians turn not to God for salvation but to each other.

Why isn't such a superior form of governance the rule rather than the exception? ('Yes,' people say, 'but these are countries with small populations and low immigration' – as though water, sunlight and soil were only good for some trees but not others.)

The 2020 US presidential election was a battle between two old dinosaurs: Donald Trump, 74, who was the oldest ever president to take office when he won the 2016 election, and Joe Biden, 78. Perhaps America, too, is ready for a president of the future rather than a relic of the past: someone smart, tough, fair, ambitious and multicultural – someone like America itself.

Six of the top-10 happiest countries have a female prime minister. These are not 'masculine protest', Iron-Lady Margaret Thatcher types but mostly energetic, well-rounded women who manage to combine caring with capitalism, super-smart, social democratically-minded, ethical pragmatists who are creating fair, functioning societies and, by all accounts, have done a much better job of responding to the coronavirus than the US or UK.

§

Humans and chimpanzees are 98.8% the same genetically. We are apes. Sometimes we are just like the chimpanzee – very violent. We are fighters. We fight to kill. Sometimes we are gorillas, devoted to our family. Sometimes we are orangutans – we want to be alone.

Occasionally we are more like bonobos. They are lovers, not fighters. Bonobo society is dominated by females. There is virtually no fighting, lots of playing, and lots of sex with lots of different partners.

Sometimes we see a lot of soul in what we call 'the wild'. The naturalist Jane Goodall observed a female chimpanzee in Gombe, Tanzania, with a malformation of her right foot that affected her mobility, but she was able to function and went on to have two infants of her own. Goodall also witnessed other chimpanzees with acquired disabilities – including from injuries and the effects of polio – survive by learning new ways of feeding and playing and moving around (1986). The mother of an infant chimpanzee with a severe disability – she exhibited symptoms resembling Down's syndrome – took extra care of her and did not allow non-relatives near; other group members 'did not show any aversive or fearful reactions to the disabled infant' (Matsumoto et al., 2016). Among Japanese macaques, researchers noted a socially neutral response to disability but did record that disabled females were bitten and chased less frequently (Turner et al., 2014).

If we humans are so similar to chimpanzees, imagine how similar we are to each other. You are just like a fellow human on the other side of the world, or your arch enemy, or that disabled bloke being winched out of a special van, or your neighbour. What is perhaps so striking about our species is not what divides us but what unites us.

We should respect each other and our planet. We should tackle common problems together. We should care about fellow humans who aren't doing so well. We might then feel compassion and concern that 70 million of our brothers and sisters are forcibly displaced people, including 26 million refugees, half of them children. Or the billion people who woke up this morning still disabled.

Nations should do what individuals should do: take responsibility. Truth, restitution, reconciliation.

We should tell a more accurate history – and a herstory: one that doesn't glorify oppression.

We are global citizens. We are a family. We should act like one. We should all take the knee.

A lot of the time we do. The shocking conclusion in Bregman's book, backed up by much research, is 'that most people, deep down, are pretty decent' (2020, p.2).

Never before have we been so in need of each other. Family and community matter more than ever. Our family is humans and our community is planet Earth. One world. United we stand, divided we fall.

It's time for humanity to rediscover itself.

To pass the Humanity Test, you must do three things. You must see yourself as a soul – and be guided by it. You must see everyone else as a soul too – all part of the same family – and respect, salute and greet the light in each person, each human brother and sister, especially if they are undertaking the Advanced Humanity Test. And finally, you must ask each group you belong to or participate in to consider its own soul and engage in its own Group Humanity Test, too.

Better to offer a hand than a fist; to listen and not just talk; to build bridges not walls; to remain curious about and respectful of the experience of others; to pursue an attitude of togethering not othering; to love not fear.

Will we choose to pass the Humanity Test? Individually, collectively, nationally, globally?

It's now or never.

References

Abrams, J.Z. (1998). *Judaism and disability: Portrayals in ancient texts from the Tanach through the Bavli*. Gallaudet University Press.

Acocella, J. (2013, January 6). Rich man, poor man: The radical visions of St. Francis. *The New Yorker*.

Agus, D.B. (2012). *The end of illness*. Simon & Schuster.

Agus, D.B. (2014). *A short guide to a long life*. Simon & Schuster.

Allport, G.W. (1954). *The nature of prejudice*. Addison-Wesley.

Althusser, L. (1971). Ideology and ideological state apparatuses (notes towards an investigation). In L. Althusser (Ed.), *Lenin and philosophy and other essays* (pp.121–176). New Left Books.

American Psychiatric Association (APA) (2013). *Diagnostic and statistical manual of mental disorders (5th ed.) (DSM-5)*. American Psychiatric Association.

Angelou, M. (1978). Still I rise. In *And still I rise: A book of poems*. Random House.

Anisfeld, L. (1993). On the therapist's disability: Opportunities for resolution of obstructed mourning in the transference. *Psychoanalytic Review, 80*, 457–473.

Arkowitz, H. & Lilienfield, S.O. (2012). EMDR: Taking a closer look: Can moving your eyes back and forth help to ease anxiety? *Scientific American Special Editions, 17*(4s), 10–11.

Aron, L. (1991). The patient's experience of the analyst's subjectivity. *Psychoanalytic Dialogues, 1*, 29–51.

Aron, L. (2000). Self-reflexivity and the therapeutic action of psychoanalysis. *Psychoanalytic Psychology, 17*(4), 667–689.

Ashworth, J. (2017). Implications of providing psychotherapy to people with neurological conditions. *Counselling Psychology Review, 32*(4), 70–77.

Bakhtin, M.M. (1981). *The dialogic imagination*. University of Texas.

Balint, M. & Ornstein, P.H. (1992). *The basic fault: Therapeutic aspects of regression*. Northwestern University Press.

Bamberg, M. (2006). Stories: Big or small: Why do we care? *Narrative Inquiry, 16*(1), 139–147.

Bamberg, M. (2011). Who am I? Narration and its contribution to self and identity. *Theory & Psychology, 21*(1), 3–24.

Barker, L.T. & Maralani, V. (1997). *Challenges and strategies of disabled parents: Findings from a national survey of parents with disabilities.* Berkeley Planning Associates.

Barrett, E.A.M. & Birdsall, C. (2008). *What it's like to live with Charcot-Marie-Tooth (CMT): The stories of those who know it best.* Hereditary Neuropathy Foundation.

Barton, J. (1998, December 13). Valley Hopping in the French Alps; Skiing for miles in the Trois-Vallees region of Savoie, with frequent stops for mountain-gazing. *The New York Times.*

Barton, J. (2014, May). Donald Trump: I'm huge! *Golf Digest.*

Barton, J. (2017, October). Love: An expert guide. *Psychologies.*

Barton, J. (2018, May). My last round. *Golf Digest.*

Barton, J. (2020). Therapy for every body. *Therapy Today, 31*(10), 28–31.

Bauby, J.-D. (1997/2002). *The diving-bell and the butterfly.* Harper.

BBC (2005, November 4). *Desert Island Discs: Boris Johnson.* BBC Radio 4.

Beebe, B. & Lachmann, F. (1998). Co-constructing inner and relational processes: Self and mutual regulation in infant research and adult treatment. *Psychoanalytic Psychology, 15,* 1–37.

Benjamin, J. (1990). An outline of intersubjectivity: The development of recognition. *Psychoanalytic Psychology, 7s,* 33–46

Benjamin, M. & Davies, N.J.S. (2021, March 5). Trump and Biden's secret bombing wars: One thing that hasn't changed. *Salon.*

Bercovici, J. (2011, June 14). Why (some) psychopaths make great CEOs. *Forbes.com.*

Berne, E. (1964). *Games people play: The psychology of human relationships.* Penguin.

Berry, E. (2017). Ghost dance. In *Stranger, baby.* Faber & Faber.

Beyond Pesticides (2021, April 14*). Lawsuits mount for Syngenta/ChemChina over claims paraquat herbicide causing Parkinson's disease.* beyondpesticides.org

Binswanger, L. (1963). *Being-in-the-world.* Basic Books.

Bion, W. (1970). *Attention and interpretation.* Karnac.

Bjork, R.A. (1994). Memory and metamemory considerations in the training of human beings. In J. Metcalfe & J.P. Shimamura (Eds.), *Metacognition: Knowing about knowing* (pp.185–205). MIT Press.

Bloom, H. (2007). *T.S. Eliot's The Waste Land.* Chelsea House Publishers.

Bloom, P. (2016). *Against empathy: The case for rational compassion.* The Bodley Head.

Bolsover, N. (2002). Commentary: The 'evidence' is weaker than claimed. *British Medical Journal, 324,* 294.

Boss, M. (1963). *Psychoanalysis and daseinsanalysis*. Basic Books.

Boswell, B., Hamer, M., Knight, S., Glacoff, M. & McChesney, J. (2007). Dance of disability and spirituality. *Journal of Rehabilitation, 73*(4), 33-40.

Bowlby, J. (1991). Postcript. In C.M. Parkes, J. Stevenson-Hinde & P. Marris (Eds.), *Attachment across the life cycle* (pp.293–297). Routledge.

BPS (2021). *Psychological interventions for people with Huntington's disease, Parkinson's disease, motor neurone disease, and multiple sclerosis*. The British Psychological Society.

Brain Research UK (n.d.). *Neuro facts*. [Online.] Brai n Research UK.

Bregman, R. (2020). *Humankind: A hopeful history*. Bloomsbury Publishing.

Breuer, J. & Freud, S. (1895/1995). Studies on hysteria. In J. Strachey (Ed.), *The standard edition of the complete psychological works of Sigmund Freud, vol. II* (pp.1–335). Hogarth Press.

Brewer, M.B. (1991). The social self: On being the same and different at the same time. *Personality and Social Psychology Bulletin, 17*(5), 475–482.

Bromberg, P.M. (2001). *Standing in the spaces: Essays on clinical process, trauma, and dissociation*. Psychology Press.

Bromberg, P.M. (2011). *The shadow of the tsunami and the growth of the relational mind*. Routledge.

Bruner, J. (1987). Life as narrative. *Social Research, 54*(1), 11–32.

Buber, M. (1958). *I and thou*. T. & T. Clark.

Buettner, D. (2010). *The Blue Zones: Lessons for living longer from the people who've lived the longest*. National Geographic.

Bugenthal, J.F.T. (1999). *Psychotherapy isn't what you think: Bringing the psychotherapeutic engagement into the living moment*. Zeig, Tucker & Theisen.

Butler, J. (1990). *Gender trouble*. Routledge.

Butler, J. (1993). *Bodies that matter: On the discursive limits of 'sex'*. Routledge.

Butler, P. (2017, August 31). UN panel criticises UK failure to uphold disabled people's rights. *The Guardian*.

Cameron, J. (1995). *The artist's way*. Pan.

Camus, A. (1942/2013). *The myth of Sisyphus*. Penguin.

Carel, H. (2008). *Illness*. Acumen.

Carel, H. & Kidd, I.J. (2020). Suffering as transformative experience. In D. Bain, M. Brady & J. Corns (Eds.), *Philosophy of suffering: Metaphysics, value, and normativity* (pp.165–179). Routledge.

Carter, G.T., Abresch, E.T. & Fowler, W.M. (1995). Profiles of neuromuscular diseases: Hereditary motor and sensory neuropathy types 1 and 2. *American Journal of Physical Medical Rehabilitation, 74*(5S), S140–149.

Casement, P. (1985). *On learning from the patient*. Routledge.

Casement, P. (1990). The meeting of needs in psychoanalysis. *Psychoanalytic Inquiry, 10*(3), 325–346.

Casement, P. (2006). *Learning from life: Becoming a psychoanalyst*. Routledge.

Chan, F., Chronister, J. & Cardoso, E.D.S. (2009). An introduction to evidence-based practice approach to psychosocial interventions for people with chronic illness and disability. In F. Chan, E. Da Silva Cardoso & J.A. Chronister (Eds.), *Understanding psychosocial adjustment to chronic illness and disability: A handbook for evidence-based practitioners in rehabilitation* (pp. 3–19). Springer Publishing.

Chang, H.J. (2012). *23 things they don't tell you about capitalism*. Bloomsbury Publishing USA.

Charmaz, K. (1995). The body, identity, and self: Adapting to impairment. *The Sociological Quarterly, 36*(4), 657–680.

Chomsky, N. (2003). *For reasons of state*. The New Press.

Chomsky, N. (2008). *Media control: The spectacular achievements of propaganda*. Seven Stories Press.

Cologon, K. (2013). *Inclusion in education: Towards equality for students with disability*. Children with Disability Australia.

Connell, R.W. (2005). *Masculinities*. University of California Press.

Cooper. M. (2008). *Essential research findings in counselling and psychotherapy: The facts are friendly*. Sage.

Cooper, M. (2012). *The existential counselling primer*. PCCS Books.

Cozolino, L.J. (2010). *The neuroscience of psychotherapy*. W.W. Norton & Co.

Cozolino, L. (2014). *The neuroscience of human relationships: Attachment and the developing social brain* (2nd ed.). W.W. Norton & Co.

Cromby, J. (2014). Depression: embodying social inequality. *Journal of Critical Psychology, Counselling and Psychotherapy, 14*(3), 179–189.

Cyrus, K. (2017). Multiple minorities as multiply marginalized: Applying the minority stress theory to LGBTQ people of color. *Journal of Gay & Lesbian Mental Health, 21*(3), 194–202.

Dahl, R. (1991). *The Minpins*. Penguin.

Damasio, A. (2000). *The feeling of what happens: Body, emotion and the making of consciousness*. Vintage.

D'Andrea, M. & Daniels, J. (2001). Expanding our thinking about white racism: Facing the challenge of multicultural counseling in the 21st century. In J.G. Ponterotto, J.M. Casas, L.A. Suzuki & C.M. Alexander (Eds.), *Handbook of multicultural counseling* (2nd ed.) (pp.289–309). Sage.

Darwin, C. (1859/1909). *On the origin of species*. P.F. Collier & Son.

Dawkins, R. (1978). *The selfish gene*. Flamingo.

Deal, M. (2007). Aversive disablism: Subtle prejudice toward disabled people. *Disability & Society*, *22*(1), 93–107. de Boer, A., Pijl, S.P. & Minnaert, A. (2010). Attitudes of parents towards inclusive education: A review of the literature. *European Journal of Special Needs Education*, *25*(2), 165–181.

Department for Work and Pensions (2020). *Family resources survey: Financial year 2018/19*. www.gov.uk/government/statistics/family-resources-survey-financial-year-201819

Dikötter, F. (1998). Race culture: Recent perspectives on the history of eugenics. *The American Historical Review*, *103*(2), 467–478.

Dion, K., Berscheid, E. & Walster, E. (1972). What is beautiful is good. *Journal of Personality and Social Psychology*, *24*(3), 285–290.

Disabled People Against Cuts (DPAC) (2015, September 7). *The IDS Files: DWP caught giving disability propaganda to Daily Mail*. https://dpac.uk.net/2015/09/the-ids-files-dwp-caught-giving-disability-propaganda-to-daily-mail-idsfiles/

Disability Rights International (DRI). (2018). *Infanticide and abuse: Killing and confinement of children with disabilities in Kenya*. Disability Rights International/Kenyan Association for the Intellectually Handicapped.

Disability Rights UK (2017, August 31). *A human catastrophe – New UN condemnation for UK human rights record*. www.disabilityrightsuk.org/news/2017/august/human-catastrophe-%E2%80%93-new-un-condemnation-uk-human-rights-record

Disabled World (2021). *Disability statistics: Information, charts, graphs and tables*. www.disabled-world.com/disability/statistics/

Dorsey, R., Sherer, T., Okun, M.S. & Bloem, B. (2020). *A prescription for action: Ending Parkinson's disease*. PublicAffairs.

Dovidio, J.F., Hewstone, M., Glick, P. & Esses, V.M. (2010). *Prejudice, stereotyping and discrimination*. Sage.

Dreifus, C. (2011, May 9). Life and the cosmos, word by painstaking word. *The New York Times*.

Drozek, R.P. (2010). Intersubjectivity theory and the dilemma of intersubjective motivation. *Psychoanalytic Dialogues*, *20*(5), 540–560.

Dube, O. & Harish, S.P. (2020). Queens. *Journal of Political Economy*, *128*(7), 2579–2652.

Dunn, D.S. (2015). *The social psychology of disability*. Oxford University Press.

Durant, W. (1961). *The story of philosophy*. Simon & Schuster.

Durkheim, E. (1897/2005). *Suicide: A study in sociology*. Routledge.

Dworkin, E. (2013). *Religion without God*. Harvard University Press.

Eagleman, D. (2010). *Sum: Tales from the afterlife*. Canongate.

Edwards, B. (2008). *Drawing on the right side of the brain*. HarperCollins.

Edwards, M.J. (2021). Functional neurological disorder: Lighting the way to a new paradigm for medicine. *Brain, 144*(11), 3279–3282. doi: 10.1093/brain/awab358

Ehrenreich, B. (2010). *Smile or die: How positive thinking fooled America and the world*. Granta.

Eigen, M. (2018). *The challenge of being human*. Routledge.

Einstein, A. (1977). Cited in H. Eves (Ed.), *Mathematical circles adieu*. Prindle, Weber & Schmidt.

Eleftheriadou, Z. (2010). Cross-cultural counselling psychology. In R. Woolfe, S. Strawbridge, B. Douglas & W. Dryden (Eds.), *Handbook of counselling psychology* (3rd ed.) (pp.195–212). Sage.

Ellemers, N., Spears, R. & Doosje, B. (2002). Self and social identity. *Annual Review of Psychology, 53*(1), 161–186.

Erikson, E.H. (1968). *Identity*. W.W. Norton & Co.

Erskine, R.G., Moursund, J. & Trautmann, R. (2013). *Beyond empathy: A therapy of contact-in relationships*. Routledge.

Fairbairn, W.D. (1952). *Psychoanalytic studies of the personality*. Tavistock Publications.

Farber, S.K. (2017). *Celebrating the wounded healer psychotherapist: Pain, post-traumatic growth and self-disclosure*. Taylor & Francis.

Feeley, J. (2021, September 13). Syngenta, Chevron could face billions in claims over weed killer. *Bloomberg*. www.bloomberg.com

Feldman, J. (2021). EPA ban on chlorpyrifos huge victory for children — but it took far too long, and we still have far to go. *The Defender*. https://childrenshealthdefense.org/

Ferenczi, S. (1932/1988). Confusion of tongues between adults and the child. *Contemporary Psychoanalysis, 24*(2), 196–206.

Fifield, P. (2020). *Modernism and physical illness: Sick books*. Oxford University Press.

Fink, B. (1999). The ethics of psychoanalysis: A Lacanian perspective. *Psychoanalytic Review, 86*(4), 529–554.

Fisher, H.E., Aron, A. & Brown, L.L. (2006). Romantic love: A mammalian brain system for mate choice. *Philosophical Transactions of the Royal Society, 361*(1476), 2173–2186.

Fiske, S.T. (2011). *Envy up, scorn down: How status divides us*. Russell Sage Foundation.

Fiske, S.T., Cuddy, A.J. & Glick, P. (2007). Universal dimensions of social cognition: Warmth and competence. *Trends in Cognitive Sciences, 11*(2), 77–83.

Fletcher, M. (2016, July 1). Boris Johnson peddled absurd EU myths – and our disgraceful press followed his lead. *The New Statesman*.

Florian, L., & Spratt, J. (2013). Enacting inclusion: A framework for interrogating inclusive practice. *European Journal of Special Needs Education, 28*(2), 119–135.

Flynn, S. (2020). Theorizing disability in child protection: Applying critical disability studies to the elevated risk of abuse for disabled children. *Disability & Society, 35*(6), 949–971.

Fonagy, P. (2001). *Attachment theory and psychoanalysis.* Karnac Books.

Ford, B.Q., Dmitrieva, J.O., Heller, D., Chentsova-Dutton, Y., Grossmann, I., Tamir, M., Uchida, Y., Koopmann-Holm, B., Floerke, V.A., Uhrig, M., Bokhan, T. & Mauss, I.B. (2015). Culture shapes whether the pursuit of happiness predicts higher or lower well-being. *Journal of Experimental Psychology: General, 144*(6), 1053–1062.

Foucault, M. (1963). *The birth of the clinic.* Routledge.

Foucault, M. (1964). *Madness and civilization: A history of insanity in the Age of Reason.* Vintage.

Foucault, M. (1980). *Power/knowledge: Selected interviews and other writings, 1972–1977.* Pantheon.

Foucault, M. (1988). *Technologies of the self: A seminar with Michel Foucault.* University of Massachusetts Press.

Frank, A. (1995). *The wounded storyteller.* Chicago University Press.

Frankl, V.E. (1946/2004). *Man's search for meaning.* Rider.

Fraser, N. (2000). Rethinking recognition, *New Left Review, 3*(3), 107–118.

Freud, S. (1899/1955). *The interpretation of dreams.* Basic Books.

Freud, S. (1913/2001). Totem and taboo. In J. Strachey (Ed.), *The standard edition of the complete psychological works of Sigmund Freud, volume 13.* Vintage Classics.

Freud, S. (1917/2001). Mourning and melancholia. In J. Strachey (Ed.), *The standard edition of the complete psychological works of Sigmund Freud, volume 14* (pp.237–258). Vintage Classics.

Freud, S. (1923a/1961). The ego and the id. In J. Strachey (Ed.), *The standard edition of the complete psychological works of Sigmund Freud, volume XIX.* Hogarth Press.

Freud, S. (1923b/1975). Two encyclopaedia articles. In J. Strachey (Ed.), *The standard edition of the complete psychological works of Sigmund Freud, volume XVIII* (pp.235–259). Hogarth Press.

Freud, S. (1930/1961). Civilization and its discontents. In J. Strachey (Ed.), *The standard edition of the complete psychological works of Sigmund Freud, volume XXI.* Hogarth Press/Institute of Psycho-Analysis.

Fromm, E. (1955/2001). *The sane society.* Routledge Classics.

Fromm, E. (1957/1995). *The art of loving.* HarperCollins.

Fry, S. (2015, January 31). Stephen Fry explains what he would say if he was 'confronted by God'. *The Independent.* www.independent.co.uk/news/people/stephen-fry-explains-what-he-would-say-if-he-was-confronted-by-god-10015360.html

Gallese, V. (2015). Which neurosciences and which psychoanalysis? Intersubjectivity and bodily self: Notes for a dialogue. *The Italian Psychoanalytic Annual, 9,*189–203.

Garland-Thomson, R. (2011). Misfits: A feminist materialist disability concept. *Hypatia, 26*(3), 591–609.

Georgakopoulou, A. (2006). Thinking big with small stories in narrative and identity analysis. *Narrative inquiry, 16*(1), 122–130.

Gergen, K.J. (1990). Toward a postmodern psychology. *The Humanistic Psychologist, 18*(1), 23–34.

Gerhardt, S. (2004/2015). *Why love matters: How affection shapes a baby's brain* (2nd ed.). Routledge.

Gerhardt, S. (2010). *The selfish society.* Simon & Schuster.

Gerrard, J. (2003). *The impossibility of knowing.* Karnac Books.

Gibran, K. (1926/1992). *The prophet.* Penguin.

Giddens, A. (1991). *Modernity and self-identity self and society in the late modern age.* Polity Press.

Gilbert, D.T. & Malone, P.S. (1995). The correspondence bias. *Psychological Bulletin, 117*(1), 21–38.

Gladwell, M. (2006). *Blink: The power of thinking without thinking.* Penguin.

Gladwell, M. (2013). *David and Goliath: Underdogs, misfits, and the art of battling giants.* Penguin.

Goffman, E. (1959). *The presentation of self in everyday life.* Penguin.

Goffman, E. (1963). *Stigma: Notes on the management of spoiled identity.* Penguin.

Goodall, J. (1986). *The chimpanzees of Gombe: patterns of behavior.* Harvard University Press.

Gould, S.J. (1981) *The mismeasure of man.* W.W. Norton & Co.

Greenberger, D. & Padesky, C.-A. (1995). *Mind over mood.* Guilford Press.

Gupta, V.B. (2011). How Hindus cope with disability. *Journal of Religion, Disability & Health, 15*(1), 72–78.

Hafiz. (2011). *The collected poems of Hafiz.* (J. Payne, trans.). Digireads.com

Hahn, H. (1985). Toward a politics of disability: Definitions, disciplines, and policies. *The Social Science Journal, 22*(4), 87–105.

Halacre, M. (2020). *Working with disability across the counselling professions.* British Association for Counselling & Psychotherapy.

Halacre, M. & Jalil, R. (2017). Holistic therapy with disabled adults from a social and individual perspective: A service evaluation feasibility study. *Counselling and Psychotherapy Research, 17*(4), 320–329.

Halperin, D.M. (1995). *Saint Foucault: Towards a gay hagiography.* Oxford University Press.

Hare, R.-D. (1993/1999). *Without conscience: The disturbing world of the psychopaths among us.* Guilford Press.

Hari, J. (2018, June 13). We need new ways of treating depression. *Vox.*

Harris, T.A. (1995). *I'm OK – You're OK.* Arrow Books.

Hastings, M. (2019, June 24). I was Boris Johnson's boss: He is utterly unfit to be prime minister. *The Guardian.*

Hay, L. (1984). *You can heal your life.* Hay House.

Heidegger, M. (1927/1962). *Being and time.* Harper & Row.

Herman, J. (1992). *Trauma and recovery: The aftermath of violence – from domestic abuse to political terror.* Basic Books.

Hillman, J. (1992). *The thought of the heart and the soul of the world.* Spring Publications.

Hinde, R.A. & Stevenson-Hinde, J. (1991). Perspectives on attachment. In C.M. Parkes, J. Stevenson-Hinde & P. Marris (Eds.), *Attachment across the life cycle* (pp.52–65). Routledge.

Hollis, J. (1992). *The Eden Project: In search of the magical other.* Inner City Books.

Hollis, J. (1993). *The middle passage: From misery to meaning in midlife.* Inner City Books.

Hollis, J. (1994). *Under Saturn's shadow: The wounding and healing of men.* Inner City Books.

Holmes, J. (2002). All you need is cognitive behavior therapy? *British Medical Journal, 324*(7332), 288–290.

hooks, b. (2004). *The will to change: Men, masculinity, and love* (Reprint ed.). Washington Square Press.

Horney, K. (1950/1991). *Neurosis and human growth: The struggle towards self-realization.* W.W. Norton & Co.

Houben, S.T., Otgaar, H., Roelofs, J. & Merckelbach, H. (2018). Lateral eye movements increase false memory rates. *Clinical Psychological Science, 6*(4), 610–616.

Howe, D. (2006). Disabled children, parent-child interaction and attachment. *Child & Family Social Work, 11*(2), 95–106.

HSE (2021). *Workplace fatal injuries in Great Britain.* Health and Safety Executive.

Husserl, E. (1927). Phenomenology. *Encyclopedia Britannic, 17,* 699–702.

Hustvedt, S. (2010). *The shaking woman or a history of my nerves*. Sceptre.

Huxley, A. (1954) *The doors of perception*. Chatto & Windus.

Hycner, R.H. (1993) *Between person and person: Toward a dialogical psychotherapy*. Gestalt Journal Press.

Illich, I. (1976/2010). *Limits to medicine. Medical nemesis: The expropriation of health*. Marion Boyars.

International Organization for Migration (IOM) (2021). *Persons with disabilities and their representative organisations in Iraq: Barriers, challenges and priorities*. International Organization for Migration.

Jabin, N. (1987). Attitudes toward disability: Horney's theory applied. *American Journal of Psychoanalysis, 47*(2), 143–153.

James, W. (1896/1956). *The will to believe*. Dover Publications.

James, W. (1902/2003). *The varieties of religious experience*. Routledge.

Janet, P. (1889/2010). *The mental state of hystericals: A study of mental stigmata and mental accidents*. Nabu Press.

Jannoff-Bulman, R. (1992). *Shattered assumptions: Towards a new psychology of trauma*. Macmillan.

Jeffers, S. (1987). *Feel the fear and do it anyway*. Random House.

Jenkins, R. (2008). *Social identity* (3rd ed.). Routledge.

Johnson, B. (2021). *PM speech at the UN General Assembly: 22 September 2021*. www.gov.uk/government/speeches/pm-speech-at-the-un-general-assembly-22-september-2021

Johnson, J.D. & Lecci, L. (2003). Assessing anti-white attitudes and predicting perceived racism: The Johnson-Lecci scale. *Personality and Social Psychology Bulletin, 29*(3), 299–312.

Johnson, J.D., Trawalter, S. & Dovidio, J.F. (2000). Converging interracial consequences of exposure to violent rap music on stereotypical attributions of blacks. *Journal of Experimental Social Psychology, 36*(3), 233–251.

Jones, L., Bellis, M. A., Wood, S., Hughes, K., McCoy, E., Eckley, L., Bates, G., Mikton, C., Shakespeare, T. & Officer, A. (2012). Prevalence and risk of violence against children with disabilities: A systematic review and meta-analysis of observational studies. *The Lancet, 380*(9845), 899–907.

Jones, M. (2007). Judaism, theology and the human rights of people with disabilities. *Journal of Religion, Disability & Health, 10*(3–4), 101–114.

Jung, C.G. (1933/2014). *Modern man in search of a soul*. Routledge.

Jung, C.G. (1957). *The undiscovered self*. American Library.

Jung, C.G. (1961/1995). *Memories, dreams, reflections*. Fontana.

Jung, C.G. (1973). *Collected works of CG Jung: The first complete English edition of the works of CG Jung*. Routledge.

Jung, C.G. (1992). *C.G. Jung letters, volume 1*. Princeton University Press.

Jung, C.G. (2009). *The red book: Liber novus*. W.W. Norton & Co.

Kalsched, D. (2013). *Trauma and the soul: A psycho-spiritual approach to human development and its interruption*. Routledge.

Karpman, S. (1968). Fairy tales and script drama analysis. *Transactional Analysis Bulletin, 7*(26), 39–43.

Kasser, T. (2016). Materialistic values and goals. *Annual Review of Psychology, 67,* 489–514.

Kattari, S.K., Olzman, M., & Hanna, M.D. (2018). 'You look fine!' Ableist experiences by people with invisible disabilities. *Affilia, 33*(4), doi. org/10.1177/0886109918778073

Kaufmann, W. (1954). *The portable Nietzsche*. Viking Penguin.

Kavanagh, A.M., Krnjacki, L., Aitken, Z., LaMontagne, A. D., Beer, A., Baker, E. & Bentley, R. (2015). Intersections between disability, type of impairment, gender and socio-economic disadvantage in a nationally representative sample of 33,101 working-aged Australians. *Disability and Health Journal, 8*(2), 191–199.

Kavanagh, P. (2004). *Collected poems*. Penguin Modern Classics.

Keats, J. (1819). *Letter to Fanny Keats*. keats-poems.com

Keats, J. (2007). *John Keats, selected poems*. Penguin.

Kleinman, A. (1988). *The illness narratives*. Basic Books.

Kohut, H. (1971). *The analysis of the self*. International Universities Press.

Kohut, H. (1984). *How does analysis cure?* University of Chicago Press.

Koshy, K.T. (1977). *Revision notes on psychiatry*. Hodder & Stoughton.

Krabbendam, L. & Van Os, J. (2005). Schizophrenia and urbanicity: A major environmental influence – conditional on genetic risk. *Schizophrenia Bulletin, 31*(4), 795–799.

Kradin, R. (2005). The roots of empathy and aggression in analysis. *Journal of Analytic Psychology, 50,* 431–449.

Krishnamurti, J. (1956). *Commentaries on living: First series*. Penguin Books India.

Kübler-Ross. E. (1969). *On death and dying*. Tavistock Publications.

Kvale, S. (1992). *Psychology and postmodernism*. Sage.

Lago, C. (2006). *Race, culture and counselling: The ongoing challenge*. Open University Press.

Lago, C. & Moodley, R. (2002). Multicultural issues in eclectic and integrative counselling and psychotherapy. In S. Palmer (Ed), *Multicultural counselling: A reader* (pp.40–56). Sage.

Laing, R.D. (1960). *The divided self*. Penguin.

Lanier, J. (2018). *Ten arguments for deleting your social media accounts right now.* Penguin.

Larkin, P. (2003). This be the verse. In *The Collected Works* (p.142). Faber & Faber.

Lasch, C. (1979). *The culture of narcissism: American life in an age of diminishing expectations.* W.W. Norton.

Laverty, S.M. (2003). Hermeneutic phenomenology and phenomenology: A comparison of historical and methodological considerations. *International Journal of Qualitative Methods, 2*(3), 21–35.

Leader, D. & Corfield, D. (2008). *Why do people get ill?* Penguin.

Lederbogen, F., Kirsch, P., Haddad, L., Streit, F., Tost, H., Schuch, P. & Meyer-Lindenberg, A. (2011). City living and urban upbringing affect neural social stress processing in humans. *Nature, 474*(7352), 498–501.

Leichsenring, F. & Steinert, C. (2017). Is cognitive behavioral therapy the gold standard for psychotherapy? The need for plurality in treatment and research. *Jama, 318*(14), 1323–1324.

Levine, P.A. (1997). *Waking the tiger: Healing trauma.* North Atlantic Books.

Levitt, J.M. (2017). Developing a model of disability that focuses on the actions of disabled people. *Disability & Society, 32*(5), 735–747.

Lewin, K. (1935). *A dynamic theory of personality.* McGraw-Hill.

Lewis, T., Amini, F. & Lannon, R. (2001). *A general theory of love.* Knopf Doubleday.

Libet, B. (1981). The experimental evidence for subjective referral of a sensory experience backwards in time: Reply to P.S. Churchland. *Philosophy of Science, 48*(2), 182–197.

Libet, B., Gleason, C.A., Wright, E.W. & Pearl, D.K. (1983). Time of conscious intention to act in relation to onset of cerebral activity (readiness-potential) the unconscious initiation of a freely voluntary act. *Brain, 106*(3), 623–642.

Lichtenberg, J.D., Lachmann, F.M. & Fosshage, J.L. (2011). *Psychoanalysis and motivational systems: A new look.* Taylor & Francis.

Lippman, W. (1922/2012). *Public opinion.* Martino Fine.

Livneh, H. (1984). A unified approach to existing models of adaptation to disability. Part I: A model adaptation. *Journal of Applied Rehabilitation Counseling, 17*(1), 5–17.

Livneh, H. (2001). Psychosocial adaptation to chronic illness and disability: A conceptual framework. *Rehabilitation Counseling Bulletin, 44*(3), 151–160.

Livneh, H. & Antonak R.F. (2005). Psychosocial adaptation to chronic illness and disability: A primer for counselors. *Journal of Counseling & Development, 83*(1), 12–20.

Livneh, H. & Parker, R.M. (2005). Psychological adaptation to disability: Perspectives from chaos and complexity theory. *Rehabilitation Counseling Bulletin, 49*(1), 17–28.

Logan, J. (2008). Analysis of the incidence of dyslexia in entrepreneurs and its implications. In *United States Association for Small Business and Entrepreneurship: Conference proceedings* (p.636). United States Association for Small Business and Entrepreneurship.

Lovelock, J.E. (1988). *The ages of Gaia*. Oxford University Press.

Luca, A., Nicoletti, A., Mostile, G. & Zappia, M. (2019). The Parkinsonian personality: More than just a 'trait'. *Frontiers in Neurology, 9*, 1191. https://doi.org/10.3389/fneur.2018.01191

Macrae, C.N. & Quadflieg, S. (2010). Perceiving people. In S.T. Fiske, D.T. Gilbert & G. Lindzey (Eds.), *Handbook of social psychology* (pp.428–463). John Wiley & Sons.

Mamdani, M. (2004). *Good Muslim, bad Muslim: America, the Cold War, and the roots of terror*. Pantheon Books.

Mann, J. (2014, September 28). British sex survey 2014: 'The nation has lost some of its sexual swagger'. *The Guardian*.

Marinelli, R.P. (2007). Foreword. In A.E. Dell Orto & P.W. Power (Eds.), *The psychological and social impact of illness and disability* (5th ed.) (pp.xxi–xxii). Springer.

Markus, H. & Nurius, P. (1986). Possible selves. *American Psychologist, 41*(9), 454–969.

Marrone, M. & Cortina, M. (2003). *Attachment theory and the psychoanalytic process*. Whurr Publishers.

Marshall, C. & Prior, M. (2022, April 1). *UK farmers call for weedkiller ban over Parkinson's fears*. BBC News.

Maslow, A.H. (1943). A theory of human motivation. *Psychological Review, 50*, 370–396.

Matsumoto, T., Itoh, N., Inoue, S. & Nakamura, M. (2016). An observation of a severely disabled infant chimpanzee in the wild and her interactions with her mother. *Primates, 57*(1), 3–7.

Mattson M.P. (2008). Hormesis defined. *Ageing Research Reviews, 7*(1), 1–7.

May, R. (1967). *Psychology and the human dilemma*. Van Nostrand.

McGilchrist, I. (2010). *The Master and his emissary*. Yale University Press.

McLeod, J. (2001). *Qualitative research in counselling and psychotherapy*. Sage.

Mearns, D. & Cooper, M. (2005). *Working at relational depth in counselling and psychotherapy*. Sage.

Mental Health Foundation (2018). *Stressed nation: 74% of UK 'overwhelmed or unable to cope' at some point in the past year*. Mental Health Foundation.

Mental Health Foundation (2021). *Men and mental health*. [Online]. www.mentalhealth.org.uk/a-to-z/m/men-and-mental-health

Merleau-Ponty, M. (1945/2002). *Phenomenology of perception*. Routledge & Kegan Paul.

Mills, J. (2005). A critique of relational psychoanalysis. *Psychoanalytic Psychology*, 22(2), 155–188.

Mind (2020). *Get it off your chest: Men's mental health 10 years on.* Mind Publications.

Misra, T. (2016, April 11). Geography and life expectancy are linked for low-income Americans. *Bloomberg CityLab*.

Mitchell, S.A. (1988). *Relational concepts in psychoanalysis: An integration.* Harvard University Press.

Mitra, S. (2018). *Disability, health and human development.* Palgrave Macmillan.

Monteith, M.J. & Spicer, C.V. (2000). Contents and correlates of Whites' and Blacks' racial attitudes. *Journal of Experimental Social Psychology, 36(2)*, 125–154.

Moore, T. (1992). *Care of the soul.* Harper Collins.

Morris, J. (2014). *Pride against prejudice: Transforming attitudes to disability.* Women's Press.

Moustakas, C.E. (1961). *Loneliness.* Prentice-Hall.

Napoleoni, L. (2003). *Terror Inc.: Tracing the money behind global terrorism.* Penguin.

Neville, B. (2012). *The life of things: Therapy and the soul of the world.* PCCS Books.

Neville, B. (2020). *The gods in a time of corona.* Carla van Laar.

NHS Digital (2020a). *Mental Health Act statistics, annual figures 2019–20.* https://digital.nhs.uk/

NHS Digital (2020b). *Statistics on alcohol, England 2020.* https://digital.nhs.uk/

O'Donohue, J. (2007). *Benedictus: A book of blessings.* Transworld.

Office for National Statistics (ONS) (2021a). *Suicides in England and Wales: 2020 registrations.* Office for National Statistics.

Office for National Statistics (ONS) (2021b). *National life tables – life expectancy in the UK: 2018 to 2020.* Office for National Statistics.

Ogden, T.H. (1994). The analytic third: Working with intersubjective clinical facts. *International Journal of Psycho-Analysis, 75*, 3–19.

Ogden, T.H. & Gabbard, G.O. (2010). The lure of the symptom in psychoanalytic treatment. *Journal of the American Psychoanalytic Association, 5(3)*, 533–544.

Oken D. (2007). Evolution of psychosomatic diagnosis in DSM. *Psychosomatic Medicine, 69(9)*, 830–831.

Oliver M. (1996) *Understanding disability: From theory to practice.* Macmillan Press.

Olkin, R. (1999). *What psychotherapists should know about disability.* Guilford Press.

Olkin, R. & Pledger, C. (2003). Can disability studies and psychology join hands? *American Psychologist, 58*(4), 296–304.

Olshansky, S. (1962). Chronic sorrow: A response to having a mentally defective child. *Social Casework, 43*(4), 190–193.

Oppenheimer, M. (2008, May 4). The queen of the new age. *The New York Times.*

Organisation for Economic Co-operation and Development (OECD) (2015). *In it together: Why less inequality benefits all.* OECD Publishing.

Organisation for Economic Co-operation and Development (OECD) (2021). *Income inequality.* [Online]. OECD. https://data.oecd.org/inequality/income-inequality.htm

Orlans, V. & Van Scoyoc, S. (2009). *A short introduction to counselling psychology.* Sage.

Ostrove, J.M. & Crawford, D. (2006). 'One lady was so busy staring at me she walked into a wall': Interability relations from the perspective of women with disabilities. *Disability Studies Quarterly, 26*(3). https://doi.org/10.18061/dsq.v26i3.717

Owens, J. (2015). Exploring the critiques of the social model of disability: The transformative possibility of Arendt's notion of power. *Sociology of Health & Illness, 37*(3), 385–403.

Paley, V.G. (2000). *The kindness of children.* Harvard University Press.

Papadopoulos, I. (2006). The Papadopoulos, Tilki and Taylor model of developing cultural competence. In I. Papadopoulos (Ed.), *Transcultural health and social care: Development of culturally competent practitioners* (pp.7–24). Churchill Livingstone/Elsevier.

Parkinson, J. (1817/2002). An essay on the shaking palsy. *The Journal of Neuropsychiatry and Clinical Neurosciences, 14*(2), 223–236.

Peale, N.V. (1952/2012). *The power of positive thinking.* Random House.

Peen, J., Schoevers, R.A., Beekman, A.T., & Dekker, J. (2010). The current status of urban-rural differences in psychiatric disorders. *Acta Psychiatrica Scandinavica, 121*(2), 84–93.

Pennisi, E. (2013, June 19). Why naked mole rats don't get cancer. *Science.* www.science.org/content/article/why-naked-mole-rats-dont-get-cancer

Peters, W. (1971). *A class divided.* Doubleday.

Pettigrew, T.F. (1979). Foreword. In G.W. Allport, *The nature of prejudice* (pp.xiii–xv). Addison-Wesley.

Phillips, A. & Taylor, B. (2009). *On kindness.* Macmillan.

Phillips, S. (2016, October 5). Sally Phillips: Society wants to stop Down syndrome babies being born – and it's wrong. *RadioTimes.* www.radiotimes.com/tv/documentaries/sally-phillips-society-wants-to-stop-down-syndrome-babies-being-born-and-its-wrong/

Piketty, T. (2014). *Capital in the twenty-first century*. Harvard University Press.

Polanyi, K. (1944/2002). *The great transformation: The political and economic origins of our time*. Beacon Press.

Polkinghorne, D.E. (1988). *Narrative knowing and the human sciences*. State University of New York Press.

Pollan, M. (2007, January 28). Unhappy meals. *The New York Times Magazine*. www.nytimes.com/2007/01/28/magazine/28nutritionism.t.html

Pop, I. & Houellebecq, M. (2018). *To stay alive – Method (Rester vivant: méthode)* (A. Hagers, E. Lieshout (Dirs.). Damned Films.

Prandota Trzcinski, A. (2018). *Advanced biological, physical, and chemical treatment of waste activated sludge*. CRC Press.

Prashad, V. (2000). *The karma of brown folk*. University of Minnesota Press.

Radford, L., Corral, S., Bradley, C., Fisher, H., Bassett, C., Howat, N. & Collishaw, S. (2011). *Child abuse and neglect in the UK today*. NSPCC.

Rawls, J. (1971/1999). *A theory of justice*. Oxford University Press.

Richardson, J.E. (2004). *(Mis)representing Islam: The racism and rhetoric of British broadsheet newspapers*. John Benjamins.

Ricoeur, P. (1981). *Hermeneutics and the human sciences: Essays on language, action and interpretation*. Cambridge University Press.

Ricoeur, P. (1984) *Time and narrative, volume 1*. University of Chicago Press.

Rieff, P. (1966). *The triumph of the therapeutic: Uses of faith after Freud*. Harper & Row.

Rodenburg, P. (2007). *Presence: How to use positive energy for success*. Penguin.

Rogers, C. (1957). The necessary and sufficient conditions of therapeutic personality change. *Journal of Consulting Psychology, 21*, 95–103.

Rogers, C. (1961). *On becoming a person: A therapist's view of psychotherapy*. Houghton Mifflin.

Rollins, H.E. (1958). *The letters of John Keats, 1814–1821*. Harvard University Press.

Ronson, J. (2012). *The psychopath test: A journey through the madness industry*. Picador.

Rosen, M. (2020). *Michael Rosen's book of play*. Wellcome Collection.

Rothschild, B. (2000). *The body remembers: The psychophysiology of trauma and trauma treatment*. W.W. Norton & Co.

Rousseau, J.-J. (1762/1998). *The social contract*. Wordsworth Editions.

Rowan, J. (1990). *Subpersonalities: The people inside us*. Routledge.

Rowan, J. (2005). *The transpersonal: Spirituality in psychotherapy and counselling*. Routledge.

Rumi, J. (1995). *The essential Rumi*. Harper Collins.

Russell, B. (2013). *History of Western philosophy: Collectors' edition*. Routledge.

Ryan, F. (2020). *Crippled: Austerity and the demonization of disabled people*. Verso.

Sacks, O. (1995). *An anthropologist on Mars*. Picador.

Sacks O. (2010, December 31). This year, change your mind. *The New York Times*.

Saeed, A. (2013). *Reading the Qur'an in the twenty-first century: A contextualist approach*. Routledge.

Safran, J.D. & Muran, J.C. (1996). The resolution of ruptures in the therapeutic alliance. *Journal of Consulting and Clinical Psychology, 64*(3), 447–458.

Said, E. (1978/2003). *Orientalism*. Penguin.

Saint-Exupéry, A. de (1943/2018). *The little prince*. Verbum.

Sanderson, C. (2015). *Counselling skills for working with shame*. Jessica Kingsley.

Sartre, J.-P. (1957/2002). *Existentialism and human emotions*. Citadel.

Savage, M. (2019). Being depressed in the 'world's happiest country'. *BBC Worklife*. www.bbc.com

Schaller, M., Miller, G.E., Gervais, W.M., Yager, S. & Chen, E. (2010). Mere visual perception of other people's disease symptoms facilitates a more aggressive immune response. *Psychological Science, 21*(5), 649–652.

Schoenberg, P. (2007). *Psychosomatics: The uses of psychotherapy*. Palgrave Macmillan.

Schopenhauer, A. (1850/2005). *On the suffering of the world*. Penguin.

Schore, A.N. (2012). *The science of the art of psychotherapy*. W.W. Norton & Co.

Scope (2019). *Disability price tag*. [Online]. www.scope.org.uk/campaigns/extra-costs/disability-price-tag/

Scrutton, T. (2020). 'My horses and hogs and even everybody seemed changed': Appreciating beauty in depression recovery. In D. Bain, M. Brady & J. Corns (Eds.), *Philosophy of suffering: Metaphysics, value, and normativity* (pp.211–226). Routledge.

Segal, J. (1996). Whose disability? Countertransference in work with people with disabilities. *Psychodynamic Counselling, 2*(2), 155–166.

Sen, A. (2003). Missing women – revisited. *British Medical Journal, 327*(7427), 1297–1298.

Sen, A. (2006). *Identity and violence: The illusion of destiny*. Penguin.

Shakespeare, T. (2018). *Disability: The basics*. Routledge.

Shakespeare, T. & Watson, N. (1997). Defending the social model. *Disability & Society, 12*(2), 293–300.

Sherif, M., Harvey, O.J., White, B.J., Hood, W.R. & Sherif, C.W. (1961). *Intergroup conflict and cooperation: The Robbers Cave experiment.* University Book Exchange.

Sherry, M. (2004). Overlaps and contradictions between queer theory and disability studies. *Disability & Society, 19*(7), 769–783.

Shy, M.E. & Rose, M.R. (2005). Charcot–Marie–Tooth disease impairs quality of life: Why? And how do we improve it? *Neurology, 6,* 790–791.

Siegel, D.J. (1999). *The developing mind.* Guilford Press.

Sikes, C. & Sikes, V. (2003). EMDR: Why the controversy? *Traumatology, 9*(3), 169–182.

Singer, P. (2011). *Practical ethics.* Cambridge University Press.

Smail, D. (2005). *Power, interest and psychology: Elements of a social materialist understanding of distress.* PCCS Books.

Smart, A. & Smart, J. (2012). *Petty capitalists and globalization: Flexibility, entrepreneurship, and economic development.* SUNY Press.

Smart, J. (2001). *Disability, society, and the individual.* Aspen Publishers.

Smith, J.A. (2019). Participants and researchers searching for meaning: Conceptual developments for interpretative phenomenological analysis. *Qualitative Research in Psychology 16*(2), 166–181.

Smith, J.A., Flowers, P. & Larkin, M. (2009). *Interpretive phenomenological analysis: Theory, method, and research.* Sage.

Smith, J.D. & Polloway, E.A. (2013). Intellectual disabilities and dystopian visions: Ayn Rand and Edgar Rice Burroughs. *Intellectual and Developmental Disabilities, 51*(3), 201–205.

Söder, M. (1990). Prejudice or ambivalence? Attitudes toward persons with disabilities. *Disability, Handicap & Society, 5*(3), 227–241.

Sontag, S. (1977). *Illness as metaphor.* Penguin.

Spinelli, E. (2006). *Tales of un-knowing: Therapeutic encounters from an existential perspective.* PCCS Books.

Spinelli, E. (2007). *Practising existential psychotherapy.* Sage.

Stangor, C. (2013) *Social groups in action and interaction.* Psychology Press.

Stern, D.N., Sander, L.W., Nahum, J.P., Harrison, A.M., Lyons-Ruth, K., Morgan, A.C., Bruschweiler-Stern, N. & Tronick, E.Z. (1998). Non-interpretive mechanisms in psychoanalytic therapy. The 'something more' than interpretation. *International Journal of Psychoanalysis, 79*(Pt5), 903–921.

Stiker, H.J. (1997). *A history of disability.* University of Michigan Press.

Stiker, H.J. (2017). Bodies lost and bodies gained: The major periods in the history of disability. In S.K. Korff Sausse & R. Scelles (Eds.), *The clinic of disability: Psychoanalytical approaches* (pp.147–162). Karnac.

Stolorow, R.D. & Atwood, G. (1992). *Contexts of being: The intersubjective foundations of psychological life*. Analytic Press.

Strachan, J.R. (2003). *A Routledge literary sourcebook on the poems of John Keats*. Routledge.

Sturrock, D. (2016). *Storyteller: The life of Roald Dahl*. Collins.

Sue, D.W. (2001). Surviving monoculturalism and racism: A personal and professional journey. In J.G. Ponterotto, J.M. Casas, L.A. Suzuki & C.M. Alexander (Eds.), *Handbook of multicultural counseling* (pp.45–54). Sage.

Sullivan, H.S. (1953). *The interpersonal theory of psychiatry*. W.W. Norton & Co.

Suzuki, S., Dixon, T., Smith, H., Baker, R. & Chadwick, D. (2010). *Zen mind, beginner's mind*. Shambhala.

Swanson, D. (2021). *US wars and hostile actions: A list*. davidswanson.org

Tajfel, H. (1969). Cognitive aspects of prejudice. *Journal of Biosocial Science, 1*(S1), 173–191.

Tajfel, H. & Turner J.C. (1986). The social identity theory of intergroup behaviour. In W.G. Austin & S. Worchel (Eds.), *Psychology of intergroup relations*. Nelson-Hall.

Tedeschi, R. G., & Calhoun, L. G. (1996). The Posttraumatic Growth Inventory: Measuring the positive legacy of trauma. *Journal of Traumatic Stress, 9*(3), 455–472.

Tedeschi, R.G. & Calhoun, L.G. (2004). Posttraumatic growth: Conceptual foundations and empirical evidence. *Psychological Inquiry, 15*(1), 1–18.

Terzi, L. (2004). The social model of disability: A philosophical critique. *Journal of Applied Philosophy, 21*(2), 141–157.

Thomas, K.R. & Siller, J. (1999). Object loss, mourning, and adjustment to disability. *Psychoanalytic Psychology, 16*(2), 179–197.

Thomas-Skaf, B.A. & Jenney, A. (2021). Bringing social justice into focus: 'Trauma-informed' work with children with disabilities. *Child Care in Practice, 27*(4), 316–332.

Tolle, E. (1999). *The power of now*. Hodder & Stoughton.

Totton, N. (2019). Different bodies: The problem of normativity in body psychotherapy. *Psychotherapy and Politics International*. Uncorrected submission. https://doi.org/10.1002/ppi.1513

Tuckwell, G. (2006). Specific issues for white counsellors. In C. Lago (Ed.), *Race, culture and counselling: The ongoing challenge* (2nd ed.) (pp.204–216). Open University Press.

Turner, S.E., Fedigan, L.M., Matthews, H.D. & Nakamichi, M. (2014). Social consequences of disability in a nonhuman primate. *Journal of Human Evolution, 68*, 47–57.

Tweedie, N. (2016, May 11). The car scam that will drive you crackers. *Daily Mail*. www.dailymail.co.uk/news/article-3585783/The-car-scam-drive-crackers-Lottery-grandmother-given-20-000-car-reveal-thousands-driving-brand-new-vehicles-paid-pretending-disabled.html

UK Government (2010). *Definition of disability under the Equality Act 2010*. https://gov.uk.

United Nations (2006). *Convention on the rights of persons with disabilities*. United Nations.

United Nations (2009). *Urban and rural areas 2009*. United Nations.

United Nations (2020). *Inequality in a rapidly changing world: World social report 2020*. United Nations.

United States Census Bureau (2014). *2014 data release*. www.census.gov/programs-surveys/acs/news/data-releases/2014.html

US Department of Justice (1990). *Introduction to the ADA*. www.ada.gov/ada_intro.htm

US Travel Association (USTA) (2019, August 16). *Study: A record 768 million U.S. vacation days went unused in '18, opportunity cost in the billions*. US Travel Association. www.ustravel.org/

Utsey, S.O., Bolden M.A. & Brown, A.L. (2001). Visions of revolution from the spirit of Frantz Fanon: A psychology of liberation for counseling African Americans confronting societal racism and oppression. In J.G. Ponterotto, J.M. Casas, L.A. Suzuki & C.M. Alexander (Eds.), *Handbook of multicultural counseling* (pp. 311–336) (2nd ed.). Sage.

Valdés, E.G., Andel, R., Sieurin, J., Feldman, A.L., Edwards, J.D., Långström, N. & Wirdefeldt, K. (2014). Occupational complexity and risk of Parkinson's disease. *PloS One, 9*(9), e106676.

Van der Kolk, B. (2014). *The body keeps the score: Mind, brain and body in the transformation of trauma*. Penguin.

Van Deurzen, E. (2012). *Existential counselling and psychotherapy in practice*. Sage.

Van Deurzen, E. & Adams, M. (2011). *Skills in existential counselling and psychotherapy*. Sage.

Vergili, G., Minciotti, I., Foschini, M., Granata, G., Schenone, A., Aprile, I., Cavallaro, T., Commodari, I., Pareyson, D., Quattone, A., Rizzuto, N., Vita, G., Tonali, P. & Padua, L. (2007). Charcot Marie Tooth Type 1A: Neurophysiological pattern is poorly related to quality of life. *American Journal of Electroneurodiagnostic Technology, 47*(4), 326–326.

Verhaeghe, P. (2003). *On being normal and other disorders: A manual for clinical psychodiagnostics*. Karnac Books.

Vidal, G. (2002, October 27). The enemy within. *The Observer*.

Vinci, P., Gargiulo, P. & Colazza, G.B. (2007). Depression and Charcot-Marie-Tooth disease. *Neurological Sciences, 28*(5), 295–296.

Vinci, P., Gargiulo, P., Panunzi, M. & Baldini, L. (2009). Psychological distress in patients with Charcot-Marie-Tooth disease. *European Journal of Physical and Rehabilitation Medicine, 45*(3), 385–389.

Voltaire (1770/1919). Letter to Frederick William, Prince of Prussia, (28 Nov 1770). In S.G. Tallentyre (Ed.), *Voltaire in his letters*. G.P. Putnam's Sons.

Wachtel, P.L. (2010). *Relational theory and the practice of psychotherapy*. Guilford Press.

Ware, B. (2011). *The top five regrets of the dying*. Hay House.

Watermeyer, B. (2013). *Towards a contextual psychology of disablism*. Routledge.

Watson, J.B. (1913). Psychology as the behaviorist views it. *Psychological Review, 20*(2), 158–177.

Westphal, J. (2016). *The mind-body problem*. MIT Press.

White A. (2011). There by the grace of… *Therapy Today, 22*(5), 10–14.

Whitman, W. (1871). *Leaves of grass: Passage to India*. J.S. Redfield.

WHO (2001). *International classification of functioning, disability and health*. WHO.

WHO (2008). *Atlas: Multiple sclerosis resources in the world 2008*. World Health Organization.

WHO (2020). *Disability and health*. World Health Organization.

Whyte, D. (2014). *Consolations*. Many Rivers Press.

Wicks, R.L. (2020). *The Oxford handbook of Schopenhauer*. Oxford University Press.

Wilde, O. (1905). *De profundis*. Victoria Institutions.

Wilkinson, R. & Pickett, K. (2010). *The spirit level: Why equality is better for everyone*. Penguin.

Wilson, E. (2015). *How to make a soul: The wisdom of John Keats*. Northwestern University Press.

Wilson, S. (2001). *Disability: Controversial debates and psychological perspective* by Deborah Marks. *Free Associations, 8*(4), 678–681.

Wilson, S. (2003). *Disability, counselling and psychotherapy*. Palgrave Macmillan.

Winnicott, D.W. (1949). Hate in the counter-transference. *International Journal of Psycho-Analysis, 30*, 69–74.

Winnicott, D.W. (1958/1992). *Through paediatrics to psycho-analysis: Collected papers*. Brunner-Routledge.

Winnicott, D.W. (1960). The theory of the. parent-infant relationship. *International Journal of Psycho-Analysis, 41*, 585–595

Winnicott, D.W. (1971). *Playing and reality*. Routledge.

Wiseman, R. (2003). *The luck factor*. Arrow Books.

Woolf, V. (1930/2002). *On being ill*. Paris Press.

World Happiness Report (WHR) (2020). *World happiness report 2020*. WHR.

Wrangham, R.W., & Peterson, D. (1996). *Demonic males: Apes and the origins of human violence*. Houghton Mifflin & Co.

Wright, B.A. (1983). *Physical disability: A psychosocial approach*. Harper & Row.

Wurmser, L. (1994). *The mask of shame*. Jason Aronson Inc.

Yale School of Medicine (2013). *Charcot Marie Tooth (CMT)*. [Online]. Yale School of Medicine.

Yalom, I.D. (1980). *Existential psychotherapy*. Basic Books.

Yalom, I.D. (2002). *The gift of therapy*. Piatkus Press.

Yalom, I.D. (2012). *Love's executioner and other tales of psychotherapy*. Basic Books.

Zimbardo, P.G., Haney, C., Banks, W.C. & Jaffe, D. (1971). *Stanford prison experiment*. Zimbardo Inc.

Zunes, S. (2003). *Tinderbox: US Middle East policy and the roots of terrorism*. Common Courage Press.

Name index

Subject index